Gay, Explained

Gay, Explained

History, Science, Culture and Spirit

Preston Grant

GUIDE

Preston Grant
Gay, Explained: History, Science, Culture, and Spirit
Guide Media, San Francisco
First Edition, June 2016

Library of Congress Control Number: 2016909249
BISAC: SOC064000 SOCIAL SCIENCE / LGBT Studies / General

All illustrations and cover, print, and electronic book
designs by the author © 2016 Preston Grant
More information and illustration digital originals
available at www.prestongrant.com

for My People —
near,
far,
gone,
and yet to come

Out beyond ideas
of wrong-doing
and right-doing,
there is a field.

I will meet you there.

~ *Rumi*

Contents

ORIGINS 1

ONE   The Names   3

TWO   Who I Am   7

THREE   Who We Are   18

ANCESTORS 29

FOUR   Ancients   31

FIVE   Shamans   37

SIX   Two Spirits   43

SEVEN   Amazons   49

EIGHT   Monks   55

NINE   Wanderers   57

TEN   Ages   61

ELEVEN   Families   68

TWELVE   Lovers   71

THIRTEEN   Suppressed   75

HISTORY 81

FOURTEEN	Greece and Rome	83
FIFTEEN	Bible	91
SIXTEEN	Renaissance	100
SEVENTEEN	Greats	108
EIGHTEEN	Heroes	116
NINETEEN	Liberation	121
TWENTY	AIDS	131
TWENTY-ONE	Now	139

NATURE 145

TWENTY-TWO	Seeing	147
TWENTY-THREE	Animal Sexuality	153
TWENTY-FOUR	Animal Gender	164
TWENTY-FIVE	Evolution	169

BODIES 175

| TWENTY-SIX | Genetics | 177 |
| TWENTY-SEVEN | Biology | 182 |

MINDS 191

TWENTY-EIGHT	Psychology	193
TWENTY-NINE	Cures	198
THIRTY	Homophobia	204
THIRTY-ONE	Healing	209

LIFE 215

THIRTY-TWO	Love and Sex	217
THIRTY-THREE	Gender	228
THIRTY-FOUR	Authenticity	239

SOCIETY 243

THIRTY-FIVE	Ethics	245
THIRTY-SIX	Military	252
THIRTY-SEVEN	Children	255
THIRTY-EIGHT	Marriage	264
THIRTY-NINE	Religion	272
FORTY	Scriptures	278

MEANING 287

FORTY-ONE	Purpose	289
FORTY-TWO	Dream	295
	Gatekeepers	301

About the Author	307
Thank You	309
Acknowledgements	311
Notes	313
Index	331

ORIGINS

ONE

The Names

There are some things
you learn best in calm,
and some in storm.

~ Willa Cather

I WAS TWENTY-NINE years old when a great quilt was unrolled across the lawn in front of the White House, and people started to read the names. As a volunteer on the grief support team I dressed in white and walked the quilt offering solace to those who needed it; and there were many. This is back when people around me were dying of AIDS. Lots of people. But it was 1989, a time when it seemed like no one else in the country cared.

To memorialize the dead and make a statement that gay lives mattered, an activist named Cleve Jones created the AIDS Memorial Quilt. Each panel was made of fabric, three by six feet, the size of a grave. Friends and family created individual panels representing the life of a departed loved one, adorning it with color, words, fabrics, and quirky memorabilia. Then each of those individual panels was stitched together with others into large squares, and those squares were stitched together with each other and with walkways, until thousands of little fabric grave sites covered the memorial lawn in front of a White House that was busy ignoring that any of us existed at all.

Off to the side of the quilt was a small white podium where parents, friends, and lovers climbed the short flight of steps to the dais, walked up to a microphone, and read the names of the dead. They each read a few names from the official list of people represented in the panels, and then, more personally, they read the names of their own loved one they had come to grieve: "...and my beloved son, Jonathan. We miss you Johnny, and think of you every day. You are forever in our hearts."

It was my job to stand at the foot of those podium stairs and help those who had just read the names. Many had supporters with them, but others came alone. Hour after hour, morning to night, people from across America came to read the names, struggled through sharing the name of their own dead lovers and sons, and then returned back down the stairs where I stood waiting as they collapsed into my arms. The majority of the people I helped were grieving mothers who shared stories of small towns where they could not tell anyone in their community how their beloved child passed, of husbands unable or unwilling to speak of the tragedy, and of their travels alone to Washington to say aloud the name of their dead child.

My technique was simple. I stood at the base of the stairs offering those coming down a hand, while simultaneously throwing out a shoulder for them to brace themselves if they needed it. I am a tall man, and solid, and when I wordlessly offered my shoulder, most of those grieving mothers took it, burying their face in my chest as they wept uncontrollably. All I could do was hold them till the sobs subsided, then turn to help the next person coming down the stairs.

After hours at this post I came to feel like a porter at some melancholy train station, taking a bit of the emotional baggage from the hands of these mothers, metaphorically lifting off some of their burdens, and putting them down on the ground as they walked away, in preparation to relieve the next grieving mother of some small piece of her sorrows. Over the hours this grief accumulated, forming a pool that felt like it was surrounding me and beginning to pull me under. Overwhelmed by it all, I had another volunteer stand in for me as I walked out onto the fresh green grass of the nation's capital, sat down on the lawn with my back to the quilt, and to the names, and to all those grieving friends and families and lovers, and wept my own tears for what was happening around me. I despaired for my country at those times, wondering at the way community disappeared when misplaced moralism took over.

There is more to discuss about AIDS in a later chapter, but I share this moment to place my life within the larger gay story. I was born a child of the 1960s, just as gay liberation was born. I grew into the confusion of my teenage sexuality during the culture upheavals of the 1970s. I came out fully as a gay adult just as AIDS hit in the 1980s. I watched with dismay as the fight for our civil rights foundered in the early 2000s, and I have ridden the waves of joy as gay lives have grown increasingly recognized, respected, and integrated into the cultural mainstream. My life paralleled the larger gay experience each step of the way. Wanting to tell that bigger story of my people, initial drafts of this book left out my own stories, but early readers convinced me that was wrong. At its root, being gay is something so intensely personal that the only story I could tell with the necessary depth was my own. The next chapter introduces me as your narrator, before launching into the bigger history of my people, the science behind how we got here, and much more.

The world today looks very different from the one I grew up in. Gay, lesbian, bisexual, and transgender people are going from success to success, our lights shining ever more brightly for all to see. There is much work left to be done, but the way ahead is clear. Now, as we enjoy these victories, it is time to pause, and gather those who love us around, and read the list of the names. Not just the names of people dead from AIDS, but the names of all the gay people previous histories bypassed, ignored, killed, and shunned. Our lives have spanned times of darkness, times of light, and times of exceptional brilliance, far beyond what I can capture in these briefest of sketches. But with each name, and each story, the thread of one life is woven with that of another, and each of those patches is then sewn together with all the others. With the addition of each piece the perspective widens, and a larger picture becomes visible. It is a picture that includes every person alive on the planet today, and everyone who has ever lived, and everyone who ever will live, all knit together into the great quilt of the human family. This book is a testament to the power of that quilt, and the importance of all those names.

Who I Am

We're here for a reason.
I believe a bit of the reason
is to throw little torches out
to lead people through the dark.

~ *Whoopi Goldberg*

MY NAME IS PRESTON GRANT, and I was born gay and Mormon. I am now an ex-Mormon, as my church excommunicated me for being gay, and I now have neither an affiliation with, nor much interest in, the Mormon church. Yet my youth as a faithful Mormon remains one of the things that defines me, and my heritage is part of me in a way that most closely resembles an ethnicity. I am a descendant of some of the original families that founded the church and built the state of Utah. My ancestors were in the first wagons that arrived in the valley of the Great Salt Lake, and I bear the last name of one of the church's great prophets. I grew up proud of my history, studied it deeply, and carried inside me the kind of confidence in Mormonism that only narrow adherence can bring. I was raised with the expectation that I would be one of the Mormon cultural elite, part of the unfolding zeitgeist of Mormon truth that was expanding and spreading and destined to take over the earth. The majority of my vast family, and most of the people I grew up with, continue to support the church. Most members of my large and extended family follow their leaders faithfully, donate their time and energy to promote Mormon culture, and fund the church through a tithe of 10% of their gross incomes to promote its global operations and expansion.

When I was ten my family moved from my native San Francisco back to our ancestral home in Salt Lake City, the place the Mormons call Zion. Decades later, as I sought therapy to help me understand what went so wrong in my childhood, a counselor guided me through a meditation where I closed my eyes and pictured myself slowly descending a staircase, moving with each step deeper and deeper into the past, until I was standing in front of a door at the bottom of the stairs. On the other side of that door would be the place where I needed to be to understand my confusion, wherever that was. At the count of three I was to open that door, look around, and report where I was, and what I saw there. One — Two — Three.

Deep in my imagination, I opened the door and walked out onto my childhood playground in Salt Lake City, just after I moved there in the third grade. The playground looked the way I remembered it — asphalt, chain link fence, surrounding trees, and the ever-present Wasatch mountains towering behind. Although I was standing there alone, with no one else in sight, I was deluged by a cacophony of voices filling my ears. Criticism. Nagging. Teasing. Disapproval. My ears rang with the sound of voices so loud I could not think. From every direction I heard voices telling me I was wrong. I was wrong in the way I walked. Wrong in the way I sat. Wrong in how much I liked to talk and wrong in what I talked about. I was wrong in what I liked. Wrong in what I cared about. I was wrong in the way I dealt with conflict, and wrong in the way I played schoolyard games. Completely alone, bereft of any companionship or support, I felt buried in the din of voices surrounding me, all telling me that every aspect of my being was bad and wrong, and making clear I was far too weird to be part of their society.

Reflecting back now, more than forty years later, I remember one story that exemplifies that time of my life. It happened one afternoon after church when I was about eleven. After returning home from Sunday services, I got a telephone call asking me to come back to the church building. Confused about why, I returned and found all the boys of my age, along with our adult leaders, gathered in a classroom. The purpose of this unprecedented meeting was to clarify the ways I was unacceptable to the group and to make suggestions on how I could improve myself. A boy a year older than I led the discussion of my failings as they listed my faults on the chalkboard, and then brainstormed things I could do to make myself more acceptable to the group. The only result I remember from that meeting was that I was supposed to be more athletic and take up jogging. The verdict against me was unanimous. I was too odd and queer for my peers, and I had to change or be rejected. No one was there to stand up for me. There were no positive attributes listed on that board. I walked home crushed by my church's official disapproval and tried jogging for a week or so, feeling as if I carried the weight of my shame with every step.

The chorus of disapproval that surrounded me through my life in Utah left lasting scars, although I will never be able to communicate fully what happened there. My recollections of those years remain scattered and chaotic, with many parts missing or incoherent. The lingering results, on the other hand, are more clear. For decades I was overly self conscious of my body, as my every move felt faulty. It also left me unsure of my thoughts and opinions, as they never seemed to mesh with anyone around me. A common legacy from trauma is an inability to simply feel what we feel when we feel it. Part of my problem came from living in a world where no one could reflect me back to myself accurately. The effect was like growing up in a funhouse of curving mirrors. The vision of who I was, displayed back by those around me, always made me into something weird and distorted.

Doing my best to survive conditions I was taught were normal, healthy, superior to mainstream society, and absolutely God's will, I came to live a life of pain. Over time I learned to contort body and spirit to try to fit in and please those around me. I cannot say that strategy was much of a success, but I had few options. My primary survival mechanism was to cringe up tight inside my body, protect my overly sensitive heart as best I could, and then try to mold my outside to fit the world I lived in.

Within a few years my body began the transformations of puberty, and I became curious about sex. Mormons of the time believed being gay was a choice, and therefore an important moral issue, but I am clear I never chose to be gay. It felt more like my sexuality chose me. It found me on a warm spring afternoon in that same schoolyard of Rosslyn Heights Elementary School when I was in the fifth grade. We were outside playing a game during afternoon recess when a sixth grader took his shirt off. With an odd awareness, I found myself staring at his athletic torso and suddenly something new happened inside me. With unnerving clarity I realized I was attracted to this boy, and more specifically, to his body. To translate for straight people, this must be something like the disruptive moment straight boys feel when a woman's breasts shift from the warmly maternal to the unnervingly erotic. Puberty's first thunderings arrived as attraction to a boy I only remember from that one searing image. And from that day on I looked at men differently.

I was not choosing to be gay. I was not giving in to an indulgent experience of decadent pleasure, as that old view of homosexuality would have it. I was only eleven. I was not even old enough, in those pre-internet days, to understand the concept of sex at all, and certainly not gay sex — a fact best demonstrated when the mean girl in class teased me for not knowing what the word "gay" meant. I was absolutely sure it meant happy, and was baffled when she laughed at my naiveté. While the debate over homosexuality pivoted on whether my sexual attractions were my choice, I cannot see how my full-bodied reaction to another boy at age eleven was something I could choose. I think it was just adolescence. Choice came later when I had to decide what to do about those feelings.

By age thirteen I had learned far too many things about sex from the bizarrely erroneous *Everything You Always Wanted to Know About Sex, but were Afraid to Ask,* and being both tall and precocious for my age, I set out to find the kind of sex described in that book. I had no idea where to meet gay men, but being a nerdish kid who lived next to a university campus I started with the college bookstore. My innovative technique for picking up a gay man who might be interested in me was to stand in the bookstore's magazine section with the newly published *Playgirl* tucked inside another magazine, and when a gay looking man stood nearby I would open my magazine wide enough that he could see it was nude men I was secretly looking at. It eventually worked, and I ended up enjoying a delightfully nervous sexual encounter with a man who was muscular and covered in furry blonde hair. Together we walked up to a forest clearing of a nearby nature preserve. The fooling around part was pretty elementary, but the thing I remember best was his silver mirrored aviator sunglasses, so popular in the 1970s, and how I nervously reached up to take them off of him so I could see into his eyes. I guess my lack of experience showed because on our walk back to campus he asked me if I was really in college, as I seemed younger than that. I did not dare tell him I was still in Junior High.

I walked home from that encounter in a daze. Having sex, out of doors, with a virile man, was a dazzling experience for a thirteen-year-old Mormon boy. I was left with the unfamiliar sensation that my actions felt both right and wrong at the same time, my first experience of what would come to be a common sensation when my internal moral compass differed so dramatically from the ethics of my religion.

A few months later, I was riding a city bus home from the downtown library when a conspicuously gay man got on. I gave him a interested look, and he chose the seat next to me. I do not remember if we talked or just flirted wordlessly, but when the bus reached my stop I got off, walked home, and forgot about him. What happened next was never quite clear to me, but somehow that man turned me in to the Mormon authorities, pointing me out to a Bishop (the Mormon equivalent of a pastor) who called me into his office to confront me about being gay. I was not quite fourteen, and what I remember best about that meeting was the way the gray walls of the Bishop's office began to quiver and melt around me as the world of my childhood disintegrated.

The Bishop told my parents, and like most members of their generation, they had no clue what to do. They showed their love for me by keeping the connection solid, but society had provided them with no guidelines for how to parent a gay child. They were of the generation where there was a specific ideal for men, and a specific ideal for women, and a defined trajectory for relationships, marriage, and family that applied to everyone equally. Homosexuality was not discussed, even by people who were clearly and obviously gay. Gender variation was not even a topic, except for the general confusion around long-haired hippies. So my parents' solution was to ask me what was going on. They would sit me down and we would discuss my "problem," and they would ask me for my feelings about it. But there was a flaw in that approach, as I did not know what I felt or why I felt it, which in retrospect is a central aspect of puberty. My adolescence as a young gay kid, long before society could discuss gay issues, left us all adrift in murky ignorance and flawed misinformation. Unfortunately for me, the Mormon church thought it did understand homosexuality, and how to handle homosexual behavior in young church members. Like many Christians to this day, Mormons believed homosexuality was curable through the application of enough effort, prayer, and negative stimulus.

Young Mormons are taught that they should not have personal boundaries between themselves and church leaders — every private thought that is not in conformance with church doctrine must be confessed to the male authorities. Withholding anything as private or personal is considered a moral flaw in resistance to God's authority. I therefore submitted to the weekly self-criticism sessions my Bishop established. Every Sunday after church I would go to his office and confess any homosexual feelings or acts from the previous week. If my level of description was insufficient, he would ask me to repeat my stories in more detail, expressing his disapproval while he was clearly fascinated to hear more. He would then declare his disgust at me, telling me I was dirty and unfit to be in association with other members of the church.

To make sure I knew how negatively God viewed me, my Bishop had me read aloud from the words of the Mormon Prophet: "Homosexuality is an ugly sin, repugnant to those who find no temptation in it," and, "All such deviations from normal, proper heterosexual relationships are not merely unnatural but wrong in the sight of God. Like adultery, incest, and bestiality they carried the death penalty under the Mosaic law."[1] The Prophet of my youth declared homosexuals unworthy of life by divine decree, a distressing thought at fourteen, but fitting in a church that routinely said homosexuality was a crime next to murder in severity. When I complained to my parents about this treatment, they deferred to the sacred authority of the church's leaders, so week after week I was sent back for more.

When strict spiritual guidance and humiliating criticism failed to cure me of my attractions towards men, I was sent to specialist. That was how, at sixteen, I ended up in aversion therapy. Long discredited outside of Utah, aversion therapy looked like the scene in the movie *A Clockwork Orange* where they pin Malcolm McDowell's eyes open and make him watch horrific movies while the nurse puts drops in his eyes. The primary difference was that

I was there voluntarily, so there was no need to hold my eyes open, and the Mormon version added a measuring device wrapped around my genitals to display my state of arousal on a dial next to the therapist's chair.

At the beginning of each session I put the plethysmograph around my privates, zipped up my trousers, and sat down in a chair with arms. The plethysmograph's wires ran out the top of my pants and back to a monitor dial mounted next to the therapist's chair and the stand holding the movie projectors. (And no, I was not wearing the Mormon sacred undergarments, as those come later in life.) The therapist then came in and placed electrodes on my arms and strapped me to the chair. Sitting back in his seat, the therapist then showed me movies depicting gay pornographic scenes, while monitoring any changes in my erection on the dial. If I had an erection, I was jolted with electricity and he switched the film to straight pornography. The theory behind aversion therapy said that by applying negative stimulus while viewing the "wrong" images, the brain would learn to avoid those specific thoughts, and by switching the film while aroused, the "correct" erotic images would be imprinted, reprogramming the mind to a more appropriate sexuality.

This was 1976, well before video tapes made pornography common, so I had never seen anything like the movies that played out on the therapist's screen from clicking reel-to-reel Super 8 projectors. The first movie I saw was of a stockily furry man wearing only jeans and leaning against a motorcycle. He seemed shy or reserved, but he slowly caressed his sculpted body, and unbuttoned his fly. The plethysmograph measured my physiological reaction, so the doctor shocked me repeatedly and then flipped to the other projector. Now a young straight couple was walking down a path in the woods holding hands, an image I was supposed to find erotic. My therapist feared showing me hard core pornography because of my young age, so all the straight pornography I saw was soft core. He did not have soft core gay pornography, as no one was making such a thing back then, so all the gay porn I saw was incredibly graphic. In the dark of that therapist's office I watched orgies of well endowed young men over and over, accompanied by more and more electric shocks that could not penetrate my awe at the imagery, alternating with straight 1970s couples fondling on a various shaggy carpets in front of all different kinds of fireplaces.

Needless to say, even this level of torture did not cure me of being gay, so buttons were added to the chair. While viewing the gay pornography and being shocked to short-circuit my body's attractions, I was supposed to push the buttons in a particular sequence. The added complexity was supposed to help override any sexual thoughts. The intensity of the shocks rose and the complexity of the required button pushing sequences increased, but nothing changed my attraction to the male sexual images. What those weekly sessions did was leave me horny, emotionally twisted, and deeply humiliated by the bright red marks that lingered on my arms as I drove around in my car for hours afterwards waiting for the redness to fade.

Church authorities said this was good for me. The therapist was a man I saw at church meetings, and my parents never asked the details of the therapy I was receiving, deferring to the supposed experts. As for me, I spoke of it as little as possible, as I was lost in a morass of internalized pain and the deepest of shame without an ally in any direction or any sense of where solid ground might lie. At some point the pain of it all grew to be too much, and after a year or so of treatment I finally pretended I was cured and quit.

Decades later, the emotional scars of that time were overwhelming me, and I finally got actual therapeutic help in sorting things out and making sense of it all. Peeling back the layers, I realized that I had an earlier violation. As a young boy I was sexually molested by a male friend of the family, a fact that scarred me deeply. I liked this man and appreciated his attention, so his violation, although not physically dramatic, was emotionally devastating. Clarity around this younger abuse helped explain why I was so sexual at such a young age. Sexually abused children are exposed to adult sexual energy, which has no place to go in a child's body. When puberty hits, the sexual wiring comes on already filled with all that energy, and acting out is common.

The combination of being sexually abused when young, and then systematic abuse by church elders, left me with at least three lasting effects. First, I learned to split my deeper self from my feelings. To survive in that social world I learned to hide the deepest sense of my truth from the mindless criticisms and cruelties of those around me. Even now, decades later, I sometimes suffer crippling body pains in my gut, down my arms, and throughout my body, along with severe bouts of PTSD, or post-traumatic stress disorder, from all that torture. At the depths of my pain I found thoughts of suicide helpful — it was comforting to know there was at least one way out of my internal hell. As an adult I thought living with a body filled with physical pain was normal. To this day, so many decades after those core experiences, panic attacks and depression remain my regular companions. At this point I view them as chronic conditions I will never be free of, but try to manage. I now live in the sunshine many days, with regular dips back into the depths to remind me of how deep the dark can be.

The second lesson I learned is something all torture victims learn, that there is some inner Me that is impenetrable to outside forces. You can hurt my body and you can hurt my mind, but there is some essential part of my consciousness that is even deeper and remains untouched, an inviolable essence of self not completely linked to my physical body or rational mind. It may have been at that point I became clear on the existence of the soul, the spirit that animates our bodies. I know from personal experience the truth of Teilhard de Chardin's saying that "We are not human beings having a spiritual experience; we are spiritual beings having a human experience."[2] It is a strange but powerful lesson to learn from torture.

The third thing I learned was that I was inalterably attracted to men. No amount of pain, shaming, or diabolical torture therapy would change that. At such a young age I did not fully understand the implications, but I knew any future would have to include the part of myself that loved men. The ideas of gay liberation were new back then and far distant from my life in 1970s Salt Lake City. My indoctrination within the Mormon world was so absolute I could not even form the thought of leaving for a very long time; but I had the vision that some day I would become an integrated person, with all the seemingly disparate parts of myself converging into a harmonious whole. I just had no idea how to make that happen.

While I never got the chance to choose, or un-choose, my sexuality, I still had to decide what to do with my life. After high school I went to a year of college, then decided to give my culture's wisdom one last great try, so I volunteered for a two-year stint serving a Mormon mission overseas. After a thoroughly religious adolescence with gay stuff running on the side, I wanted to commit completely to my church's teachings, run the experiment fully, and see what happened. So for two full years, from nineteen to twenty-one, I lived a life of prayer, service, religious study, complete submittal to authority, and absolute celibacy. The result was a profoundly enlivening cultural and linguistic experience living in Tokyo, Japan and a profoundly unfulfilling experience serving as a door-to-door salesman for the church. Most importantly, this most intensive attempt to shift my sexuality left me utterly clear that the experiment failed. There was no effective path from where I was to where the church said I was supposed to be. So I gave up on being Mormon, moved to Washington, DC for graduate school, found a boyfriend, and started to live as an open and honest gay man. The church followed up by officially excommunicating me for the crime of being gay and honest about it.

Because every gay person has to find their own path through life, outside of the societal norms, it is part of our culture to share our coming out stories. When I told other gay people I was writing this book, the most common response was, "Well you should hear my story!" Almost every one of us has a significant story to share, filled with pathos, joy, and powerful insights into the human condition. And now you know mine.

This book is the voice of a single individual. I write from my experience as a fifty-something, white, American, relatively masculine, gay man. I celebrate all of who I am, but that also means my ability to speak for women, younger, older, gender variant, bisexuals, people of different races, and many others is limited. My hope is that honesty about my own experiences will help reveal the deeper truths universal to us all. This book is my attempt to share what I have learned about the great distinction that separated me from the mainstream, the signature quality that marked me as unique, different, special, eccentric, and queer — the fact that I was born gay.

It was only well into the project that I realized how directly the roots of this book date back to my troubled youth. I remember long lonely nights sitting in my bedroom, lost in sadness, looking out my window at the street below and feeling baffled that no one had ever traveled this road before and left me a trail of breadcrumbs to help me find my way out. In the midst of that teenage despair I swore that if I ever made it through to the light, I would mark the path for others. Although I did not realize it when I started writing, this book is my fulfillment of that teenage commitment. I have been in the dark forest. I have found my way out. And now I have marked the path.

A couple of quick notes: I describe people of the "opposite sex" as the other-sex, both to mirror the term same-sex and because men and women are not opposites in any meaningful way. I use the term "gay" to represent the LGBT and related communities, as well as for animals and other natural phenomena because it is easier than the alphabet soup of the fullest possible inclusion, and is the word most often used in common speech. All scriptures are King James Version unless otherwise noted. And finally, I use the word

God to honor the sacred and transcendent. Read it as figurative or literal and the meaning should remain the same.

And so the most personal chapter of the book comes to an end. The remainder is a diverse collection of topics divided into short chapters. Wanting to warm up a work that could seem too serious, I created icons and illustrations to illuminate and enliven the text. I hope you enjoy them. The next chapter expands into my community as a prelude to discussing some of the diverse stories that help explain what it is to be gay, and how our existence affects everyone in the human family.

Who We Are

> When we remember
> we are all mad,
> the mysteries disappear
> and life stands explained.
>
> ~ *Mark Twain*

WHEN I STEPPED OUT of the narrow Mormon world of my youth I entered the raucous cacophony of the gay community, and I have considered myself gay ever since. Yet all these years later, I still cannot define with precision what it means to be gay. The realities of life are so much more complex than any single label can communicate.

Personally, I like the term gay as an umbrella category, without too much attachment to exactly what it means. In my ears the word sounds positive and joyful, with a touch of a smirk embedded into it. I have the image of a "gay" man being someone who is expressive and effusive in whatever way seems appropriate to the moment, without the constraints many straight men seem to feel.

Over time the implication that gay referred to men became a problem, as gay men tended to hog the spotlight. As I remember the story, we separated out Lesbians back in the 1980s so that gay women would be acknowledged more explicitly and not as some women's auxiliary to the men's club; and then we added Bisexuals to cover the middle ground. That made us the Gay, Lesbian, and Bisexual community. While that more or less covered sexuality, it left out the interrelated issues of gender, or the ways individuals relate to their own masculinity and femininity, so the GLBs added the T to represent trans-gender people and all the other gender variations, and putting women first, we became the LGBT community.

Even thus defined, it remains an odd sort of club. By circumstances of my birth, I am a part of a community formed by drawing a circle around everyone who feels a mainstream sense of sexuality and gender, and then declaring solidarity with everyone born outside that circle. While there are endless divisions and sub-groups within the LGBT community, at our grandest we are a group of people defined by our inclusiveness for the excluded.

Wanting to make sure every variation felt welcome, we kept adding letters. We added Q for Queer people who were simply different, and another Q for Questioning people who were wondering about their true sexuality. For those who were loving but not sexual we added an A for Asexual. For those born physically outside the male-female norms we added an I for Intersex. We tried to honor every gender or sexual variation in the human experience with its own letter, but acronyms like LGBTQQAI were such tongue twisters that most of us retreated back to the simplicity of saying gay, LGBT, LGBTQ, or increasingly, queer. There may never be a singular label that covers such a disparate community, so the most important thing is the welcome offered to anyone who wants in. If you feel you are part of the club, or just have affinity for the rest of us non-mainstream folk, then consider yourself welcome, and call us by whatever name works best for you.

I like labels, and consider them important. They are useful little tags that help sort out different kinds of people: funny, Flemish, pedestrian, liberal, Lutheran, quadriplegic, motherly, Eagle Scout, plumber, redhead, wise, short, rich, acerbic, girly, suburban, Hindu, intelligent, centered, African, kind, athletic, American, and obstinate. Of course any label can also be offensive when used to hurt, and labels are only valid when their limitations are respected, so no one label ever tells the whole truth about a person. Applying the label Mormon or even ex-Mormon to me, for example, does not begin to convey the complexity of my story. The same is true for the label gay. I am gay, but the image conjured in someone's mind when they hear that label may not match the real me. I am my labels, and I am so much more, and so is everybody else.

The core nature of humanity is probably pretty consistent over time, but as the collective understanding of the human condition grows and changes, the labels must evolve as well. The concept of heterosexuality, for example, was invented in the late 1800s. Heterosexual sexuality had always existed, but it was only in the Victorian age that people decided they needed a label for people attracted to the other sex. This conceptualization of heterosexuality arrived as the corollary to the equally new idea that some people could be labeled homosexual, another new social label for a timeless sexuality. Both of these labels came from the period when science was trying to name and categorize everything in the natural world, a process led by people like Charles Darwin and Sigmund Freud.

Originally, the homosexual label was used as a description of a mental illness-like malady, as the medical establishment considered homosexuals sick and deviant. That began to change in the twentieth century as gay people gathered in large cities and started sharing our stories with each other. Together we developed a collective sense of who we were and what made us different, and began pushing back against the prevailing norms. Over time we became clear that we experienced our homosexuality and sense of gender as inborn parts of ourselves, and therefore society was wrong to label those variations a sickness. With that shift in perspective came the need for a new label, so we dropped the clinical sounding homosexual, and started calling ourselves gay.

No one really knows when the word gay first came to mean someone who loves another person of the same sex. The word originally meant carefree or uninhibited, and someone being extremely carefree and uninhibited was probably doing something immoral. Chaucer used the word gay in that sense in the 1630s.[1] In his time a gay woman was a prostitute, so maybe a gay man was a roughly equivalent breaker of sexual rules.

By the 1920s the word gay was showing up among homosexual men in New York, but it was not the most common term of the time. In describing pre-World War II culture in his wonderful book *Gay New York,* historian George Chauncey noted that newspaper and court records routinely used three different terms for men who had sex with men: fairies, queens, and trade.[2] Fairies were the obviously and outwardly gay, mincing and lisping and often considered low class figures living outside of polite society. Queens were the secretly gay men who could pass as straight in public, often living with their wives and children and conducting their gay relationships in private on the side. Trade is the category most unfamiliar to modern Americans, as trade were straight men who occasionally had sex with gay men, usually in the "masculine" sexual position. The classic image of trade was the sailor on shore leave looking for a little sexy something before a long sea voyage, and better the sexual ministrations of another man than nothing at all.

This layered conceptualization of human sexuality solidified into a singular gay identity in the 1970s as the gay community became adamant that anyone who ever had any sexual contact with anyone of the same sex was gay, and straight American men stopped fooling around in the gray zones for fear of being tarred with a negative label. As part of early gay liberation, gay came to mean a singular identity, inborn and intrinsic for an identifiable minority of the population, a label to be worn as a declaration of a proud and positive sense of self. Today that meaning has softened, and usage varies by community and speaker.

This idea that everyone who had sex with a same-sex partner must be gay was a culturally-defined boundary. In much of the world it was considered normal for a man to have sex with other men once in a while. Gay friends in Brazil, for example, tell me that most straight Brazilian men are available for male-male sex, as long as it is discreet. Gay travelers to parts of the outwardly anti-gay Muslim world bring back stories of secretive male-male behavior so common it can feel threatening. Some of the best stories of this hetero-flexibility, to use the modern term, came from British gay men who enjoyed dalliances with "straight" American soldiers in the darkened alleys of London during the Blitz of World War II.[3] Their heightened sense that life could end at any moment stripped away many soldiers' traditional inhibitions.

Gender studies scholar Eve Sedgwick provided a framework for understanding these various perspectives by defining two ways of looking at being gay, the minority view and the universal view.[4] The minoritizing view declares gay people a distinct minority with definable traits, while the universalizing view sees sexuality as a continuum where everyone has a bit of heterosexuality and homosexuality in them, varying from full-on queer to barely a whiff.

The more activist members of the gay community tended to prefer the minoritizing view. Defining ourselves as a well-delineated group made us into a class of citizens who could be researched and protected, and gained us clear analogues with other racial and ethnic minorities. It simplified the discussion to say that some people are gay, some are not, and leave it at that. Many individuals found it comfortable to claim these labels in a similarly rigid way, as it was easier to identify as 100% straight or 100% gay and ignore any fuzzy bits around the edges.

Comforting as that kind of black and white thinking can be, the minoritizing view fails in its ability to define a clean bright line separating who belongs in which category. The universalizing view solves that problem by declaring sexuality a spectrum, placing everyone somewhere on a gay-straight continuum. As societies became more honest about sexuality, this perspective seemed to be gaining, as it helped explain the straight guy who had a man crush in college and the straight woman who wondered if she loves her female friends more than her husband. Seen from this universal perspective, the idea that homosexuality only exists in some easily definable minority group is nonsense, as there is a little sugar in all of us.

Psychologist Lisa Diamond added a helpful distinction in her book *Sexual Fluidity*, as she teased out ways the traditional gay-straight distinction worked differently in women. Diamond found that many women did not sort so easily into the gay-straight-bi categories of the LGBT paradigm. In fact, she suggests that the whole idea of a persistent sexual orientation that can be labeled L, G, or B may be more of a male paradigm than a female one. As Diamond describes it, many women have attractions that are clear and un-choosable in the moment, but may be more fluid over time.[5]

Diamond's descriptions of a fluid female sexuality fits the commonly heard stories of women who live their lives happily married to a man, but when that marriage ends, find themselves in love with a woman. I recently met a middle-aged woman who had married a man, and liked sexual relations with men, but had a lingering sadness that her most emotionally intimate relationship had been with another woman earlier in her life. I find it astonishing how many straight female friends tell similar stories, and how few men.

It should not be surprising that the cycles of male and female sexuality can be different. Women and men are physically different, emotionally different, and differently socialized. To give one concrete example, men shown pornographic images while hooked up to machines that measure arousal displayed strong responses to pictures of either one sex or the other. Even men who claim to be bisexual tend to show physical arousal to only one of the sexes. Women's bodies, on the other hand, showed sexual arousal to both sexes. So it appears that men's minds and bodies have a more focused and targeted sexuality, while women are more generally sexual.[6] Women's sexual preferences also seem to broaden as they age, while men's narrow.[7]

Having brought up bisexuality, I should note that I seldom use the term, but that is not because I consider it invalid. Quite the opposite. I tend to find the universalizing view more useful, so I see everyone on a spectrum. That means that for me the term bisexual applies to so many people, to such widely varying degrees, and in so many different ways, that I find it difficult to use meaningfully. To illustrate the problem, sex researcher Alfred Kinsey used a six-point scale for sexuality, from one for perfectly and completely heterosexual to six for perfectly and completely homosexual. That means from the moment a person steps off of one, all the way until they arrive firmly on six, they are in bisexual territory. In addition, a lot of young gay people call themselves bisexual for a time. It is a more socially neutral term than gay, and it may be a more accurate description of the state they are in as their bodies and souls work out the nature of their still-emerging adult sexuality.

All of that said, truly bisexual people do exist. Tests of pupil dilations in response to male and female imagery have proven that bisexual men have a clearly biological response to both genders.[8] Analyzing people's personal behaviors online, however, the dating site OKCupid found that only 23% of declared bisexuals actually sent messages to both sexes.[9] Add in the previously mentioned data that bisexual men are typically aroused by just one of the sexes, and it appears that the nature of human attractions is complex indeed.

To get out of this tangle of labels, younger people often use the word queer. Older people tend to cringe at the word for its stings of schoolyard bullying, but younger generations are adopting it as a generalized and affirming umbrella label for everyone whose sexual or gender life is outside the mainstream. It is a great example of reclaiming a hate word and putting a positive spin on it. Personally, I like the word, as I love embracing the traditional meaning — that someone queer is curious, funny, eccentric, different, singular, odd, or surprising, all descriptions I proudly claim for myself. Queer people are the ones who live beyond the normal boundaries, playfully deviating from what is usual and expected. To my ears, the word has an edgy political spin with a tang of defiance about it, while remaining broadly inclusive, a nice combination to my way of thinking.

One nice thing about the word queer comes from the fact that it does not infer anything particular about a person's sexuality or gender. It just means they are different. To say someone has a queer spirit, for example, means they have the depth and insight to see the quirks of life from broader and deeper perspectives than the mainstream, without implying anything more.

Another great but underused word is homophile, meaning same-loving, which stands in contrast to homosexual, which means same-sexual. To step outside the stand-off between the sex-obsessives and the sex-phobic, I think homophile, and the related terms homophilic, heterophile, and heterophilic, could communicate more clearly the difference between love and sex, a valuable distinction. Maybe someday.

Straight, on the other hand, is a rather strange term because of its judgmental origins. Straight came to mean heterosexual because a straight person did not deviate from the usual, normal, and conventional. Someone who "goes straight" after a life of crime or drug abuse becomes ethical, honest, and honorable. Gay people, by contrast, were considered bent, twisted, and immoral. As with the word queer, I hear straight differently now. To me it means the people who walk the default path, while the non-straight are the sinuous folk who celebrate curlicues, meanderings, spirals, and curves — the road less traveled, if you will.

And while celebrating all the diversity in humanity, I also want to honor straight people, and everyone who considers themselves to be normal or average. It is OK to be straight. It is a beautiful thing to be a feminine woman or a masculine man. It is wonderful to love someone of the other sex. Marriages between one man and one woman are powerful commitments and an important part of the social structure, to be honored and celebrated whenever possible. I take those truths as givens, important and integral norms that define the bulk of society, and I say hurrah to each and every person who fits comfortably into the mainstream. I am even a little jealous. I cannot imagine a life where I fit easily into society's expectations without struggle, thought, or effort. It must be a wonderful feeling to feel "normal," devoid of variations that cause hate and disgust in the people around you. But I do not begrudge those who can live happily in the slipstream of life. Oh heck no — I celebrate your sexuality, your relationships, your families, and your lives! There is nothing that is true about my life that could possibly rob you of what is honorable and beautiful about yours. This is not a contest with winners and losers. It is life, where the more who thrive, the more life there is to celebrate.

Having considered some of the variations that make up the LGBT community, persistent questions remain about our numbers. It can be hard to get an accurate count of the gay population because not everyone agrees on what is being counted. In the biggest survey of LGBT people ever conducted, Gallup asked over 120,000 Americans one simple question: "Do you, personally, identify as lesbian, gay, bisexual, or transgender?" Out of the entire population, 3.4% said yes. More interestingly, the answer among eighteen to twenty-nine year olds was 6.4%, and among women of that age group 8.3% said yes.[10] As the closeted generations fade and more people are honest, it looks like those numbers are going to rise. Summarizing the studies to date, *Time Magazine* concluded that 5% of the population is LGBT. They also noted that a third of millennials do not consider themselves strictly straight or gay, but rather somewhere in the middle.[11] That is part of the change now unfolding, as people learn to include all of who they are, and not just the dominant parts.

In this book I use the 5% number as it is important for another reason: voters. According to exit polling from America's 2012 elections, when confronted by a pollster with a clipboard outside of voting booths, 5% of the American electorate self-identified as LGBT.[12] That is 5% of actively engaged citizens, so it is a number that matters. By comparison, the US Census says Mormons are 1.9% of the population, Jews are 1.7%, and Southern Baptists are 6.7%. Latinos make up almost 17% of the country, while Blacks are 13% and Asians 5%.[13] At 5%, the population of gay Americans equals the populations of Wyoming, Vermont, North Dakota, South Dakota, Alaska, Delaware, Montana, Rhode Island, New Hampshire, Maine, Hawaii, Idaho, West

Virginia, Nebraska, and New Mexico combined. In any random group of twenty Americans, one is LGBT.

Equitable distribution, then, would say that one in twenty television kisses should be between two people of the same sex, one in twenty families in advertising should be LGBT, and one in twenty Senators should be gay. If the loose coalition we call the gay community constitutes 5% of humanity, then of seven billion people alive today, 350 million of us are gay, or one third of a billion souls. That means there are more gay people on the planet than there are citizens of the United States. We are many.

Yet even that is not every queer person, as pretty much every human being is unique in some special way. There is something that makes every person an individual, something about every one of us at least a teeny tiny bit... queer. For some it is our sexuality or relationship to gender, but for others it may be the brightness of our eyes, that funky part of our bodies, the pain of past relationships, sadly tangled family histories, or our idiosyncratic paths to peace, success, and meaning in life. As I get older I increasingly realize that no one feels completely normal, free of momentary doubts or insecurities, and the ones most puffed up and rigid about their "normalcy" tend to be the most fragile on the inside. While 5% may be a nice round number for the LGBT community, pretty much 100% of human individuals vary in some discernible way.

Every quality I can use to define the gay population exists in even larger quantities among straight people. When I try to define gay lives, what I am pointing to are propensities, the likelihood a trait will show up in a particular group. Very little of it is exclusive. As Bill Clinton said, "There is no them; there's only us."[14] It is my deepest hope that every reader — straight, gay, or other — will be able to see aspects of themselves mirrored in almost everything discussed in this book. At its root this is simply the stuff of life.

In the end, the numbers of who is gay and who is straight do not matter. The arguments about what makes a person gay, or even what defines gay, do not matter. The labels do not matter. What matters is the sanctity of a human life, and the value of the person living it. For a visceral experience of this truism, I recommend the TED talk of the artist iO Tillett Wright, called *Fifty Shades of Gay,* available at www.ted.com. Not only does she articulate the complexity of this thing called gay in a delightfully personal way, but more importantly, she links the abstract concepts of this conversation to specific photographs of individual faces in a way that is both enlightening and empowering. The only way to understand this experience of being human comes from seeing all that is true about unique individuals while grasping what is true about the greater mass of collective humanity at the same time.

ANCESTORS

Ancients

> The further back you look,
> the further forward you can see.
>
> ~ *Winston Churchill*

MODERN GAY PEOPLE have a backstory. We have a history. Some of our stories were documented and are still visible in the historical record, but more often we were left out. It is said that history is written by the victors, so the common people, the less powerful, and the vanquished got left out. In a world where straight people dominated, the stories of gay lives were often neglected or ignored. Even when our histories were chronicled or represented through art in more tolerant and inclusive times, that evidence was later destroyed by disapproving cultures. As a 1979 flyer for the San Francisco Gay History project declared: "Our letters were burned, our names blotted out, our books censored, our love declared unspeakable, our very existence denied."[1] Until recently, most of the great repositories of culture — the libraries, museums, archives, and universities — rejected the records of our existence. Even now the scant documentation, photographs, and personal memorabilia from the early years of gay liberation are being lost as the last survivors of that pivotal generation fade away with little evidence archived before their passing.

Because the records of our lives were so systematically ignored and destroyed, it can appear as if the world has always been straight, with only the occasional sightings of anyone different. Without the knowledge that gay people existed in other times and places, homosexuality seems like another fad of the 1960s, like lava lamps or bell-bottom pants. Knowing that we are a people with a history can shift that perspective as it becomes clear that what happened in the 1960s was not just a revolution in sex, but also a change in the culture's ability to speak truthfully about sex, including variations that have existed across all time.

Depictions of same-sex sexuality date back to the earliest art drawn on the walls of caves by primitive humanity. Twelve thousand years ago, humans entered the darkness of the Addaura caves in Sicily and carved ritualistic scenes on the cavern walls. The drawings showed men in bird masks with genitals displayed, dancing in a circle. In the center of the circle were two men, the erect penis of the man above connected by parallel lines with the buttocks of the man below. Modern tour guides describe the figures as acrobats, as if the men of 10,000 BC went deep into dark caves, circled up, pulled out their erections, and did cartwheels together. The cave's original discoverer offered the likelier but more controversial explanation, that they were drawings of homoerotic initiation rituals.[2]

If that incredibly ancient example remains open to interpretation, more blatant sexual graffiti was recently found on a remote Greek island. Scrawled on the rocks there are two large phalluses and an inscription written in bold letters: "Nikasitimos was here mounting Timiona."[3] Loud and proud from 2,500 years ago.

An even more intriguing example comes from petroglyphs found in the remote deserts of northwest China. Carved into rock more than 3,000 years ago, the Kangjiashimenji petroglyphs portray over a hundred figures in one of humanity's oldest representations of sexual intercourse, and the participants include some rather obviously two-gendered people.[4] Drawn like fancy stick figures, some larger than life size, each individual is depicted with their arms stretched out, every one of them with their right arm bent up and their left arm bent down. The males have triangular bodies, often with distinct erections, while the females have hourglass figures, often with explicit vulvas. Along with males and females are numerous bi-gender figures combining male and female elements, with female headwear and dress along with erections, possibly indicating gender-variant shamans. The gender and sexual combinations depicted in these ancient petroglyphs are fascinating. A clearly female body has a large penis. A female figure is shown giving birth to a series of smaller figures next to a bi-gender figure who was about to penetrate a female. A female is being penetrated by a male and a bi-gender while men with erections dance along with another bi-gender figure. And these kinds of depictions were not unique to western China, as similar dual-sexed figures occur in Neolithic and Bronze Age petroglyphs around the Mediterranean.[5]

A more tangible example of gender variation came from a tribe of early Bronze Age people living five thousand years ago near modern Prague in the Czech Republic. Their custom was to bury their men on their right sides with their heads facing east along with weapons, tools, and flint knives, and buried their women with their heads facing west with their jewelry, pets, and distinctive egg shaped jars. In 2011, archaeologists dug up a male skeleton buried in the female position, without weapons, but with household jugs and the egg shaped jar at his feet.[6] There is no way to know how this man lived his life — if he was gay or lived his life as a woman. All we know is that when he died, his people gave his male body a respectful burial in the manner of a woman, probably reflecting something about how he lived his life.

Humanity invented written language about five thousand years ago, and among the oldest literature is the ancient Sumerian *Epic of Gilgamesh*. Found in fragments of cuneiform on ancient clay tablets, the epic tells of the adventures of King Gilgamesh and Enkidu, the wild man he loved. Both men were sexual with women, but they formed a lasting bond with each other from the time they met. Most of the surviving fragments center on the king's grief after Enkidu's death, describing in long and poetic detail the king tearing his hair and clothes, wearing animal skins, and journeying far from his kingdom in grief and terror over his own mortality. Bereft at the loss of his friend's body, the gods finally allowed Gilgamesh to speak to his dead friend, who tells the grieving monarch: "That which you cherished, Enkidu then confided, that which you caressed and which brought happiness to your heart, now, like an old garment, it is devoured by the worms. That which you cherished, that which you caressed and which made your heart glad, is today covered in dust. It is all plunged to dust."[7]

If *Gilgamesh* is the oldest human story, the earliest portrait of a same-sex couple is even older. Early Egyptians rarely portrayed sex. The most intimate figures on the walls of Egyptian tombs depicted couples with faces turned nose to nose, arms holding each other in that wonderfully stiff Egyptian style. In a tomb where two males were found buried together in the custom of a married couple, a portrait on the wall showed the two men holding each other, arms intertwined and nose to nose. Their names reveal their bond, as one is named Niankhkhnum which means "joined to life" and the other is Khnumhotep meaning "joined to 'the blessed state of the dead.'" So together their names mean "joined in life and joined in death."[8] No "till death do us part" for this couple.

For a more evocative story, one night in 2300 BC, Pharaoh Neferkare left his palace and walked to the house of a general named Sisene. Standing outside in the street, the records say that Neferkare tossed a stone at the house and stamped his foot until a ladder was lowered for him to climb up for the evening. The story mentions love, but also clarified that the king was motivated to see the general "because there was no woman [meaning wife] there with him."[9] What a crazily visual scene that makes — a Pharaoh roaming darkened streets over 4,300 years ago in search of intimacy with another man.

A millennia and a half later a more complex story unfolded around the famous figures of King Tutankhamen, Queen Nefertiti, and Pharaoh Akhenaten. Nefertiti, as portrayed in a limestone bust discovered in 1912, is considered one of history's most iconic beauties. She was married to Pharaoh Akhenaten, who was often depicted with curving feminine hips, thick rounded thighs, and pronounced sagging breasts. Akhenaten may also have been the father of King Tut, an otherwise unimportant boy king made famous by his tomb of well-preserved art, although the familial connections remain uncertain. In the fourteenth year of Akhenaten's reign, Nefertiti's name disappeared from the official records and a new male figure named Smenkhkare appeared as Akhenaten's co-ruler and apparent lover. Images of the two show them physically intimate. In one image the older king caressed young

Smenkhkare's chin, and in others the youth poured the king wine or sat in the king's lap.

While there is no definitive version of the story, Egyptologists used to think Smenkhkare was Akhenaten's son, but the records list only daughters. Tomb objects were inscribed "Smenkhkare beloved of Akhenaten" and "Akhenaten beloved of Smenkhkare."[10] Another theory hypothesized that Queen Nefertiti became co-Pharoah and took the male name Smenkhkare to enhance her legitimacy. A more straightforward answer may be that the androgynous Akhenaten fell in love with a young man named Smenkhkare and left Nefertiti behind. If it is true that Akhenaten openly loved a young man named Smenkhkare, then they are the earliest gay couple in history whose proper names are known to us today.

Much more is known about another Egyptian Pharoah who lived blatantly across gender lines. Pharaoh Hatshepsut was born female, rose to the throne around 1479 BC, and was considered one of the most successful rulers in all of Egypt's long history. As part of her claim to traditionally male power, she often donned the accoutrement of male rulers. The monolithic statues honoring her reign sometimes depicted her as male, sometimes as female, and often as a mixture of both, including a false beard. The sprawling Temple of Hatshepsut is one of the greatest monuments of ancient Egypt, still standing strong on the banks of the Nile at Luxor, bearing witness that gender shifting is a very old tradition indeed.

All of these stories come from thousands of years ago. Long before modern labels like gay, straight, and transgender existed, people drew depictions of gender variations and same-sex sexuality on cave walls and ancient tombs, displayed their respect for human variations in their burial customs, wrote the stories of same-sex love in the earliest epics, and recorded our existence in the oldest human records; yet none of these people were gay in the modern sense. For them, same-sex sexuality and gender variations were just another part of human existence. As pre-modern gay people they loved whom they loved, and lived how they lived, and left a trail of evidence for later generations to decipher. Once that code is unlocked around the way these gay lives are represented in such ancient times, the entire lesbian, gay, bisexual, and transgender spectrum is revealed, even when those terms were still thousands of years away.

Pre-modern gay people were not so visible because they lived in villages. People today think cities are normal, as half the world's population now lives in urban areas, but that is a recent phenomenon. Classical Athens had around sixty thousand adult male citizens, and ancient Rome at its height had less than half a million people. By 1800, the two largest cities on Earth were London and Beijing with around a million people each.[11] So until about a hundred-and-something years ago, pretty much every human being lived in a village-like social structure of five to thirty families, or seventy-five to 150 people, numbers consistent across European forests, African savannas, and Pacific islands.[12] In small human clusters, the 5% who varied, in often subtle ways, may not have been so visible. In a community of one hundred, one might have been a married bisexual woman, another an effeminate older man, a third an androgynous teen, a fourth an unmarried lesbian, and a fifth a newborn child. In that scenario, there is no way for those people to see a common thread in their life experiences. It was only later when humanity gathered into larger cities that these more subtle variation patterns became more visible.

As gay people we form a sort of loose tribe, for lack of a better term. Seldom related by blood, we are not an ethnicity, a religion, or a racial group. What differentiates us from the mainstream is not family heritage, spiritual beliefs, skin color, eye folds, or nationality. The entire concept of using sexuality and gender as a way to categorize people is distinctly modern, yet we have always existed with shared experiences and a shared history. Nature made us different, but our experiences bring us together. When I consider all those people living their varying lives across time and geography, I think of them as my queer ancestors. They are the ancient members of my tribe, the misty progenitors of my modern life.

Having covered some of the oldest examples, the next chapters discuss a diversity of archetypal ways we show up in historic and modern lives, a collection I think of as my village people: shamans, two spirits, Amazons, monks, minstrels, and married couples, among others, a variety of gay manifestations that helped create the world we live in today.

Shamans

Earth's crammed with heaven,
And every common bush afire with God:
But only he who sees takes off his shoes.

~ *Elizabeth Barrett Browning*

BEFORE THE ARRIVAL of large organized religions, the intermediaries between humanity and the larger everything-else were called shamans, and many of those shamans were gay. One of my favorite stories from this tradition comes from an African shaman named Malidoma Somé, who goes by his first name which means "friend of the enemy-stranger." Malidoma is an amazing man. After finishing his education in France, the elders of his tribe told him to leave the village and his people and go live in the West, taking their spiritual traditions abroad to help heal the ailing modern cultures, declaring, "The village will be reborn in the heart and soul of the culture that is destroying the village."[1]

I had the good fortune to meet Malidoma, an energetic and charismatic man with an incredible life story he shares in his book, *Of Water and the Spirit*.[2] Born into a family of shamans in the Dagara tribe of Burkina Faso, Malidoma was kidnapped at four years of age by French Jesuits who raised him to be a priest. The priests gave him a Western education in French and banned all knowledge and discussion of his native language and culture. At fifteen Malidoma escaped and made his way back to his village. On his return, his elders viewed him as an outsider because of his strange upbringing. From their perspective, his Westernized education had left him with so little soul in his body that they feared he could not survive the traditional initiation rituals that marked the passage of young men into adulthood.

With great difficulty, Malidoma passed his initiation, a series of tests and experiences led by a group of men the Dagara call gatekeepers. In their otherwise open culture, only the gatekeepers were allowed to operate in secret. According to the Dagara's traditions, gatekeepers were essential to the health of the overall community, standing in the doorways between this life and the spirit worlds, keeping the gates open for the energies to flow back and forth. Once a year, the gatekeepers went out of their village to do the sacred rituals that made them gatekeepers. Rituals so important, the Dagara believed, that if the gatekeepers did not go out and do them, the village might not survive another year. Rituals so sacred and secret that the gatekeepers had the right to kill any outsiders who observed them.

As a young adult, Malidoma went to Paris to attend the Sorbonne university for the first of his several doctorates. While living in Paris he met gay people, and as he puts it, he recognized their vibrations. On a return visit to his village Malidoma went to the gatekeeper who had guided him through his initiation and asked the gatekeeper if he had sexual attractions to other men. The man was shocked, asking back, "How do you know that?!" adding, "This is *our* business as gatekeepers."[3] Gay people existed in Malidoma's village society, and even had their own socially-recognized grouping, but they were not called by the LGBT names we use in the West.

In the traditional world Malidoma grew up in, everyone married and had children. There were no "gay people" in the modern sense, but there were children born with slightly different vibrations, a quality that allowed the elders to identify those children as gatekeepers. They were like any other child on the outside, but a young male gatekeeper vibrated female energy and a young female gatekeeper vibrated male energy. In the Dagara world it was those vibrations, and not genitalia, that determined gender. They were just regular people with differing vibrations that allowed them to connect with the planet's highest vibrational points, the places where the gates between worlds were located. In the cultural understanding of these ancient people, gatekeepers were essential to the health and survival of the planet. Only by caring for the gatekeepers, and making sure they were at their posts, could the earth and humanity survive.

The Dagara had a cultural understanding of gay people that transcended individual villagers' lifetimes, carrying a deeper understanding across generations. My heart sighs at the idea of grandmothers experienced at identifying their gay children, parents with the cultural knowledge of how to raise those children into their unique strengths, and circles of gay adults who gathered to nurture those strengths in each other. I cannot imagine how different modern society will be when cultural institutions like churches and schools recognize the children who vibrate a little differently, and know how to teach those children to understand where they fit into life, society, and the greater forces of the universe.

Malidoma's story also illustrates how difficult it can be to map same-sex sexuality across cultures. Some of my queer ancestors thrived as a respected subset of a prominent African tribe, but they were labeled with spiritual and social labels that did not automatically ring the LGBT bell. Even Malidoma and the people of his village, who knew each other's lives intimately, did not view their gatekeepers through the gay-straight lens. But not wearing a modern label does not mean they were not there, an important fact to remember when political and religious leaders claim there are no gay people in their cultures. We are always there, even when our neighbors cannot see us.

[For the full interview with Malidoma Somé, see Gatekeepers on page 301.]

Stories of African shamans can feel foreign, as Judaism, Christianity, and Islam moved the gods out of the earth, animals, and plants and consolidated the divine into a single supreme deity living in the sky. Understanding the magic of this earlier world, however, is essential to understanding the importance of shamans. In his breathtaking essay, *The Ecology of Magic*, David Abrams explained this ancient paradigm in ways that resonated strongly for me as a gay person, starting from his first-hand experience with the shamans of Bali in Indonesia.[4] As he tells the story, Balinese shamans live on the edge of their villages, or just outside of the community, and are viewed as a little scary. This physical distance and fearful respect kept people from bothering the shaman too much with their petty needs, but also represented the role they played.

I have always thought of shamans as mediating between this world and the spirit world, more in the way Malidoma describes. But the concept of spirit is problematic, as each individual carries their own definition or understanding of what it means. In Abrams's explanation, shamans lived at the balancing point between the world of humanity and the world of everything else — nature, animals, crops, weather, the land, and the forces beyond. Illness in this traditional world was believed to be rooted in an imbalance, and it was the shaman's job to live at the edge and ensure the human life force and the natural energies flowed back and forth in a balanced manner, for the wellness of both and the overall prosperity of the people. Scholars of pre-modern religions like Mircea Eliade pointed out the importance of androgyny and varying sexuality in identifying those with shamanic energy.[5]

Standing at the border of masculine and feminine, gay and differently gendered healers understood the relationship between human lives and the rest of nature, and between human beings and the supernatural, in a different way than anyone else in the tribe. As the medicine women and men, we were often the village healers. Working through magic and dance, song and touch, journeying and trances, we bridged the worlds and healed souls, bodies, and the earth. As the people who walked between worlds, we looked across energetic divides and wove the disparate elements together into a healthier life for everyone.

With their God up in the heavens, later religions needed people who could mediate between this earthly life and their God above, so gay people became the priests and nuns. Our sensitivity to human needs informed our earthly ministries, and our healing compassion and bridging natures connected our flocks to the higher truths. As an added bonus, we excelled at theater and marketing, making us particularly effective in organized church services and hierarchical religious structures.

Tragically, those of us born today with this kind of shamanic understanding can find ourselves blocked from using these gifts by the dissociations of modern life. To manage the disconnect between the cold world we live in and the deeper truths we feel, the sensitive often turn to the coping mechanisms of modern culture like drugs, alcohol, sex, and materialism. Looking at the modern gay community I see the social problems but I also see a community of people denied their birthright and doing the best they can. "In a society that is profoundly dysfunctional," Malidoma explained, "what happens is that peoples' life purposes are taken away, and what is left is this kind of sexual orientation which, in turn, is disturbing to the very society that created it." He called out Christianity in particular for making gay people into "a disempowered person, a person who has lost his job from birth onward, and now society just wants to fire him out of life. This is not justice. It's not justice. It is a terrible harm done to an energy that could save the world, that could save us. [...] The gatekeepers have been fired from their job. They have been fired! They have nothing to do! And because they have been fired, we accuse them for not doing anything. This is not fair!"[6]

For those who have the powers to see, gay people are much more than our sexuality. I once drew a picture of myself standing on the earth, but bent over sideways at the waist. One arm stretched far up into the sky until it touched the highest point of the heavens, while my other arm stretched down into the earth until it touched the deepest dark of the underworld. That is what it feels like to hold that shamanic energy, spanning the light and the dark at the same time. A healthy humanity includes all the light and all the dark, which makes the people who can span those contradictions essential, in opposition to the forces that threaten to rip us apart.

Anyone can have this power to span contradictions. It is not a gay or straight quality, but it is a gift many gay people have — this willingness to wrap our arms around all that is sacred, and all that is profane (meaning the not-sacred, or earthy), and then attempt to balance through the ebbs and flows of life. That is the shamanic energy. That is the power many gay people, and queer spirits of every different kind, have running through our bodies. If the earth and society are out of balance, then it is time to draw on some of humanity's most ancient wisdom, and give the shamanic people their jobs back.

One very different example of the shamanic temperament is hidden in fairy tales. In many old European tales there is a self-empowered individual who lived outside the village circle, balancing light and dark energies, known for healing and other powers, but routinely labeled evil because she was a woman who threatened the all-male power structure. The stories always start the same way: Once upon a time… a wrinkled old woman lived in a crooked little house in the deep dark of the forest. She lived there alone, far from the other people of the village, which was daring and brave in those dangerous times.

For reasons usually unstated in the story, this was a woman confident in her own strengths, using the fears of others to gain some independent living in much the way Abrams noted in Balinese shamans. These women, derided as evil witches by the ignorant, lived without a man, a powerful clue to her true nature. The modern tellings often made her ugly, but in older versions she could be beautiful and seductive, but indifferent to men. Most importantly, the stories tell of her powers in potions and healing, and how she was someone people, and often other women, would go to as a last resort in times of trouble.

Taking off the fairy tale glasses and putting on modern lenses, many of these "witches" were lesbian or women profoundly queer in some other way. In response to their powers, the Christian churches demonized them, made them into figures of scorn and fear, and burned them alive.[7]

Disney's films did a lot to popularize this single-minded picture of the witch as evil, but even Disney Corporation is now embracing fuller versions of the archetype in recent movies like *Maleficent* and *Into The Woods*. These newer witches remain unmarried and childless and can still be careless with their hair, but they retain their powers and are thoughtful, passionate, and strong. As the narrator declares at the end of *Maleficent*, the story behind the witch in Sleeping Beauty: "In the end, my kingdom was not united by a hero or a villain as legend predicted, but by one who was both hero and villain."[8] That is the world that I live in, where powerful people meld the light and the dark energies to benefit all, a quality honored in the archetype of the shaman.

Two Spirits

Nothing is as strong
as gentleness,
Nothing as gentle
as real strength.

~ *St. Francis De Sales*

IN THE SPRING OF 1886, President Grover Cleveland formally received a representative from the Zuni nation of the American Southwest, a "princess," as the newspapers called her, named We'wha (pronounced WAY-wah). On arriving in Washington she was presented to members of the Senate, the Congress, and the Supreme Court and became friends with the speaker of the House and his wife.[1] Over the summer she spent there, We'wha gave demonstrations of Zuni weaving and consulted with anthropologists at the

Smithsonian Institution. She had much to teach, as she was considered one of the greatest living experts on the Zuni religion. And We'wha was born physically male.

In the Zuni tradition, there was a place for people who differed from the gender norms, people they called two spirits. Not only was We'wha an elegant woman, she was also six feet tall and square jawed, with a sturdy build. Photos of We'wha show her as strong, dressed in traditional clothing that mixed male and female elements, along with the traditional female Zuni hair style and elegant jewelry. Anthropologists used to use the offensive French term *berdache* for third gender North American natives, but today two spirit is preferred.

Some people of the time said We'wha was a man trying to pass as a woman, as if being two spirit was some kind of trick. Americans of the time lived in a world that recognized only two human genders, but in We'wha's world being a two spirit was a blessing, the result of divine intent. She was honored by her tribe, serving as a mediator and as the Kolhamana Kachina who brought rain and good fortune, before becoming a cultural ambassador to white America.

In a way nearly incomprehensible to many people even today, We'wha was not considered either a man or a woman in her culture, as she represented a third category altogether. While believed to embody male and female elements, two spirits were often larger and stronger than other men, and could be fierce warriors, notably aggressive and even hyper-masculine. Lakota and Ojibway warriors thought it pumped up their masculinity to have sex with a two spirit to take in some of that excess masculinity,[2] and the early Spanish explorer Álvar Núñez Cabeza de Vaca wrote that he saw among the natives in Florida: "a man married to another. Such are impotent and womanish beings, who dress like women and perform the office of women, but use the bow and carry big loads. Among these Indians we saw many of them; they are more robust than the other men, taller, and can bear heavy burdens."[3]

There is no place to map this Native American conceptualization of a third gender into the modern West's dualistic views of gender and sexuality because third gender people were neither male nor female, and neither straight nor gay. The best way to understand is to consider an indigenous American male partnering with a male-born two spirit. Neither partner would then be considered homosexual because their coupling was between a man and a third gender, and not between a man and another man.[4]

The power of this tradition arose in cultures that knew how to nurture their variant children. The Tohono O'odham, or Papago, of the Sonora desert would notice if a boy was not interested in typical boyish play and give him a test. They constructed a circle of brush, putting a man's bow and a woman's basket in the center. The boy was then told to go in and retrieve one of them, and when he did, the bushes were set on fire. If he brought out the women's object, he was deemed a two-spirit.[5] The Mojave did a similar test through a community ritual of song and dance. A hidden singer would sing the ritual songs, and if the boy danced in the manner of a woman, he was a two-spirit. If it was in his nature, they believed, "he cannot help it."[6] Anthropologist Will Roscoe has identified at least 150 tribes across North America who honored their two spirits including the Lakota, Mohave, Crow, Cheyenne, Zuni, Pueblo, and Navajo.[7]

Women too could be two spirits, adopting male roles and serving as warriors. One famous example was a woman named Pine Leaf, born to the Gros Ventre tribe in 1806. After her twin brother was killed by the Blackfoot tribe, she swore vengeance and became such a successful warrior that she continually rose in rank until she became part of the Council of Chiefs of the Crow people where she was known as Woman Chief, leading the Crow from 1830 to 1851. She even hired other women to do the female duties that did not interest her. White Americans who met her were confused by this powerful woman, and called her the Absaroka Amazon, *absaroka* being the native name for the sparrow hawk mistranslated as "crow."

In the southern Mexican state of Oaxaca there are Zapotec indigenous communities where the two-spirit tradition survives to this day. Referred to as *muxes*, a word derived from the Spanish *mujer* for woman, *muxes* are physically male but dress and live as a third gender, mixing male and female elements. Not only do they find employment in traditionally female fields, but they are accepted by their communities and valued by their families because of their tendency to stay home and care for their parents.[8]

Outside of cultural considerations, a child's body at birth can place some people in the category of third gender, as they are born with ambiguous genitalia, or the genitalia of both sexes, a physical condition called intersex. In traditional India, intersex people formed an entire caste called *hijras*, another label without Western counterpart. As part of their third gender identification, it was traditional for *hijras* to remove any vestigial male genitalia. Like North American two spirits, South Asian culture viewed *hijras* as neither male nor female, but a third gender category of their own, but unlike the Native American reverence for two spirits, India's *hijras* were rejected by mainstream society. Shunned by their families and villages, *hijras* formed their own communities for solidarity and support.

To understand their world, consider an intersex baby born with ambiguous genitalia among the poor of India or Pakistan. Given a baby whose body did not fit the gender norms, parents might abandon their newborn on a local *hijras'* doorstep. Although usually extremely poor and of low social status, the *hijras'* tribal solidarity drives them to take these children in as one of their own, feed them, and help them learn to live their life performing ceremonies, begging in the streets, and serving as sex workers.[9]

Given the timelessness of their tradition, it was exciting news recently when India's Supreme Court, which was not generally favorable to gay rights, honored the historic role of *hijras* in their culture and ruled for transgender rights, allowing them to legally identify as third gender, ruling: "It is the right of every human being to choose their gender," and, "...the Constitution states that all citizens shall have the right to freedom of speech and expression, which includes one's right to expression of his self-identified gender. Self-identified gender can be expressed through dress, words, action or behavior or any other form."[10]

I find the way these terms and categories from various cultures resist easy translation fascinating, as one culture's understandings of gender is transported to another culture and changed along the way. A famous example is the Buddhist bodhisattva, or enlightened being, named Guanyin. I first fell in love with her as a white porcelain statue sitting in the roots of a tree next to my favorite hot springs, which was perfect as she represents compassion, mercy, and healing. In the typical depictions in Chinese art, Guanyin was an elegant woman in beautiful flowing robes, but in India, where her legend started, Guanyin was a male figure called Avalokitesvara, who was depicted as an androgynous young man. As the images and stories of Avalokitesvara moved east with the spread of Buddhism into China, they entered a culture that lacked the concept of a third gender, so the Chinese mistook the feminine androgyny of the male Avalokitesvara for a woman. Classical

Chinese also considered compassion and mercy to be feminine virtues, so in East Asia Guanyin became a woman, making her the only female Buddhist deity. To this day, the figure of Guanyin is one of the most popular in Asia, and because of her story, some transgender people consider her their patron saint.[11]

Most of my own experiences of distinctly third gender people in other cultures were with the *kathoey*, or ladyboys, of Thailand, a group that has been part of that culture for centuries. I have met ladyboys who varied from highly effeminate men to others who seemed to have a more complex transsexual or intersex nature. Travelers to Thailand often note that many ladyboys are authentically effeminate and lovely. The first ladyboy I met in Thailand was working in a suburban market in Bangkok and was more like We'wha, tall and broad shouldered but impeccable in her conservative dress and makeup, and deeply shy. I later got to know a more gregarious ladyboy working as a waitress at a beachside restaurant after she became smitten with me when I showed her kindness. I felt bad when she was crestfallen after I confessed I did not in fact have a thing for ladyboys in the ways she had hoped.

In contrast to every stereotype, one of Thailand's most famous *kathoey* was Nong Tum, who became a national celebrity as a champion kickboxer in Muay Thai, one of the world's fiercest fighting forms. The movie *Beautiful Boxer* tells his inspiring story of rising through the fighting world to get out of rural poverty and win enough money for sexual reassignment surgery. Nong Tum now lives her life as the beautiful woman she felt she was born to be.[12]

Another culture famous for honoring its third gender people is visible in the South Pacific's *fa'afafine* tradition of the Samoan islands. Usually born male, *fa'afafine* means "in the manner of a woman" and the *fa'afafine* balance masculine and feminine elements. Like other third gender people, they were not necessarily gay or homosexual in the Western sense, but live in another third gender category altogether.[13] Traditional *fa'afafine* were considered an essential part of Samoa's large communal family system where their combination of masculine strength and feminine skills were highly valued, and to honor their importance, the Prime Minister of Samoa, Tuilaepa Sailele Malielegaoi, recently declared to a group of *fa'afafine*: "You are just another shining example of the glorious miracles and creations of our Lord."[14]

A similar tradition existed in the islands of Hawaii where the in-between people were called mahu and considered part of the spiritual tradition of aloha, embracing love and respect for all.[15] Although largely suppressed after the arrival of Christian missionaries, the concept of the mahu remains striking. Imagine a large and powerful Polynesian native Hawaiian, born male or intersex and enlivened by a culture that honored her embodiment of all the masculine and feminine energies. Picture her standing strong on a warm sand beach, wrapped in a sarong with a flower in her hair, dancing and teaching the interweaving hand motions, steps, and undulations of the hula beneath a setting tropical sun. For me that scene embodies the power of the two spirits, reaching out to us today in a language that is exotic, primal, elegant, and delicately beautiful, all at the same time.

Amazons

Well-behaved women
seldom make history.

~ *Laurel Thatcher Ulrich*

AFTER CONQUERING THE INCAS from the Pacific, the Spanish conquistadors crossed the Andes mountains and descended into the great jungle basin that fills the center of the South American continent. Finding the region inhospitable, and food growing scarce, a group of fifty men including a Dominican priest named Gaspar de Carvajal, built boats and set off down the river in search of food.[1] After traveling downstream for a few days they realized they had gone too far and would not be able to get back up the river, so they decided to keep going downstream and see where it led.

Along the way, the explorers saw vibrant villages lining the river's banks, and heard stirring tales of warrior women. On June 24, 1542, the Spanish group was raiding a local village to steal their food supplies when they suddenly met and fought the female warriors for whom the Amazon is named. It is not known how much of the Spanish account was true and how much embellishment, but De Carvajal described those fighting women as the fiercest warriors they encountered. He said they were tall and white, robust, and mostly naked, living under a queen named Coñori.

The Spanish captured a local man who explained that the warrior women lived days away from the river but ruled over his people through superior strength. When these amazon women wanted to procreate they went out in raids and captured local men to impregnate them before releasing the men back to their homes. Their male children were killed or sent back to their fathers. He said they lived in stone houses with doors, not thatched homes, and their ruling class ate on plates of gold and silver. By the captured man's count there were over seventy villages of amazon women to whom his people sent regular tributes.

There is no way to know the sexuality of these amazons, although as a female-only tribe it seems likely female-female sexuality was part of their relationships. More important than their sexuality, amazons represent the power of gender appropriation. These women took on the traditional powers of men and claimed them as their own, an archetype that resonates to this day.

Surviving the attack, the Spanish expedition continued downriver to the South Atlantic where they were rescued by passing ships. Sadly, it was twenty years before another European expedition dared to make that same journey down the Amazon, and by that time, nearly all the civilizations described by De Carvajal were gone. Historians were left doubting the veracity of De Carvajal's account, disbelieving the Amazon ever supported those kinds of populations, but that presumption may be wrong. In the book *1491*, author Charles Mann lays out the evidence that the pre-Columbian Amazon was richly farmed and populated. The Amazon warriors of De Carvajal's stories, and all those civilizations they encountered, were never seen again, presumably wiped out by the European diseases carried by De Carvajal's group. But to this day the world's largest river, the world's largest rainforest, and the vast basin that makes up 40% of South America are all named for those warrior women.

One other place in the Americas named for female amazons is my home state of California. A Spanish writer named Garcia Rodríguez de Montalvo wrote a fictional story around 1500 about Queen Calafia who ruled an island of black warrior women called California. They flew into battle on the back of winged griffins to fight alongside the Muslims defending Constantinople against the invading Christian crusaders. The book was popular for decades and well known to Hernán Cortés and his men as they explored North America's west coast. On discovering what they thought to be a great island, they named it California, a place that remains semi-mythical to this day.

The word Amazon comes from the records of the ancient Greeks and Romans who told stories of warrior women living on the fringes of their civilizations. While the ancients told these stories as fact, modern historians discounted their tales as romantic mythology, but recent evidence proves the Amazons of Central Asia were real. Archaeologists who dug up warrior remains used to assume that bodies were male if they were found with obvious battle wounds and buried with armor, swords, spears, and bows and arrows. DNA testing of those bodies revealed that over a thousand of these warrior graves across the steppes, from Bulgaria to Mongolia, were female, making up almost 40% of the dead in some sites. This evidence proves the Greek stories placing Amazon cultures to the north and east of the Black Sea were right.[2]

As with two spirits, the subject of amazon women revolves around gender and gender roles, a subject separate from, but interrelated with, sexuality. To tease out the difference, consider an all-female tribe that only used men as tools of procreation and certainly had some lesbian relations, versus powerful warrior women who took on male roles and powers but preferred hetero-sexual relationships. The ancient Greek stories of Amazons never mentioned homosexuality, even though they were profoundly comfortable discussing the topic. For the Greeks, the stories of the Amazons were about gender roles, as the classical Greeks relegated women to confined dress and social roles. Empowered Amazon women, able to face men as their equals or better, became a Greek fascination and one of the favorite subjects in their art. Greek heroes who desired Amazon companions had to prove themselves in battles or physical contests in order to win their affections as no Amazon woman would accept a man who was not her equal.

Stories of female warriors and military leaders exist around the globe, from Egypt, Libya, Siam, Java, and beyond. The Chinese have stories dating back to Fu Hao or "Lady Good," their first recorded female general in 1200 BC,[3] and including Princess Pin Yang who wore men's clothes and formed their first all-female army around 600 AD.[4] And then of course there was Mulan, a name made famous by the animated movie. Born somewhere around 500 BC, Mulan was one of the greatest female warriors in all of China's history. She never married, but she fought for many years, riding her "flying" horse across thousands of miles as part of the Great Wall's defense from the steppe peoples. The steppes are an interesting geographic feature of Eurasia, forming grasslands that run from the mouth of the Danube in Eastern Europe, across central Asia and north of the Himalayas, and almost all the way to the Pacific. That means that while the Greeks were reporting Amazons on the western end of the steppes, warrior women like Mulan were fighting Amazon warriors on the far eastern edge.[5]

Only one amazon culture survived into the modern period, an all-female military regiment of the Fon people in what is now the West African nation of Benin. Europeans called them the Dahomey amazons and early anthropologist Sir Richard Burton referred to them as "black Sparta." A noted chronicler of their history remarked on the difference: "Spartan women kept in shape to breed male warriors, Dahomean amazons to kill them."[6]

For all the tales of amazonian women, perhaps the single most famous female warrior came from Christian history in the form of a peasant girl named Joan of Arc. The Hundred Years' War had decimated France. Royal governance was shaky, and French armies were failing as much of France fell under English control. Into this leadership vacuum stepped a sixteen-year old girl who approached the military commanders with her claim that she received holy visions telling her to drive the English out of France, take the young prince to the throne, and predicting a French military victory at Orléans. Joan ended up convincing the royal court to let her travel with the army to Orléans, dressed and outfitted as a knight, where she led the armies of France to victory, turning the course of the war. Confident that God was on her side, Joan rallied her troops with religious vigor, ignoring the cautious male leaders and leading her army from conquest to conquest, finally capturing Reims and fighting up to the walls of Paris. While Joan cried out for repeated assaults to retake the city, the male political powers weakened.

Joan then received visions she was going to be captured, and on May 23, 1430 she was surrounded by Burgundians, taken into captivity, and sold to the English. A trial ensued where she was accused of heresy, her accusers declaring her visions a lie because God would never speak to a woman. When she would not admit to her crime, they tortured her. Unable to make their accusations of heresy stick, Joan's inquisitors convicted her of cross-dressing based on the Bible's edict that: "The woman shall not wear that which pertaineth unto a man, neither shall a man put on a woman's garment: for all that do so are abomination unto the Lord thy God."[7] Convicted of violating God's laws, Joan of Arc was burned alive for the biblical gender crime of wearing pants.

Looking at Joan of Arc through a modern lens, nothing is known about her sexuality or even her personal sense of gender, but she dramatically claimed a leadership role that her culture reserved for men. In essence she was an amazon, a woman doing typically male tasks, and because she fought from horseback she claimed the right to wear the same clothing and gear as every other horse-mounted warrior. In that sense Joan was a defiantly queer spirit, in touch with her own sense of divine guidance and willing to confront the male-dominated powers of her day. As the Hungarian freedom fighter Lajos Kossuth famously said, "Consider this unique and imposing distinction. Since the writing of human history began, Joan of Arc is the only person, of either sex, who has ever held supreme command of the military forces of a nation at the age of seventeen."[8]

As a quick aside on the topic of dresses versus pants, wrapping a cloth around the body is a pretty timeless form of attire, a fact equally true for men and women — picture Egyptian loincloths, Greek tunics, Roman togas, Scottish kilts, Asian sarongs, and Japanese Kimono, to name a few. Pants, on the other hand, require more complicated tailoring, so they only became popular with the rise of horseback riding cultures, where sitting with one leg on each side of the horse was essential.[9] Given how fundamental a wrap of cloth is to clothing the human body, the persistence of the Western taboo against a man in a "dress" remains a mystery to me, but it does demonstrate the power of cultural gender norms. To illustrate the oddness of this cultural presumption, try imagining the historical Jesus giving up his flowing robes for a shirt tucked into his pants.

The word Amazon resonates across time as one of humanity's great archetypes of women who were beautiful, powerful, and the equals of men. H.L. Mencken famously said, "Every normal man must be tempted, at times, to spit upon his hands, hoist the black flag, and begin slitting throats."[10] I am grateful I live in such a peaceful culture where I will never have to kill another human being, but I must also be a fairly normal man because I know exactly what Mencken was talking about, and so do plenty of women, now and across history. If the archetype of the two spirit is of men blending in the beauty of the feminine, then the archetype of the Amazon is its corollary — of women bringing in the masculine and blurring the boundaries of gender in the fiercest possible ways.

Monks

> At the still point
> of the turning world.
> Neither flesh nor fleshless;
> Neither from nor towards;
> at the still point,
> there the dance is.
>
> ~ *T.S. Eliot*

SOME OF MY ANCESTORS were born too sensitive for traditional village life. They did not fit in the everyday tumult. They were too quiet and too tapped into the knowing fields of the universe to synchronize with the mundane activities of everyday life. Those too queer and different to live among other human beings withdrew into seclusion on the tops of mountains and the insides of caves, preferring solitude over societies where they did not fit. Some of those retreating ancestors formed monastic communities of nuns or monks, an option that offered status and legitimacy while removing the sexual pressures to marry and procreate.

Not every monk or hermit was gay in the sense that I live a gay life, of course, but it should be no surprise that many men and women who chose celibacy had something atypical in their sexual natures. Proof of the number who were queer in some way was revealed when living as an openly gay person became more acceptable. Lifelong retreats into celibacy became a lot less appealing and the number of nuns and priests dropped sharply. Understanding the sexuality of those who retreat into religious abstinence is difficult. Anecdotally I have heard many stories of gay and differently gendered monks who speak of their experiences with frank acknowledgment of a sexual, or asexual, component now that they are allowed to feel their inner truths more freely.

For those who were not so spiritual it was possible to live under a bridge, as a ferryman at a distant crossing, or as the hermit in a mountain cave. Throughout history, some of us have sought ways to retreat from the social tumult. However we managed it, queer spirits of every stripe sought our own quiet niche where they could live our lives in peace. Straight, gay, or asexual, I happily include these more monastic lives within my family of queer ancestors. And of course I honor anyone with the fortitude to let go of society's noise and diversions and genuinely embrace the gifts of silence, solitude, and communion with the transcendent aspects of life.

Wanderers

If the center of the culture is missing,
you will find it at the edges.

~ *Michael Meade*

NOT EVERYONE WHO LEFT the village retreated into quiet, as some of my queer ancestors exploded into boisterous parades of wandering entertainers, performing and busking for money to make their way. Filled with color and life, these entertaining people lived as minstrels, musicians, singers, balladeers, poets, bards, puppeteers, and troubadours, wending their way down the forested roads of Europe, across the dry Sahel of Africa, through the jungles of Mesoamerica, and over the Silk Road of Asia. Some of us were born with theatrical spirits — too colorful, melodic, and dramatic to fit in with the ordinary. We liked spangly clothes and funny hats and made all the world our stage. For queer children trapped in claustrophobic towns, the sounds of flutes and cymbals approaching on the country road were the sounds of our hearts. Watching the puppet shows, hearing the ribald tales, seeing the magic and theatrics of the traveling shows, we knew we were meeting our true people.

Running away with the circus meant finding a place where the queer, freakish, and different were welcomed, or at least employed. Such options could be life-saving for a bearded lady or someone with a half-male, half-female body. Looking around San Francisco's gay community today it is easy to picture many of my colorful gay brothers and sisters as bawdy entertainers brightening the pre-media world. This same tradition persists in Hollywood, Broadway, Bollywood, the East End, and everywhere the colorful gather to entertain with their talent, sparkle, and fountains of merriment.

And merry we were. Think of Robin Hood's band of men living as pranksters in the woods without women. Modern minds can now imagine what kind of men would gather in a community together outside of society. The delightful Friar Tuck, for example, first chose the male-only priesthood of the church, and then a male-only gang in the forest, which left me wondering about him as a kid. Certainly the Merry Men made merry with each other once in a while. One woman, Maid Marian, appeared in some later versions of the stories, but she played little active role.

Men who wanted same-sex companionship and a life of adventure joined the military, serving shoulder to shoulder over long campaigns with their sworn brothers in battle. Sailors and explorers set out to map the globe with other men, far from their wives and children. I always wonder about the sexuality of men in the old stories who left home and traveled for years, and on return, turned around and left again. They certainly lived a very different life on the road from the one they had at home, and their actions showed which one they preferred.

In one of the greatest population movements in American history, the California Gold Rush drew a thousand men a week from around the world in search of new wealth, resulting in a city with fifty thousand men and eight hundred women. It should be no surprise that many of those men found comfort in each other's arms through the foggy San Francisco nights. As a later chronicler wrote of the mining camps in the Rocky Mountains, "Amid the companionship of his friends a man could relax, play cards, have a drink, sample from the free lunch counter, conduct business, or do well-nigh anything within reason that he desired. This stronghold of masculinity was seldom breached by the opposite sex."[1] And while Texas cowboys were portrayed as mythically heroic figures by 1950s Hollywood, the truth was more often like the awkward loners of the movie *Brokeback Mountain* or the pseudo-macho types Willie Nelson sings about in *Cowboys Are Frequently Secretly (Fond of Each Other)*, a song well worth listening to if you have never heard it.

And all those men out in the Wild West needed entertainment. As historian Alexander Saxton described the period, "Minstrelsy had become mass entertainment in the decade of war against Mexico and the California gold rush. Shows were generally performed by males before largely male audiences. Frontier settlements had few females, and contemporary accounts tell of men dancing in saloons and hotel dining rooms dressed as women."[2] There is a wonderful old photograph of Mormon Prophet Brigham Young's stocky son Brigham Morris Young cross-dressing as his alternate persona, the Italian opera diva Madam Pattirini who performed across Utah. It is said he sang a rather convincing falsetto.[3] This same spirit survived into the movies from World War II where servicemen entertained each other by dressing as women. For some a mop of a wig, coconut breasts, and a grass skirt were just humorous props for their ukulele playing, but for others it was a brief taste of freedom.

The Wild West freed women as well, as stories of women dressing in men's clothing and passing as male were not rare. As historian of drag Evelyn Schlatter wrote, "They crossed the boundary between male and female not so much to stretch the limits of nineteenth-century roles but rather to escape the restrictions of womanhood and to seek opportunities available to westering men."[4]

As for sailors, Hollywood got it right in casting Johnny Depp as a flamboyant pirate in the *Pirates of the Caribbean* movies, as many of the Caribbean's pirates, both male and female, were gay. To tell just one of the many stories, Anne Bonny of Ireland dressed as a man and pirated around the Caribbean in the 1700s. At one point their ship, the Vanity, captured another ship and a crew that included Mary Read, a female sailor raised as a boy in London who sailed dressed as a man. On meeting the two fell in love, joined forces, and pirated together, gaining a reputation for bloodthirsty ruthlessness. Finally captured and sentenced to death by the British, they won reprieves because they were both pregnant. It is not clear what happened next, but one rumor claimed they escaped to French Louisiana where they raised their children together.[5]

Flamboyance is one of the most notable traits in some gay people as we unleash our desire to strut the stage and dazzle the crowds. While most gay people live quieter lives under the radar, it is only natural the eye is drawn towards the sparkles, music, and roars of applause. Some of my queer ancestors lived large — dominating the sea lanes, settling new territories, emoting theatrically across stage and screen, and playing music both loud and sweet — playing a variety of roles as we trumpeted culture across the land.

Ages

Crazy old men
are essential to society
because young men
need role models.

~ *James Broughton*

MOST OF MY ADULT life has been spent in committed relationships. If I were to line up my ex-partners they have little obvious in common, ranging from introverted and intellectual to extroverted and social, pale white with red hair to dark black and bald, tall and slim to short and stocky. I have always laughed at the diversity of my taste, but the one commonality they shared was their age. All the men I dated were my contemporaries. I just never found myself attracted to men much older or younger than myself. And then the gods laughed, as they tend to do, and my most recent companion, with whom I shared a relationship and friendship over the years I was writing this book was a dynamic and provocative young man more than thirty years my junior. He was twenty when we met, while I was fifty-one. I liked him from the moment we met, but as I confessed to him later, the extreme youthfulness of his body was not seductive for me. I often had to stare directly into his eyes to see him clearly. As I joked with friends at the time: my previous lover was from Brazil, while my new one was from the '90s. The cultural distances seemed about the same.

Gay people appear most clearly in the historical record in two different ways: in the gender distinctions of third gender people like the two spirits, and in age asymmetrical relationships. For reasons I do not understand, it seems common for straight men to prefer much younger female companions (ask first wives about that one), but the desire for age-differing relationships seems less common in modern gay life. My experience was therefore an outlier, but it taught me some interesting things about why men in the past often chose this dynamic. It can be hard for two male egos to find a balancing point. While some gay relationships have one stronger and one weaker partner, more like the dominant male-submissive female paradigm of traditional heterosexuality, most gay relationships are more equitable. Personally, I need a companion who can stand up to me, push back when I am wrong, and share the journey in a way that feels more equally yoked. In sharing my life with a partner who was young but powerful, we ended up balanced in a way that was growth-inducing for both of us.

History's most famous older-younger same-sex relations were in ancient Greece, in a configuration called pederasty. A word easily confused with pedophilia, pederasty was not older men having sex with children, although pedophilia certainly existed back then. Pederasty was a cultural practice that promoted the formal pairing of a young unmarried man with a teenager who had hit puberty. Arranged and approved by the parents of Athens' privileged classes, the couple was formed by a young man in his early twenties taking an adolescent youth to mentor and protect, providing the youth with a nurturing partner until it was time for the older partner to marry at around thirty. Their coupling provided them both with an emotional connection and a sexual outlet that would not result in unwanted pregnancies.[1] It was the responsibility of the older partner to spend that time teaching the younger how to become a man, educating him in the ways of Greek life, love, and adult responsibilities. Intriguingly, in high class society their sex was limited to one position, called intercrural sex, meaning between the legs, where one man slid his erection between the other man's thighs as they embraced.[2]

While formal pederasty was practiced by a wide variety of cultures around the world, older-younger gay relationships often formed for the simpler reason that two men of differing ages fell in love. My favorite story of this dynamic is of Zahir-ud-Din Babur and the love he found with a boy from the market. Babur was a powerful man who founded the Mughal empire that ruled much of India for centuries. He was a direct descendant of Genghis Khan and predecessor to Shah Jahan who built the Taj Mahal. Babur was such a robust figure that he would put one man over each shoulder and run up hills as a workout, but he was shy towards women. He was married by family arrangement, but avoided his wife. Describing his marriage in the 1500s: "In the first period of my being a married man, though I had no small affection for her, yet, from modesty and bashfulness, I went to her only once in ten, fifteen, or twenty days. My affection afterwards declined, and my shyness increased; in so much, that my mother...used to fall upon me and scold me with great fury, sending me off like a criminal to visit her once in a month or forty days."[3]

Uninterested in sex with a woman, Babur then met a young man who changed his life, a story best told in his own words: "...during this time there was a boy from the camp market named Baburi. Even his name was amazingly appropriate. I developed a strange inclination for him — rather I made myself miserable over him. Before this experience I had never felt a desire for anyone, nor did I listen to talk of love and affection or speak of such things." In Baburi, Babur found something different. "I was so bashful that I could not look him in the face, much less converse with him. [...] There was no possibility of looking at him or of speaking coherently." With the discovery that his true affections were for another man, Babur's emotional world blossomed. "When I fell in love I became mad and crazed. I knew not this to be part of loving beauties."[4]

I can imagine a variety of possibilities for Babur's attraction to this younger man. It may have been that the young Baburi was so distant in class, age, and expectations that Babur could let himself relax into love. The obvious power differential could have been part of the attraction, making the younger man subservient to the domineering Babur. Or maybe the beauty of their relationship came in the feelings of love that transcended the obvious divides. It could be the younger man was delicately effeminate and womanly in a way that complemented Babur's macho spirit but let him overcome his shyness. Or maybe the young man was tough and scrappy in a way that let him stand eye-to-eye as Babur's emotional equal, even as other parts of their lives differed so greatly. As modern readers it is impossible to know the basis for their attractions, but history records, in his own words, that one of humanity's great conquerors, and founder of an empire that lasted for centuries, found his great heart-opening love in the arms of a younger man.

Invoking a Muslim man's same-sex love may sound strange to those who know the version of Islam commonly heard today, but the historian Raymond de Becker claimed that almost all Muslim, Arab, and Persian poetry had a tinge of homosexuality, a strong indication of its earlier acceptance across Islamic cultures.[5] Some of the greatest Arab poets praised the beauty and love of boys, and the Persians, like the Greeks, found young men's beauty a source of inspiration, equating their affections with a higher spirit. The renowned Arab-Persian poet Abu Nuwas wrote openly of his love of men around 800 AD. He called the bath-house a palace of pleasure, describing the handsome buttocks and shapely torsos there, adding, "In the bath-house, the mysteries hidden by trousers, are revealed to you."[6]

One of the history's greatest poets, the Persian known as Hafiz, was a devout Muslim who wrote verses that wove together the base and the sublime:

His mop of hair tangled, sweating, laughing and drunk,
Shirt torn, singing poems, flask in hand,
His eyes spoiling for a fight, his lips mouthing "Alas!"
Last night at midnight he came and sat by my pillow.
He bent his head to my ear and said, sadly,
"O, my ancient lover, are you sleeping?"
...The cup's smile and the wine boy's knotted curl
Have broken many vows of chastity, like that of Hafiz.[7]

One Thousand and One Nights, known as the Arabian Nights in English, is famous for stories of Aladdin's magic lamp, the voyages of Sinbad, and Ali Baba and the Forty Thieves, but it also includes stories of same-sex sexuality. To pick one, in the tale Treasures Without End a young male slave whose beauty shone like the sun brought the Caliph red wine in a cup made from a single ruby. The Caliph drank the wine, and as he handed it back to the radiant slave boy, realized the cup was still full. The Caliph then drank again, and as he handed the cup back to the boy, it was full again. Love for a young man, according to this ancient Arab story, was perpetual intoxication.[8]

As the *Encyclopedia of Islam and the Muslim World* explained: "Whatever the legal strictures on sexual activity, the positive expression of male homoerotic sentiment in literature was accepted, and assiduously cultivated, from the late eighth century until modern times. First in Arabic, but later also in Persian, Turkish and Urdu, love poetry by men about boys more than competed with that about women, it overwhelmed it."[9] In a way it makes sense, as traditional Muslim males are kept apart from unrelated women. The only place unmarried young men filled with sexual vigor could focus their energy was on other men.

An Afghan-American friend once shared with me his belief that the strict sexual segregation and taboos of the Taliban were a distorted form of bisexuality or homosexuality combined with a fearsome misogyny. His comments were confirmed after 9-11 when the foreign press started paying more attention to Afghanistan. A PBS Frontline documentary called *The Dancing Boys of Afghanistan* revealed in disturbing detail the world of *bacha bazi*, or "playing with boys."[10] It seems that even in modern Afghanistan, it is not uncommon for young men to dress and dance as women for male audiences who are otherwise denied female entertainment. This *bacha bazi* tradition is ancient, dating back at least as far as Classical Greece's pederasty, yet is so persistent that a recently published Taliban rulebook stated Rule Nineteen: "Mujahideen [warriors] are not allowed to take young boys with no facial hair onto the battlefield or into their private quarters."[11] It must be a pretty common problem if it is number nineteen in the rulebook.

The *bacha bazi* example raises the issue of child abuse in other times and places. Modern ethics says that adults, straight or gay, should not have sex with children. Reading these historical examples of adult-youth gay relations, I view them through the same lens I apply when reading of heterosexual equivalents. History is full of men having sex with girls and marrying child brides, often with societal approval or indifference. The older-younger dynamic in historical gay relations seems morally equivalent to me. For modern people, though, the morals of other periods can be complicated. Today's Afghanistan, for example, represents a culture standing with one foot in modernity and another in antiquity. The way forward is to strive for cultural understanding while still pushing for proper rights and protections for all children, male and female, in every culture.

Traditional Japanese Samurai *bushido* ethics, or "way of the warrior," offer a different example of older-younger relations in a highly formalized society, more like Greek pederasty. In the Japanese custom though, the younger man chose the older, an intriguing shift in dynamics. This tradition was practiced among warriors and in Buddhist monasteries,[12] and because Japanese culture balanced power with aesthetics, homosexuality was widely celebrated in art and literature. As one author described Samurai *shudo*, or "way of youth," in 1653: "It is natural for a samurai to make every effort to excel with pen and sword. Beyond that, what is important to us is not ever to forget, even to our last moment, the spirit of *shudo*. If we should forget it, it will not be possible for us to maintain the decencies, nor gentleness of speech, nor the refinements of polite behavior."[13]

The world's first novel, the *Tale of Genji*, was written by a Japanese noblewoman in the early 1000s, and included older-younger male-male affection. After being spurned by a woman, Genji, the son of an Emperor, chose the woman's younger brother. "The boy was delighted, such were Genji's youthful charms. Genji for his part, or so one is informed, found the boy more attractive than his chilly sister."[14]

With the opening to the West in the Meiji Restoration of the late 1800s, Japan came under the influence of modern Christian ethics, including its negative views on homosexuality. As a result, the traditional views were suppressed, and homosexuality is not widely discussed in modern Japan. Tokyo, the world's largest city, has no significant gay pride celebrations. The same-sex traditions of *bushido* that survived into the late 1800s are now lost to time.

Along with the Greeks, Romans, Arabs, Persians, Mughals, Afghanis, and Japanese, age-differing relationships were found throughout the world, from casual relationships to formalized cultural structures. Strangely enough, pederasty is a male social structure across the globe, while no formal cultural pederasty among women has ever been found.[15]

People fall in love. Sometimes love comes in the form of couples who choose nearly identical companions for the journey of life. And sometimes love finds its zest in the differences, falling across boundaries of class, race, religion, nationalities, and ages. Straight or gay, modern or ancient, love finds a way, even across our apparent differences.

Families

> I am certain of nothing
> but the holiness
> of the heart's affections
> and the truth of imagination.
>
> ~ *John Keats*

WHEN I WAS YOUNG and trying to puzzle out life as a gay man, I often wondered how I would have lived if I had been born in the simpler times of the traditional village. It may be surprising to hear, but the answer seems obvious to me. I believe I would have successfully followed the default path and married a woman, had decent sex with her resulting in a passel of children, and we would have formed a loving family together. That was the only socially acceptable path available in most traditional cultures, and I have little doubt I could have made it work.

For my queer ancestors, and many gay people today, traditional marriage meant a gay person marrying a straight partner of the other sex. Of course marrying someone of the other sex did not make a gay person straight. It made them a gay person having straight sex. And yet I imagine many of those relationships were a success, muddling through just fine, partly because these marriages occurred inside a different cultural paradigm than the one people live in today. In the traditional world, family bonds centered more on community, rules, and necessity. Love, if it arrived, was a lucky by-product rather than a requirement. I am sure many mixed straight-gay couples made wonderful parents, as long as the friendship side of their relationship remained strong and neither party grew too bitter about the physical and emotional deficits.

For a case study of an older society's approach to these traditional gay-straight marriages, consider one of history's most structured and formalized cultures, Confucian China. According to the philosopher Confucius, relationships were the central element of a moral society. Each individual lived within strictly defined relationships based on obligations: ruler to ruled, father to son, husband to wife, eldest brother to younger brother, and friend to friend. Within that structure, every person was supposed to play their designated roles fully and virtuously. A husband, therefore, had a duty to care for his wives, have children, and be a good steward of the family. But once those responsibilities were fulfilled, what he did with his private time was his own business, unrelated to any sense of morality or obligation. Having a mistress or homosexual relations on the side were not a problem, as long as it did not interfere with his higher obligations. Rather than focusing on the morality of sex acts in the way of Western cultures, Confucian values focused on the individual's duties to others. This is part of why China did not experience the high profile persecutions of homosexuality seen in the West until the later Western values of communism took hold with its anti-gay biases.

In low trust societies, now and in the past, the traditional blood ties of family offered the securest bonds. Modern cultures, on the other hand, rely on institutions like banks, insurance companies, laws, police, and the courts. This change reduced family from the core of a vast and embracing social structure down to the nuclear family, meaning the two parents and their children. Modern ethics tend to say that parents and families exist for the children, while in the traditional world it was the opposite. Children existed to support their parents and provided their only social security, which is part of why people wanted so many. The imperative for children as a component of survival decreased as individual wealth and empowerment grew and economies matured and stabilized.

Even in the traditional world, not everyone reproduced, but almost everyone lived inside the family structure. Survival of the species does not result from every couple producing the maximum number of babies. Evolutionary success comes from the most children possible growing into healthy adults who can reproduce and repeat the process, and having a few extra adults around can help. Because of that, traditional families were sprawling, diverse, and multi-generational. By contrast, modern nuclear families are just two people and their progeny, without much room for varying familial roles or a diversity of support from outside. There is a famous quote attributed to an Australian Aboriginal elder who said, "You white people are so strange. We think it is very primitive for a child to have only two parents." In truly traditional families there were plenty of spots for the treasured aunts, uncles, or cousins. The legacy of these larger families can be seen in the plantation homes of the South, brownstone townhouses of New York, and sprawling farmhouses of New England, as those massive homes with their many bedrooms were not built for nuclear families. They were built in a time when family still meant a small community of people that included the single cousin from the country and the unmarried servants in the attic, all clustered together in service of a larger conceptualization of family.

Many of my gay ancestors married other-sex spouses and had children, conforming to traditional norms and doing the best they could. Some of my ancestors were part of their families in other supportive ways, from the spinsters of old English novels to the *fa'afafine* of Samoa. For those who did not fit into the traditional couplings, families had alternative spaces and roles. Individuals vary, and healthy families have room for them too.

TWELVE

Lovers

Love all,
trust a few.
Do wrong to none.

~ William Shakespeare

SOMETIMES MY GAY ANCESTORS simply fell in love. There was a day, for example, back around the time of Christ, when a Chinese emperor named Ai was asleep with his male lover Dong Xian. When Emperor Ai woke he found that Xian was asleep on his robe's long hanging sleeve, so rather than wake him, the emperor cut off the sleeve. When Ai came into public view with his cut robe, the imperial court so honored the couple's love they adopted the cut sleeve style, and to this day homosexual love in Chinese is called the "love of the cut sleeve." On another day in another time, a duke named Ling loved a male court official named Mizi Xia. One day Xia was eating a peach so delicious he offered half to Ling, who responded with surprise: "How sincere is your love for me! You forget your own appetite and think only of giving me good things to eat!" For the next two thousand years another Chinese euphemism for gay love was the "love of the shared peach."[1]

Mirroring the Roman Emperors of the same period, every Emperor of China's Han dynasty had at least one male lover.[2] Homosexuality was considered a normal part of society through much of China as late as the end of the Ming dynasty around the late 1600s. According to historian Arno Karlen, Arab travelers to China in the ninth century reported from their Muslim perspective: "The Chinese were addicted to sodomy and even performed it in their shrines."[3] Some of the first European descriptions of China came from Dominican friar Gaspar da Cruz who reported in 1569, in language dripping with his Christian disapproval, that he found there: "a filthy abomination, which is that they are so given to the accursed sin of unnatural vice, which is in no way reproved among them."[4] Translated into modern speech, he saw a world where gay life was common and not seen as a problem. Applying his Christian perspective to the natural world, Da Cruz blamed one of the most devastating disasters in history, the Shaanxi earthquake of 1556 that killed over eight hundred thousand people, on God's punishing the Chinese for the sin of homosexuality.[5]

This Chinese tendency to accept sexuality as part of the human condition dates back to the dawn of history. The Yellow Emperor, the ancestor of the Han Chinese and founder of Chinese civilization, lived around 2700 BC and was credited with inventing clothing, boats, the wheel, math, astronomy, and the magnet. He was an important figure in Taoism, and like King Solomon of the Bible, he had hundreds of wives and concubines. He was also the earliest recorded Chinese man to take another man into his bed.[6] Founder of civilization indeed. The long history of China's literature makes clear how casually common homosexuality was in traditional Chinese life. Historian Louis Crompton notes that stories of same-sex love from China are depicted as part of everyday life, in contrast with Western and Arabic traditions where same-sex love was seen as inspiring, ennobling, and distinctly separate from the norm.[7]

The last of China's emperors, like its first, loved men. Anyone who has seen the movie *The Last Emperor* knows Puyi's story: the strangely pampered childhood after his rise to the throne at age two, his mentoring by the Imperial household's eunuchs, his weak government overthrown by the invading Japanese who made Puyi their puppet, and his forced "reformation" under the communists turning the last Emperor of China into just another citizen of the People's Republic. Unlike his portrayal in the movie as a man romantic with his wife, however, Puyi was widely believed to have been gay. He was mocked from youth for his feminine figure and his preference for men. His own sister-in-law wrote in her memoirs that he lived with pageboys as his concubines, and it is not clear he ever consummated his marriages.⁸ His family's version of the story is a fascinating view of an amiable and gentle man caught in the pincers of historical change. In a recent interview, one of Puyi's nieces told reporters that he was such a playful person that as children they felt "he was just like one of the kids," and could not believe such a humble man as their uncle had ever been the emperor of China.⁹

Going back to the origins of Western culture, the ancient Greeks told a delightful story explaining the variations in ways humans love each other. According to this ancient myth, the original humans had four legs, four arms, two sets of genitals, and two faces looking opposite directions, so they looked like two modern people zipped together back to back. These early humans could walk upright, but even better, they could roll really fast with all eight limbs flying around them as they went. As is often the case in these origin stories, early humanity grew arrogant and threatened the Gods. Fearing humanity's collective power, Zeus cut the humans in half, which is why humans today have only one face facing one direction, with two arms, two legs, and only one set of genitals. As Plato told this story in *The Symposium*, those original humans had three sexes. The children of the sun were male on both sides, the children of the earth were female on both sides, and the children of the moon were male on one side and female on the other. Love was described as the feeling every person carries for their missing half. According to Plato, couples who found their missing halves threw their arms and legs around each other in an attempt to meld back together and heal the division rendered by the Gods, or as he put it: "When a man meets the half that is his very own, then something wonderful happens; the two are struck from their senses by love, by a sense of belonging to one another, and by desire, and they don't want to be separated from one another, not even for a moment. These are the people who finish out their lives together and still cannot say what it is they want from one another."¹⁰

Across millennia, across religions and customs, women loved women and men loved men. The stories vary, but knowing the feelings of modern gay people it is not hard to deduce how ancient people felt for each other. They fell in love, kissed, held each other, had sex, made commitments, sacrificed, lost loves, and worked their way through relationships just as human beings do today in every corner of the world. The archetype of the lovers lives on in people like me who seek to give and share love with another human being, just as people have been doing since the beginning of time. Long before the modern concept of gay existed, some of my queer ancestors fell in love. Simple as that.

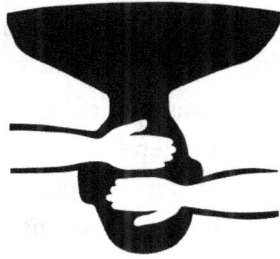

Suppressed

A man should look for what is,
and not for what he thinks should be.

~ *Albert Einstein*

TRAGICALLY, ONE OF THE WAYS my queer ancestors show up most clearly in history is in the records of our oppressors — the cultures that suppressed, persecuted, tortured, and killed us. To choose just one sprawling example from humanity's long and bloody history, consider what happened when Christian Spain spread its conquest across the Americas.

Christopher Columbus landed in the Caribbean in 1492, and the first European account of the Americas was written by the expedition's doctor, Diego Álvarez Chanca. In the highly biased language of his time, Chanca described the Caribes people's custom of castrating young boys to feminize them and use them for sodomy. Of course, it is impossible to trust this kind of reporting filtered through medieval Spanish eyes, so the result is a record that indicates there were openly gay relationships on the islands where Columbus landed, but we have little insight into the true nature of those relationships.

Spanish reporting of that time was particularly suspect because of their own issues around homosexuality and gender, as Spain was plummeting into one of history's darkest religious frenzies. On defeating the Islamic Emirate in Granada, Spain was completing the *Reconquista*, or re-conquest of the Iberian Peninsula for Christianity, after seven hundred years under Muslim rule. To ensure Christian orthodoxy across their realm, King Ferdinand and Queen Isabella, the same royals who funded Columbus's expeditions, initiated the Spanish Inquisition, a reign of terror purging the country of heretics, Muslims, Jews, and homosexuals. According to historian Louis Crompton's research, the Inquisition may be most famous for burning heretics, but court records show the largest group of people killed were gay.[1]

Queen Isabella had her own issues with homosexuality, as her father King John II had an older male lover, Álvaro de Luna, which may have led to the king's nickname, John the Impotent. And when John died, Isabella's gay brother Henry IV took the throne, but it seems he was so gay he failed to consummate his marriage, so was probably not the father of his wife's children, setting up Isabella for ugly struggles to gain the throne.[2]

Because of the Inquisition, the Spanish conquistadors came from a culture where gay people were routinely tortured and killed in the streets of their home cities. When these Spaniards then met and reported on gay and third gender people in the Americas, they viewed them with those same cultural values. As Hernán Cortés reported from Mexico, "We know and have been informed without room for doubt that all [of the natives] practice the abominable sin of sodomy."[3] Francisco Pizarro sent home reports that the South American Incas had sacred male temple prostitutes, or as he put it, "The devil has introduced his vice under the pretense of sanctity. And in each important temple or house of worship, they have a man or two, or more, depending on the idol, who go dressed in women's attire from the time they are children, and speak like them, and in manner, dress, and everything else they imitate women. With them especially the chiefs and headmen have carnal, foul intercourse on feast days and holidays, almost like a religious rite and ceremony."[4] How I wish for a less biased record of what those religious ceremonies were like. I imagine many sexualized religious ceremonies, straight and gay, were decadent and frenzied. I imagine many more as earthy, infused with meaning and symbolism connecting human sexuality with the cycles of the earth, the seasons, and the fertility of plants and animals.

As their conquest spread, Christian Spaniards slaughtered the two spirits and gay people wherever they found them. When Vasco Núñez de Balboa crossed Panama he "saw men dressed like women; Balboa learnt that they were sodomites and threw the king and forty others to be eaten by his dogs," a scene described as, "a fine action of an honorable and Catholic Spaniard."[5] The Spanish in Cuba castrated the native "sodomites," coated the severed testicles with dirt, and made their victims eat them.[6] They burned "effeminate" sodomites as they did in their homelands and sentenced others to an island in Havana's bay called Cayo Puto, or Island of the Faggot. In Mexico City authorities of the Holy Inquisition feared that a culture of sodomites was thriving, so they marched the accused "sodomites" through the streets to the bizarre Christian execution festival called the *auto da fé*, or "act of faith." The church officials spent the day strangling the accused in front of the crowds, and then burned their bodies at night.[7]

We know so little about the pre-Columbian peoples because they died in such vast numbers, first from the unintended genocide of Eurasian illnesses and then through the systematic destruction of their cultures as the Europeans tore down the temples, burned the libraries, and banned the traditional religions. As a result we know little of pre-Columbian philosophers and literature, of their Platos and Da Vincis, or of their myths, science, or technology. Worse, perhaps, we know far too little about their everyday lives. To justify the morality of their ongoing slaughter and conquest, Spanish Catholics exaggerated their reports of cannibalism, human sacrifice, and of course sodomy.[8] Lost to these conquerors was the fact that many of these "sodomites" were sacred people, the healing people of their communities, the shamans and the medicine people, and the keepers of the oral traditions who told the old stories and sang the old songs to teach the young the sacred ways of their people. Of course, to the extent the Christian authorities did understand that these peoples were the carriers of traditional culture, it only made their annihilation more urgent.

Among the stories that survived the conquest, we know that the first people the Europeans met on the American continents, the Mayan people of

Mexico's Yucatan peninsula, incorporated homosexuality into their lives. One of their nature gods was a dwarf named Chin who introduced homosexual relations to the people.[9] The Mayan ruling elite gave their sons handsome younger men from the lower classes as their sexual partners, preferring their sons had pederastic sexual relations than premarital heterosexual intercourse.[10] Some Mayan same-sex partners were even considered legally married.[11] The Maya also practiced transvestism and accepted adult homosexuality as a private affair, and those beliefs show up in their art and religious practices.

The Aztecs, on the other hand, were known for their aggressive machismo, and male homosexuality was not honored. They did however respect masculine women, known as *patlacheh*, who joined with men in battle. Men who were the passive partner in homosexual sex were given harsh punishments, as the offender's bowels were pulled out through his anus, before burning him to death.[12] Friar Bartolomé de las Casas, a historian of the Americas in the 1500s, noted that in Aztec culture: "The man who dressed as a woman, or the woman found dressed with men's clothes, died because of this."[13]

In trying to understand these difference between cultures, one theory says this kind of anti-gay government arose from the way advanced states were formed. The Aztecs and Incas were empires moving into a more modern phase of military and bureaucratic control that saw shamans, and there-fore gay people, as a threat to their centralized power. The earlier Maya, on the other hand, allowed more local control to thrive. Their communities remained closer to nature, the land, and to their community shamans.[14] It appears that rejecting gay people maybe be part of the process of moving away from the earth and embodied spirituality and into more consolidated power structures.

The Aztecs did, however, retain their older traditions of same-sex sexual ceremonies in their temples and a god named Xochiquetzal, who had both male and female sides. The male side of this god was called Xochipilli, who was the Flower Prince and the god of art, beauty, dance, male homosexuality, and male prostitution.[15] As his twin sister she was Xochiquetzal, the goddess of fertility, birth, and female sexual power. Xochiquetzal gave birth to mankind, but after being raped she became the goddess of non-procreative sexuality. Even more powerfully, Aztec history tells of an earlier Age of Flowers when women warriors ruled and men had same-sex relationships and focused on the arts.[17] What a shame the records of that magical time are lost to human history.

How interesting it would be to meet these American "sodomites," read their literature and philosophies, or at least have more neutral reports of how they lived. Because so many of the cultural traditions respectful of gay people were later annihilated and our records expunged, the records of our existence were often written by the hands of our destroyers. Hated and feared by hierarchical powers and religions, sometimes all that is left to show we existed are the stories of our persecution, torture, and extermination.

HISTORY

Greece and Rome

Myth is what we call
other people's religion.

~ *Joseph Campbell*

ANCIENT GREECE STANDS OUT as the root of Western civilization, and no culture in history celebrated homosexuality like the Greeks. Plato, student of Socrates and one of the greatest minds ever, loved men. He never married and declared the love between males the highest form of love, as it was the love between equals. Plato saw the love of a man for a woman, by contrast, to be simply lust, useful only for procreation. As Plato described in his *Symposium*, the bond between men was so powerful that an army of same-sex lovers would be invincible, as they would fight to the death to defend each other on the battlefield.

The Greek belief that homosexuality was normal went all the way up to the great god Zeus, the father of many other gods and men, a status he achieved by having a lot of sex with a lot of different women, divine and mortal. Zeus also loved Ganymede, prince of Troy and described as the most beautiful of mortals. Zeus so enjoyed Ganymede that he took him up to Mount Olympus and granted him eternal youth. In the eyes of the ancient Greeks, the love of Zeus for Ganymede resounded as the archetype for older-younger male relationships.

The name Apollo rings across time as the classically powerful and beautiful young man. Portrayed as the *kouros*, the beardless athletic youth idealized by the ancient Greeks, Apollo was the god of the sun and light, prophecy, healing, music, and poetry. And like so many beautiful young men, he was known for his sexy ways. Among his many loves, Apollo fell for a beautiful young man named Hyacinth. One day they were playing discus together as Zephyr, the god of the west wind who also loved Hyacinth, watched and grew jealous. When Apollo threw the discuss high into the air, Zephyr blew the discus back at Hyacinth's head, killing him. As Hyacinth's head hung from his broken neck, it drooped like a flower blossom from its stalk, and his blood spilled onto the earth. On that spot a beautiful flower sprang up which was named the hyacinth, most probably the flower we now call the iris.

Apollo's twin sister Artemis, called Diana by the Romans, was one of the most important deities of ancient Greece and Rome. As the goddess of the moon, birthing, and the hunt, she represented female power. She lived as a virgin, a maiden hunter with no need for a man. As such she was worshiped by the Amazons. Diana is often portrayed holding a bow with a quiver of arrows over her shoulder or showing her affections for the princess Callisto. She never married and lived as a "sworn virgin" in the woods surrounded by her nymphs — hunting, bathing, and dancing together. Semi-erotic depictions of Diana and her nymphs appear repeatedly in Renaissance art and sculpture, including paintings by Titian and Rubens, and references to Diana appeared frequently in Shakespeare's plays.

Hercules was a massive hunk and such a stud that there is no count of how many women he had sex with. The records claim he bore five hundred children, and the historian Plutarch records that Hercules had male lovers beyond counting. His most famous stories were the labors Hercules performed for King Eurystheus, included cleaning the Augean stables in a day, and in some versions it was same-sex love that motivated Hercules to please Eurystheus.[1] Beyond that, the male lovers of Hercules included Philoctetes, Nestor, Admetos, Iphitos, Euphemos, Elacatas, Abderus, Iolaos, and most consequentially, Hylas.[2]

In Homer's story of Jason and the Argonauts and their quest for the Golden Fleece, Hercules fell in love with the young Hylas. As the poet Theocritus described their love in 300 BC, "We are not the first mortals to see beauty in what is beautiful. No, even [Hercules] loved a boy — charming Hylas, whose hair hung down in curls. And like a father with a dear son he taught him all the things which had made him a mighty man, and famous. And they were inseparable, being together both day and night. That way the boy might grow the way he wanted him to, and being by his side attain the true measure of a man."[3] Hercules helped row the ship Argo, but was so strong that he broke his oar. When the ship next landed, Hercules went off to find a strong tree to make a new oar while Hylas went for water at a famous spring. There Hylas met nymphs who fell in love with his beauty and captured him, possibly dragging him into the water to drown. When Hylas did not return, Hercules was so distraught that when the Argonauts sailed on, Hercules stayed behind to search for Hylas, abandoning the expedition for same-sex love.

To quickly tell just three more from Greek mythology, Dionysus was the god of wine, ecstasy, poetry, and love. Described as womanly, he was lovers to both Adonis, the male god of beauty and desire, and the two-sexed Hermaphroditus. Hermes and Aphrodite had a beautiful son who fell so deeply in love with a female water nymph that the gods combined the two of them, creating the androgynous Hermaphroditus. Usually depicted with a female body and male genitalia, his name was a meld of his parent's names, from which we get the term hermaphrodite. Lastly, Pan is a favorite of mine as he was the half-man, half-goat god of music and nature who lived in Arcadia and chased after women and men with his erect penis, while playing his pan flute, of course. Pan is a wonderfully visual figure who shows up in all kinds of playful art.

As mythology emerges into history, the stars of the *Iliad*, Achilles, invincible but for his heel, and his partner Patroclus, went on adventures around the ancient world, and for nine years they fought the Trojan war together. They were both married, and Achilles fell in love with other men as well, but his commitment to Patroclus remained throughout his life. As Achilles wearied of the war, Patroclus waged a siege against Troy without Achilles at his side and was killed. Achilles was so distraught at the death of his lover Patroclus that he would not let the body be buried, laying with it for days, unsleeping and wailing, "You had no consideration for my pure reverence of your thighs, ungrateful after all our frequent kisses."[4] After cremating Patroclus, Achilles ordered his bones kept in a gold vase, to be intermingled with his own bones when he died, and then to be placed in a single mausoleum.

While Athens represented the love of art and culture, Sparta represented warrior masculinity. Sparta was so powerful it went undefeated in battle for four hundred years, conquering much of Greece. And when Sparta was finally beaten, it was by an army of gay men led by a gay general named Epaminondas. Epaminondas commanded the armies of the Greek city-state of Thebes, was known for his intellect and athleticism as well as his music and dancing, and was said to be so honest he would never lie, not even to joke. I fell in love with Epaminondas on seeing an etching of his handsome profile, and the Roman orator Cicero proclaimed that Epaminondas was "perhaps the most outstanding figure in Greek history."[5] He never married, but he did have a male lover who was considered so brave that when he died, the Greeks hung his shield at the temple of Delphi.[6]

Following Plato's belief that no warrior would fight harder than one defending his lover at his side, Epaminondas gathered one hundred and fifty gay male couples from his armies to form a single fighting unit named to honor the depths of the men's bonds: the Sacred Band of Thebes. Sparta's army was three times larger than the army of Thebes, and the Sacred Band was sent in to battle against Sparta's toughest flank. The Sacred Band fought with such ferocity, killing the Spartan king in the process, that Sparta's army collapsed. Epaminondas then fought Sparta city by city across Greece, liberating the country from Spartan rule and reestablishing citizen democracy as he went. In the end he drove the Spartan army all the way back to their city walls — the first siege of Sparta in six hundred years. Given that this battalion of gay men went undefeated for thirty years, it is a source of bafflement to me that the names of the Sacred Band and their leader Epaminondas are largely lost to history. No story better represents the fighting spirit so many gay men possess.

In later battles, the Sacred Band fought against the Macedonian armies led by Philip II and his eighteen-year-old son, Alexander. Vastly outnumbered, most of the Theban army fled while the Sacred Band fought on, but in the end, Macedonia won. According to legend, 254 of the lovers died, while forty-six survived. Excavations of the battle site in 1903 discovered the cremated dead of Macedonia, and 254 skeletons laid out in seven neat rows, confirming the veracity of the legend of the Sacred Band.[7]

The survivors of the Sacred Band remained important, however, as young Alexander of Macedon went on to become Alexander the Great, possibly the greatest conqueror in the history of the world. At the height of his power, Alexander controlled most of the known world including Greece, Egypt, Persia, and across South Asia to the Indus River in India. Having seen the prowess of the Sacred Band, Alexander incorporated the survivors into his own personal army. Like Epaminondas, Alexander the Great had his own reasons for trusting an army of male lovers, as Alexander became the model for every world conqueror with the help of his own male lover, Hephaestion.

Married twice, Alexander had difficulty producing an heir, but had multiple male and female lovers, including a young Persian eunuch named Bagaos in Babylon and an Afghani princess named Roxanne. Alexander's greatest love, however, was for his childhood friend Hephaestion, a general Alexander trusted so deeply that Alexander gave Hephaestion control over half of his armies so they could perform dual movements together. Alexander even had a special name for Hephaestion, "Philalexandros," meaning lover of Alexander or Alexander's dear longtime friend. The love between Alexander and Hephaestion was so great that they made a special trip to Troy together to honor the tomb of Achilles and Patroclus, a site that represented same-sex love for the people of the ancient world.

Later, as they were returning from India through Persia, Hephaestion died unexpectedly. Alexander, the great conqueror, was overwhelmed with grief. He laid on top of Hephaestion's dead body for a day and a night, and when friends finally pulled him away he sat silent in tears for three days. When he finally arose, Alexander ordered all the manes and tails cut from the horses, all the ornaments broken off the city's walls, the city's shrine destroyed, all music banned, the sacred fires extinguished, and a period of mourning throughout his empire. Then he shaved his head and laid a lock of his hair into dead Hephaestion's hand as his soldiers wept. Alexander then ordered the most expensive funeral in the history of the world to mourn the loss of his friend.[8] Abandoning his military leadership, Alexander went on a prolonged drinking binge and grew increasingly sick. Eight months after Hephaestion died, at the age of thirty-two, Alexander the Great was dead.

One other gay person who stands out boldly in Greek history was a lesbian woman named Sappho who was considered one of the nine greatest poets of the classical world, the only woman in that exalted company. She was a lyrical poet, a style where poetry was recited while accompanied by the lyre, and she was considered one of the greatest musicians of antiquity. Sappho was so famous in her day that her face appeared on coins, and Plato elevated her to rank of Muse.[9] Calling Sappho a lesbian, though, is ironic, because the very word lesbian comes from her homeland, the Greek island of Lesbos. The word sapphic also comes from her name and refers to both the meter of her poems and sexual relations between women. One surviving fragment makes clear the nature of Sappho's attractions:

> For that girl, that beautiful girl; her dresses'
> clinging makes you shake when you see it,
> And I'm happy.[10]

Another fragments shows her obsession with another woman, and the jealousy she felt for any man who drew close to her object of desire.

> He seems to me to be like the gods —
> whatever man sits opposite you
> and close by hears you
> talking sweetly
> And laughing charmingly, which
> makes the heart within my breast take flight;
> for the instant I look upon you, I cannot anymore
> speak one word,
> But in silence my tongue is broken, a fine
> fire at once runs under my skin,
> with my eyes I see not one thing, my ears buzz,
> Cold sweat covers me, trembling
> seizes my whole body, I am more moist than grass;
> I seem to be little short of dying...[11]

The only complete poem of Sappho's still in existence is the *Hymn to Aphrodite* where the author beseeches the goddess of love to help her win over a reluctant woman. There were scholars who read Sappho's work and concluded she was just expressing sisterly fondness for other women, or affection for her female pupils, but that seems a bit deluded and disrespectful of such feminine passions.

In another of history's great tragedies, the importance of Sappho's work did not prevent its loss. The Library of Alexandria had nine volumes of her poems that did not survive the fire, and collections of her works held in Catholic libraries in Rome and Constantinople were ordered burned by Pope Gregory VII in 1073. Most of what exists today come from segments quoted by other authors, and pieces of papyrus found in the deserts of Egypt, including a 1906 discovery of papier-mâché coffins made from scraps of Sappho's poems.[12] Even in the scraps her power shines through. Let the memory and greatness of Sappho resound in the truth of her poetry:

> Although they are
> Only breath, words
> which I command
> are immortal[13]

Or as she told her female companions thousands of years ago: "Someone, I tell you, in another time, will remember us."[14] Two thousand six hundred years later, I can say with confidence: she was right.

Rome followed Greece and built one of the world's most successful and lasting empires, and almost all of the Roman emperors took male lovers. Some loved out of affection, and some with the decadence of emperors like Caligula and Nero. Even the great military man, Julius Caesar, had a relationship with another man, King Nicomedes IV of Bithynia. The two spent so much time together that Caesar's soldiers sang "Caesar conquered Gaul, but Nicodemes conquered Caesar," and Caesar's enemies started calling Nicodemes the "Queen of Bithynia."[15]

While tragically little evidence remains of everyday Roman lives, the ruins of Pompeii revealed how common homosexuality was in their culture. The art of the Suburban Baths include sixteen sex scenes, one of them male-male, another female-female, one of a threesome with two men penetrating a woman, and another of a threesome of a man who is penetrating a woman while being penetrated by another man.[16] While no equivalent erotic art survived in other locations, the casualness of its display in Pompeii shows how inoffensive the Romans found such imagery. The graffiti of Pompeii are equally revelatory, ranging from the confessional "I have buggered men," to the accusatory "Secundus likes to screw boys," to the playful lamentation on the walls of a brothel: "Weep, you girls. My penis has given you up. Now it penetrates men's behinds. Goodbye, wondrous femininity!"[17]

The fall of Rome came four hundred years later, long after its most decadent period. Rome only fell after 150 years of Christian rulers enforcing the new religion's anti-sex attitudes and the suppression of the traditional religions, alienating the populace. Rome fell for complex reasons including an over-reliance on mercenary armies and falling tax revenues, yet there persists an odd tradition of blaming gay people for Rome's demise, and then using that fable as a morality tale for all nations. As an example, prominent Christianist Pat Robertson said, "Any country that openly embraces homosexuality throughout the history of mankind has gone down into ruin. That's history. That's the historical record. Whatever nation embraces this so-called lifestyle, it ends up in the garbage heap of history."[18] Given that all nations and empires eventually founder, it is equally true that every nation that wore shoes or lived in houses eventually failed. Only the anti-gay fixations of Robertson's followers could make that statement sound perceptive. The ironic truth is that Christianity was far more responsible for the fall of Rome than homosexuality.[19]

With the fall of Rome's empire, power was centralized in the Christian church, and the Dark Ages began. For the next thousand years, little thought was allowed outside of that approved by the clerics and authorized by the Bible. Art, science, medicine, and human progress ground to a crawl across Europe, and most of humanity's great achievements shifted to other great cultural centers within Islam and China. Only with the rise of a different kind of thinking, led by people like Martin Luther, Copernicus, and Galileo, did Western Culture begin to flower again in a period now called the Renaissance.

Bible

I pointed out the stars to you
but all you saw
was the tip of my finger.

~ *Swahili saying*

A FAGGOT IS A BUNDLE of sticks used to fuel a fire. How faggot became the term for a gay man is unknown, but it may have been a derogatory term for the bent old women who gathered those sticks that was then applied to gay men, meaning we were like bent women. Faggot may also have gained its current meaning because faggots were thrown onto the fire.[1] Through much of Western history, gay people were burned alive, or killed first and then burned.

The best illustration of this history comes from Venice, that most fabled of European cities. Modern visitors arriving from the mainland can travel up the Grand Canal by boat, finally arriving at Venice's one great open space, the Piazza San Marco, or Saint Mark's Square. The view from that square is immortalized in countless snapshots, gondolas bobbing in the waves, the waters of the lagoon framed by two monumental columns. On one of those columns stands the city's patron Saint Theodore with his crocodile and on the other a bronze lion with wings, the symbol of Venice itself. For people like me those columns do not look so noble, as the records show that more gay people were killed between those two columns than anywhere else in Europe until the Holocaust.[2]

Venice was able to build such an opulent city because it was rich from the wealth gained by its fleet's control of the Adriatic. From there the Venetians built a trading empire so powerful they could send emissaries like Marco Polo as far east as China in search of trade. Unfortunately, Venice was vulnerable. Built at sea level on the sediment of a natural lagoon, Venice was constantly threatened by floods and destruction by nature.

As Christians, the medieval Venetians consulted their Bible for lessons on how to protect their precarious city from devastation, and the great biblical story of civic destruction was the story of Sodom. According to the Bible,[3] the people of Sodom were so wicked that God rained down fire from the heavens, destroying the city, and in the view of those medieval Christians, the sin of Sodom was homosexuality. Fearing the wrath of the elements and believing weather calamities were controlled by an angry God, the Venetians protected themselves from God's wrath by killing the gay people, burning them alive between those magnificent pillars. Over the years the screams and death cries of the burning gay people became too unnerving for the bureaucrats working in the surrounding palaces, so as a humanitarian gesture towards those workers, the city beheaded its victims first.[4] For hundreds of years Venetians pursued and killed their gay children and neighbors to ensure that the city's wealth and prosperity would continue under divine protection.

This is not a mindset lost to history. There are Christians today who still view the story of Sodom as the principle morality tale of sexuality and correlate all great acts of destruction with the existence of gay people. After both the terrorist attacks of 9-11 and Hurricane Katrina's devastation of New Orleans, some of America's most prominent Christianists rushed to their televised pulpits to blame gay people.[5] Here in California it seems as if every earthquake and flood leads some Christian leader to blame the gay community for the catastrophe.

If you have ever wondered why so many Christians can overlook murder, rape, slavery, and genocide while maintaining that gay marriage will destroy society, the answer lies in the story of Sodom, as this is the singular story that underpins those fears. Given that importance, it is worth spending a little time to consider what the Bible's story actually says, as it is so different from the way it is commonly portrayed.

The scene begins with Sodom's one good man, Lot, sitting near the gates of the city as two angels arrived disguised as men. Lot took the strangers in, offering them food and a place to sleep in his home, powerful hospitality in a dangerous world lacking safe roads and lodging. Then, as the biblical narrative describes it, "But before they lay down, the men of the city, even the men of Sodom, compassed the house round, both old and young, all the people from every quarter: And they called unto Lot, and said unto him, Where are the men which came in to thee this night? bring them out unto us, that we may know them."[6]

To "know them" is a biblical euphemism for sex, so going with the common interpretation, all of the men of Sodom, every single one, was a rampaging homosexual rapist. While that certainly sounds horrible, and scary, it also is an event unknown in all the rest of history. Outside of this one myth, as old as the tales of Noah's flood and the tower of Babel, I have never heard of aggressive gay sex mobs attacking the innocent. I do not know why people hold so strongly to this old myth when this kind of thing never actually happens. Plus it is illogical to believe that this story proves all the men of the city where homosexual. If that were true, then God would have had no need to destroy the city, as it would be gone in a generation for lack of procreation.

Women's rights advocates know the likelier explanation. Rape is an act of violence, not lust, and those Sodomite men were threatening male-on-male rape. The men of Sodom did not rampage to Lot's house to have sexy good times with strangers. They wanted to hurt them. To give two recent examples of this phenomenon: New York City cops did not sodomize an arrested man with their baton because they thought it was hot. They did it to humiliate him.[7] Rebels in Congo's civil wars did not rape hundreds of thousands women and men because their country was caught up in some kind of erotic frenzy; they did it as an act of war.[8] Men have used rape as a weapon across history, against women and men. Many people in Central and South Asia are named Khan because of the raping skills of Genghis Khan and his family, and Latinos are lighter skinned than most Native Americans because of the raping skills of Christian conquistadors. Maybe some of these men found rape erotically satisfying, but to confuse the act of rape with love is sick. The scriptures give no evidence these Sodomite men were gay. A little wine and nice music would have been more effective if the goal was a night of tender love making. The likelier explanation is that these attackers were straight men threatening violence and therefore more like the New York cops and Congolese rebels.

For evidence from the Bible that these men were not gay, consider what Lot did next. Lot lived in Sodom, so I presume he knew his neighbors, and yet he responded by saying to the mob: "Behold now, I have two daughters which have not known man; let me, I pray you, bring them out unto you, and do ye to them as is good in your eyes: only unto these men do nothing; for therefore came they under the shadow of my roof."[9] Along with being surreal that the most ethical man in town is offering his virgin daughters to be raped, that was not much of a solution if the men of Sodom were gay. Fortunately for Lot's daughters, the men of Sodom did not take their father's offer. Again, they wanted to hurt the strangers, not have an orgy. The angels then saved Lot from the mob and told him to leave the city with his family and never look back. Lot took his family and left, but his wife looked back at the destruction of their city, and was turned into a pillar of salt.

So to recap, no sex occurred in the story of Sodom. No anal sex. No oral sex. No gay sex of any kind. No gay, lesbian, bisexual, or transgender people had sex. In fact, the only sex acts in the story of Sodom occur after the city's destruction when Lot's daughters get their father so blind drunk they can have sex with him on repeated nights and get impregnated so their incestuous family can live on feeling morally superior to everyone else.[10] Yet it is this story of Sodom that has whipped Christians into anti-gay fear and hysteria for centuries based on the threatened rape of two men, or more accurately, of two angels disguised as men. It saddens me when women who have suffered actual rape tolerate male church leaders declaring this threatened male rape as one of history's greatest sins.

People in antiquity interpreted the sin of Sodom as the threatened violence against the guests, a sin of gross inhospitality with no clear analog in our modern times. As Jesus himself described the sin of Sodom, "If anyone will not welcome you or listen to your words, leave that home or town and shake the dust off your feet. Truly I tell you, it will be more bearable for Sodom and Gomorrah on the day of judgment than for that town."[11] Or consider how the prophet Ezekiel described it: "'Now this was the sin of your sister Sodom: She and her daughters were arrogant, overfed and unconcerned; they did not help the poor and needy."[12] The Gospel of Jude also mentions Sodom, condemning the men there of craving "strange flesh,"[13] but given that the visitors of Sodom were angels, they were strange flesh indeed. Crazy as it sounds now, Christians used to consider angel lust a real problem, which is why women used to cover their heads in church, protecting them from the lusty angels overhead. As the Bible says in First Corinthians: "For this cause ought the woman to have power on her head because of the angels," the power in this case being a veil or covering.[14] As Paul wrote in Hebrews: "Be not forgetful to entertain strangers: for thereby some have entertained angels unawares."[15] It wasn't until Saint Augustine wrote *The City of God* in 412 AD, thousands of years later, that the sin of Sodom was clearly declared to be sexual sin, and even then it was not exclusively focused on homosexuality.[16]

Part of the problem for modern Christians reading an English language Bible comes from the medieval mistranslation of the term "sodomite." The original word was *qadhesh*, the ancient term for temple prostitutes, a sacred function of the Jewish people's neighboring religions.[17] The word "sodomites" in the King James version of the Bible did refer to people who had male-male sex, but it was not a reference to the people or events of Sodom, confusing English language readers ever since.

Because this story persists as the singular parable for anti-gay hate, I want to make something very clear: I have never committed the sin of Sodom, as I have never committed or threatened rape. Just as prohibitions against heterosexual rape have nothing to do with heterosexual marriage, love, and affection, the story of Sodom has no moral message applicable to my same-sex affections, loves, or relationships.

For a change of tone, consider the Bible stories that do address same-sex affection. The most famous is the story of David and Jonathan. This is the same David who stands today as the world's most iconic naked man in Michelangelo's magnificent marble sculpture. David comes into the historical record three thousand years ago when the twelve tribes of Israel gathered into a unified kingdom under a king named Saul. But King Saul was troubled by evil spirits, and seeking peace through music, one of his servants recommended a harp player named David, a shepherd from Bethlehem described as "cunning in playing, and a mighty valiant man, and a man of war, and prudent in matters, and a comely person, and the Lord is with him."[18] So he was brave, well-spoken, spiritual, fierce, and handsome. He was also a hunk, or as the scriptures put it, "ruddy, and withal of a beautiful countenance, and goodly to look to."[19] So Saul invited the strong, sensitive, and hunky David to his court, and "when the evil spirit from God was upon Saul, that David took an harp, and played with his hand: so Saul was refreshed, and was well, and the evil spirit departed from him."[20]

The Israelites of that time were at war with the Philistines, whose greatest warrior, the giant Goliath, challenged the Israelites to choose a warrior for a one-on-one battle. David took the challenge and slew Goliath with one stone from his slingshot. In victory, David cut off Goliath's head and took it to Saul. (And if that sounds weird, David returned from a later battle presenting Saul with over 200 foreskins of the men he killed.[21] What a strange post-battle scene that must have been.)

When David showed up in Saul's court, the king's son, Jonathan, fell instantly in love, or as the Bible puts it, "the soul of Jonathan was knit with the soul of David, and Jonathan loved him as with his own soul." Swept up in a moment of passion, "Jonathan stripped himself of the robe that was upon him, and gave it to David, and his garments, even to his sword, and to his bow, and to his girdle."[22] (Girdle meaning belt.) Given this story occurred before the invention of underwear, that left Jonathan naked in front of the man he had knit his soul with. From that day David became part of the royal household, and Jonathan was so smitten that he declared that if he and his father were to die, David should inherit the throne. Apparently Jonathan was not planning on having sons, which sets up the next twist to the story.

Over time the king soured on David, partly because of his son's infatuation. As Saul said to Jonathan: "...do not I know that thou hast chosen the son of Jesse [David] to thine own confusion, and unto the confusion of thy mother's nakedness? For as long as the son of Jesse liveth upon the ground, thou shalt not be established, nor thy kingdom. Wherefore now send and fetch him unto me, for he shall surely die."[23] Saul realized Jonathan was not sexually interested in women and was not going to produce grandchildren while David was around, so Saul planned to kill David. When Jonathan told David of his father's plan, "they kissed one another, and wept one with another — until David exceeded."[24] No one is quite clear what the Bible meant by that last phrase.

The wars continued, and soon Saul and Jonathan were killed in a battle, making David king of Israel. David was heartbroken and sang in response, "I am distressed for thee, my brother Jonathan: very pleasant hast thou been unto me: thy love to me was wonderful, passing the love of women."[25]

David went on to unify Israel, and in another of those dark twists that make the Bible such a colorful read, David then fell in love with his neighbor's wife Bathsheba, got her pregnant, and killed her husband so he could marry her. Obviously David also liked women, a lot. One of David and Bathsheba's sons became the famously wise King Solomon, who was also a steamy sexual figure with 700 wives and 300 concubines, women a man owned and had sex with but did not marry. Even then, God promised David that the Messiah would be his descendant, so a thousand years later Jesus was born "of the House of David" …on his mother's side, of course.

Interpreting the story of David and Jonathan from a modern perspective, Jonathan comes across as profoundly gay, while David is more complex. There is a Hollywood quality to David, all dashing and brave, while tender and flawed, but triumphing in the end, and the audience leaves happy as long as they do not think about the implications too much. This story is important because those same-sex affections had a profound effect on biblical history. David became king of Israel and one of the most important figures in the Bible because of another man's love.

Women do not get much coverage in the Bible, but one notable exception is David's great-grandmother Ruth. Ruth is one of the few women named in the lineage of Jesus, as all those so-and-so begat so-and-so's in his genealogy are male. Ruth married into an Israelite family and after the death of her husband, grew close to her mother-in-law, Naomi. Over time they grew so close that Ruth's declaration of commitment to Naomi is famous to this day: "Where you go I will go, and where you stay I will stay. Your people will be my people and your God my God. Where you die I will die, and there I will be buried. May the Lord deal with me, be it ever so severely, if even death separates you and me."[26] I imagine few of the heterosexual couples who use this beautiful verse in their wedding vows realized this was one woman's pledge of love and commitment to another woman.

The Bible's fragments say nothing about a sexual relationship between Ruth and Naomi, and of course it is impossible to know the intimate details from thousands of years ago, but it does clarify that they were more than just friends. Two different scriptures say, "Ruth loved Naomi as Adam loved Eve,"[27] so either Adam and Eve loved each other like hand-holding soul sisters, in which case there would be no human race, or Ruth and Naomi really did share something special.

One last Bible story is not about sex, centering instead on a fabulously queer spirit: the story of Joseph and his coat of many colors. Joseph was Israel's eleventh of twelve sons, from whom we get the twelve tribes, but he was the firstborn of Israel's first wife Rachel. Biblical marriages rarely fit the "one man, one woman" formulations seen on bumper stickers. Realizing there was something special about Joseph, his father gifted him a coat of many colors, shocking apparel in their world of homespun cloth. Apparently Joseph's father realized there was something especially "colorful" about his son, as evinced by Joseph's shamanic abilities with prophetic dreams. So Israel recognized his special son Joseph and honored him with a coat that was... flamboyant.

Joseph's brothers resented something about their favored younger brother, whether it was their father's attention, Joseph's vibrant spiritual gifts, or something else not explicitly named but so bothersome they tried to kill him. At the last minute, the brothers changed their minds and sold Joseph into slavery. The Bible teaches an important lesson here — that insecure men have always been murderous towards the sensitive and colorful.

The enslaved Joseph ended up in the household of Egypt's Pharaoh, where he rejected the sexual advances of a woman because he was so pious, or maybe because he was not so heterosexual, even as that rejection landed him in prison. Meanwhile, Pharaoh was troubled by dreams of seven lean cows coming out of the Nile and eating seven fat cows. Joseph interpreted the dream as meaning Egypt would see seven years of abundance followed by seven years of famine. Pharaoh then put Joseph in charge of stockpiling Egypt's grain reserves, which saved Egypt when the long famine did arrive seven years later. His new employment as Pharaoh's favorite led Joseph to bring his family to live with him, which is how the Jews ended up in Egypt. This sets up the story of the plagues and subsequent exodus lead by Moses, the event that Jews everywhere continue to celebrate as Passover. Again a decidedly queer figure stands at a pivotal point in the biblical saga.

David and Jonathan. Ruth and Naomi. Joseph and his flamboyant coat. Some of the pivotal stories in the Bible center on the clearly declared love between people of the same sex and queer spirits with magical gifts. Yet it is the story of Sodom, with its unfulfilled threat of male-on-male rape, that sticks in the minds of the pious when they think of same-sex love. Yet even that story defies moral reductionism for those who actually read it. The Bible, like life, is more complex than that, which is part of what makes it such an enduringly important book, even if certain specifics are a little tough to apply to modern lives.

Renaissance

One does not discover new lands
without consenting
to lose sight of the shore
for a very long time.

~ *André Gide*

CHRISTOPHER COLUMBUS SET OUT to prove that sailing west from Europe was the quickest route to Asia. What he found was something else entirely — the American continents filled with civilizations and peoples largely cut off from the rest of humanity since the end of the previous Ice Age. That moment of surprise in 1492 was one of the first great examples of what we now call the scientific method: develop a theory, run the test, observe the results, and be prepared for unexpected discoveries. From that one great experience and the mind shifts occurring across Europe at that same time, the Dark Ages began to end. Twenty-five years after Columbus, Martin Luther began the reformation of medieval Christianity's corruptions by nailing his *Ninety-Five Theses* to the church's door. Fifty-one years after Columbus, Nicolaus Copernicus published his theory that the earth was part of a moving solar system. By 1615, Galileo had proven that humanity was not the center of creation, demonstrating that we live on a spinning planet in a great revolving universe, directly contradicting the Bible that declared: "[God] set the earth on its foundations; it can never be moved."[1]

"We live," as the scientist Carl Sagan said, "on a hunk of rock and metal that circles a humdrum star that is one of 400 billion other stars that make up the Milky Way Galaxy which is one of billions of other galaxies which make up a universe which may be one of a very large number, perhaps an infinite number, of other universes."[2] Earth's human population is the center of the human story, as far as we know, but humanity is only one infinitesimally small part of the great revolving cosmos.

Along with these realizations came an awakening from superstition and fear, and Europe flowered into the Renaissance, meaning rebirth. With the opening of medieval minds, Europe looked back to the wisdom of the Romans and Greeks and began relearning the ancient traditions of science and rational thought, and in their reading, they found the classical Greek and Roman writings on same-sex love. Unsurprisingly for those who understand the roles of gay people in creative societies, gay life flowered during the Renaissance. Both of the iconic Renaissance men, Leonardo da Vinci and Michelangelo, had same-sex relationships, and along with other queer spirits, helped lead humankind into modernity.

Leonardo da Vinci practically defined his age. Not only did he paint the *Mona Lisa* and *The Last Supper*, but he also drew up plans for aircraft and a submarine, charted the human circulatory system, and in *Vitruvian Man*, produced the most famous image of human proportions. As the art historian Bernard Berenson noted: "Leonardo is the one artist of whom it may be said with perfect literalness: Nothing that he touched but turned into a thing of eternal beauty. Whether it be the cross section of a skull, the structure of a weed, or a study of muscles, he, with his feeling for line and for light and shade, forever transmuted it into life-communicating values."[3]

Beyond his transformative genius, Da Vinci was described by his contemporary biographer Giorgio Vasari as well loved and witty. "In appearance he was striking and handsome, and his magnificent presence brought comfort to the most troubled soul; he was so persuasive that he could bend other people to his will. He was physically so strong that he could withstand violence and with his right hand he could bend the ring of an iron door knocker or a horseshoe as if they were lead. He was so generous that he fed all his friends, rich or poor."[4] He was also known as a skilled musician, a strong horseman, and such a respecter of nature that he lived as a vegetarian.

Early in life, Da Vinci lived and apprenticed in the workshop of the artist Verrocchio, the studio that began the tradition of painting handsome boy angels.[5] After painting *The Baptism of Christ* together, Verrochio was so overwhelmed by the beauty of the young male angel Da Vinci painted that Verrochio never painted again.[6] Court records also show that at twenty-four, Da Vinci was accused, along with several other men, of committing sodomy with a seventeen year old named Jacopo Saltarelli, an event that may have greatly affected his life.[7]

While known for his many friendships, Da Vinci was also secretive, famously keeping his personal notes in code, and part of his secret may have been his sexuality. He never married, but at thirty-eight he formed a relationship with a ten-year old named Gian Giacomo Caprotti whom Da Vinci nicknamed Salai, or "the little devil." The historian Vasari described Salai as "a graceful and beautiful youth with fine curly hair." Leonardo said he was "a thief, a liar, stubborn, and a glutton."[8] Over their twenty-six years together, Salai spent Leonardo's fortune on clothes, including, at one point, twenty-four pair of shoes. When Leonardo died he left the *Mona Lisa*, an extremely valuable piece even then, to Salai.

Leonardo had another relationship with Count Francesco Melzi, who was apprenticed to Leonardo at fourteen and remained with him to his death. Leonardo left his notes to Melzi with instructions for publication. Troubling for those who want to believe Leonardo was gay, there are no hints of sex or romance in all those notes, although he does reveal his discomfort with heterosexual sex: "The act of procreation and anything that has any relation to it is so disgusting that human beings would soon die out if there were no pretty faces and sensuous dispositions." Historians have argued about Leonardo's sexuality ever since. Personally, it strikes me as odd to think this powerful and creative man could have been as sexually and emotionally suppressed as some biographers insist. He had lifelong intimate associations with beautiful younger men and close friends ranging from street ruffians to the King of France, who is said to have held Leonardo's head as he died. Looking back centuries later, Sigmund Freud famously said of Da Vinci that he was "like a man who awoke too early in the darkness, while the others were all still asleep."[9]

If Leonardo da Vinci was the original Renaissance Man, Michelangelo Buonarroti followed and became what many consider the greatest artist of all time. Michelangelo sculpted the *Pietà* and the *David*, painted the ceiling and *The Last Judgment* in the Sistine Chapel, and completed the building of St. Peter's Basilica, the centerpiece of the Vatican. The power of his art was so overwhelming that he was called *Il Divino*, or the divine one, and his work was described as *terribilità*, or having frightening power.

In contrast to the impressive presence of Leonardo da Vinci, Michelangelo was rough. He ate and drank only what he needed to survive and often slept in his clothes and boots.[10] According to his biographer Paolo Giovio: "His nature was so rough and uncouth that his domestic habits were incredibly squalid, and deprived posterity of any pupils who might have followed him." As Michelangelo told an apprentice: "However rich I may have been, I have always lived like a poor man."[11] Prone to melancholy, Michelangelo lived a withdrawn life, but not without passion. He was so hot tempered another sculptor broke Michelangelo's nose in a fight.

As with Da Vinci, Michelangelo's private sexual life can never be known, but in contrast to Da Vinci, he left clear records of his love for men. Of Gherardo Perini he wrote, "Here, my love ravished my heart and life. Here his fine eyes promised me succour, yet took it away from me. Here, in infinite sorrow, I wept and saw the departure of this stony-hearted man who had revealed me to myself and no longer wanted me."[12] Michelangelo wrote the first modern love poems from one man to another for Tommaso dei Cavalieri, when Michelangelo was fifty-seven and Cavalieri twenty-three.

> I feel as lit by fire a cold countenance
> That burns me from afar and keeps itself ice-chill;
> A strength I feel two shapely arms to fill
> Which without motion moves every balance.[13]

And even more clearly:

> The love I speak of aspires to the heights;
> woman is too dissimilar, and it ill becomes
> a wise and manly heart to burn for her.[14]

Cavalieri wrote back: "I swear to return your love. Never have I loved a man more than I love you, never have I wished for a friendship more than I wish for yours."[15] Lamenting their age discrepancy Michelangelo wrote, "It is an infinite sorrow to me that I cannot give you also my past, so that I could serve you longer for the future will be short: I am too old."[16] In sum Michelangelo described his beloved Cavalieri as "light of our century, paragon of all the world."[17] On the death of another male friend, Cecchino dei Bracci, Michelangelo wrote:

> The flesh now earth, and here my bones,
> Bereft of handsome eyes, and jaunty air,
> Still loyal are to him I joyed in bed,
> Whom I embraced, in whom my soul now lives.[18]

Like Leonardo, Michelangelo never married. Later in life he loved and wrote poems to a woman named Vittoria Colonna who was a close friend for years, but their relationship did not seem physically intimate. After Colonna's death, Michelangelo told a friend that he loved her so much that "his only regret was that, when he went to see her as she was departing from this life, he did not kiss her forehead or face as he kissed her hand."[19]

It is easy to see how much Michelangelo loved men by looking at his art. In *The Rape of Ganymede* an eagle wrestles with a muscular naked man in the air. In *The Punishment of Tityus* an eagle wrestles with a muscular naked man on the ground. In *The Fall of Phaeton* a muscular naked man falls from his flying chariot. In the magnificent *The Dream* a cherub descends from above the heavens, blowing his horn as it touches the forehead of a muscular naked man. In each we see evidence of Michelangelo's passion for Cavalieri, as Michelangelo gave at least four of those groundbreaking works to Cavalieri as gifts and scholars believe Cavalieri was the model for the muscular naked man.[20]

Michelangelo's contributions to the Sistine Chapel were particularly disturbing to his more repressed contemporaries. Sprawling across the ceiling and front wall of a chapel deep in the Vatican, Michelangelo painted voluptuous and masculine male figures, and profoundly masculine female figures as well. I remember hearing that some of his women looked like men with cantaloupes strapped to their chests. Researchers at the University of Pisa believe the scenes from *The Last Judgment* came from the Roman baths Michelangelo frequented, where men got massages and medical treatment, and found both male and female prostitutes.[21] The naked images of the chapel were considered so tawdry at the time that Biagio da Cesena, the Pope's Master of Ceremonies said, "that it was a very disgraceful thing to have made in so honorable a place all those nude figures showing their nakedness so shamelessly, and that it was a work not for the chapel of a Pope, but for a brothel or tavern."[22] In response, Michelangelo painted Da Cesena's face at the bottom as Minos, judge of the underworld, complete with donkey ears. When Da Cesena complained to the Pope, the pontiff replied that hell was outside his jurisdiction, so the portrait stayed.

The nudity of Michelangelo's Sistine Chapel represented a crossroads in Western culture. In defiance of the primness that came before him and centuries of wooden-looking Medieval figures, Michelangelo's art idealized the human body. His renditions of blatantly exposed flesh expressed the emerging humanist beliefs that the human body represented its own beauty, its own exalted ideal, beyond church-mediated control. Clergymen fighting to retain the church's power were outraged, and eventually the Council of Trent ordered the genitalia of the *Last Judgment* painted over, and their awkward draperies and fig leaves remain to this day.

While Leonardo and Michelangelo were exemplars of same-sex love in the Renaissance, they were hardly alone. Gay male love in Renaissance Florence became so common that the word *Florenzer*, or Florentine, became German slang for homosexual.[23] Court records show that as many as half the men of Florence were accused of same-sex connections, and some historians believe most males participated.[24] In response, the municipal government created a special sodomy police called The Office of the Night. The records of that office provide abundant documentation on the centrality of homosexual relations to this period of cultural awakening.

As famous as Italy was for its homosexuality, the most famous author in the English language, William Shakespeare, wrote 126 sonnets to a "Fair Youth," an unnamed young man. The lines from Sonnet 13 that ask, "Shall I compare thee to a summer's day? Thou art more lovely and more temperate," were written by Shakespeare to another man, or as he called him in Sonnet

18, his "master-mistress." Of course Shakespeare was also married to Anne Hathaway and they had three children, so he may be best described as bisexual.

The most famous book in the English language, the King James Version of the Bible, was named for a gay English king. First published in 1611, this most elegant of translations affected the English language for centuries. James himself lived apart from his wife and was praised for his chastity, while in truth he had a variety of relationships with men. This fact was so well known that Sir Walter Raleigh, the man who led the colonization of American Virginia, publicly declared: "Elizabeth was King, now James is Queen,"[25] a reference to the effeminate James following the powerful Virgin Queen, Elizabeth I. One of James's long rumored same-sex relationships was confirmed by the recent discovery of a secret passage connecting James's palace bedroom to the bedroom of George Villiers, one of his favorites.[26] When James wrote to Villiers he called himself "dad and husband" and Villiers "my sweet child and wife," saying, "Christ had John, and I have George,"[27] a reference to Jesus's affection for John the Beloved. King James died with Villiers at his side. It is beyond ironic that modern Christians wave their King James Bibles in the air as they condemn homosexuality, and King James loved men.

Another famous same-sex loving European was Richard the Lionheart, the pretender to the English throne who Robin Hood and his merry men paid allegiance to while Richard was crusading to conquer the Holy Land. Richard, meanwhile, when not killing Muslims for Christ, was spending quality sexy times with the king of France. As a contemporary biographer, Roger of Hoveden, told it, "Richard, duke of Aquitaine, the son of the king of England, remained with Philip, the king of France, who so honored him for so long that they ate every day at the same table and from the same dish, and at night their beds did not separate them. And the king of France loved him as his own soul; and they loved each other so much that the king of England was absolutely astonished and the passionate love between them and marveled at it."[28]

There are so many stories of gay people in the histories of European royalty I cannot possibly list them all here, but to note a few... The great English king William the Conqueror had an openly homosexual son, William Rufus, who was a bully and a tyrant, and ended up shot in the back, while

Edward II was a flamboyantly gay man much as he was depicted in the movie *Braveheart*. Richard II was gay, befriended Chaucer, loved the arts and fine clothes, and invented the hanky. (Seriously. The man invented the handkerchief.)[29] He also married twice without having children, but spent quality time with Robert de Vere, Ninth Earl of Oxford. A contemporary said their relationship was "obscene, and not without a degree of improper intimacy."[30] Queen Anne had famously close relations with her handmaiden Sarah Churchill, the Duchess of Marlborough, who had the delightful title Lady of the Bedchamber. Swedish Queen Christina never married or had sexual relations, commented on her body throughout her life, and had such distinctly manly features and masculine dress that modern scholars assume she was intersex.[31] She also set Paris fashion on fire when she wore a man's hat with feathers. And then there was Frederick the Great, King Ludwig II, Tsar Alexander I, and I am not even going start on the famously flaming French court or all those gay popes. (Although Catholic Popes had a strong incentive to keep their sexuality hidden, the curious can start their explorations with John XII, Benedict IX, John XXII, Paul II, Sixtus IV, Julius II, Leo X, Julius III, and maybe even the recent Benedict XVI. One gay friend of a devoutly Catholic nature told me the inner sanctum of the Vatican was the gayest place he had ever seen, so not much has changed there it seems.)[32]

The narrow perspectives of the medieval world broke open when some of history's greatest men, many of them gay, led Western civilization out of the dark and through a period of rebirth, planting the seeds of modern life. That is often the role of gay people, getting out ahead of the crowd and opening visions of new possibilities for the betterment of all. With the flowering of the Renaissance, the world began to change, and the dawning of the Enlightenment was nigh.

Greats

The one thing in the world of value
is the active soul.

~ *Ralph Waldo Emerson*

ONE OF MY FAVORITE phrases in American literature comes from Walt Whitman's 1855 *Leaves of Grass*: "I sing the body electric."[1] Whitman realized long before most observers that both democracy and the sacred are experienced through the body, and the only way individuals could survive the divisive onslaught of modernity was to ground themselves in nature and the physical experiences of life. Out of Whitman's earthy celebrations rose a love of America seldom rivaled. "The United States themselves," he wrote, "are essentially the greatest poem."[2] He believed American greatness arose from its newly implemented experiment in democracy, or governmental power rooted in individual citizens. As Whitman described it, "The whole theory of the universe is directed unerringly to one single individual."[3]

Integral to Whitman's poetry was his love for men, or as he tenderly wrote,

> The one I love most lay sleeping by me under the same cover in the
> cool night,
> In the stillness, in the autumn moonbeams, his face was inclined
> toward me,
> And his arm lay lightly around my breast —
> And that night I was happy."[4]

For Walt Whitman, this love between men was core to what made America great:

> Come, I will make the continent indissoluble;
> I will make the most splendid race the sun ever yet shone upon;
> I will make divine magnetic lands,
> With the love of comrades,
> With the life-long love of comrades.
> I will plant companionship thick as trees along all the rivers of
> America, and along the shores of the great lakes, and all over the
> prairies;
> I will make inseparable cities, with their arms about each other's
> necks;
> By the love of comrades,
> By the manly love of comrades.[5]

Well over a hundred years before modern gay culture and self-identification, Walt Whitman named the feelings that underlie the gay identity, leading Historian Rictor Norton to declare Whitman the Prophet of Gay Liberation.[6] How much Whitman was gay in the modern sense remains unknown, but he spent much of his life immersed in the world of the working class men he loved, and he selected his emotional companions from their ranks. His most famous relationship was with a nineteen-year-old horse-drawn omnibus conductor named Peter Doyle, whom Whitman met when he was in his forties. They lived intertwined lives for the rest of their days, but never lived together. A photograph shows Whitman and Doyle sitting in facing chairs, so close they are touching, a lovely portrait of their affections. For Whitman love could be very small and personal:

O you whom I often and silently come where you are, that I may be with you;
As I walk by your side, or sit near, or remain in the same room with you,
Little you know the subtle electric fire that for your sake is playing within me.[7]

From hanging out with ferry boat operators to volunteering with wounded soldiers in Civil War hospitals, Whitman did everything he could to be close to men and male bodies. Reports from doctors and others said he was an amazing presence, calm and healing for those who interacted with him,[8] and he wrote about his experiences with a modern sense of honesty. As Henry David Thoreau said of *Leaves of Grass*: "he has spoken more truth than any American or modern I know."[9]

If the prudish cringe at hearing too much truth from Walt Whitman, discussing Abraham Lincoln puts them right over the edge. While Lincoln was certainly America's greatest president, it also clear that he loved men. While the rebuttals to such an assertion are instantaneous, consider the evidence. As a young man Lincoln wrote a little ditty about his extended family that became infamous in his community:

I will tell you a joke about Jewel and Mary
It is neither a joke nor a story
For Rueben and Charles has married two girls
But Billy has married a boy...[10]

As an adult Honest Abe was a very tall man who spent a lot of nights in very small beds with other men. Apologists say this was because beds were rare at the time, but his choice of sleeping companions may have been more affectionate than practical. As Herman Melville wrote in *Moby Dick* around that same time, "No man prefers to sleep two in a bed. [...] I don't know how it is, but people like to be private when they are sleeping."[11] And yet one of Lincoln's steady bedmates and longtime friends, Billy Greene, said of the future president, "He was at that time well and firmly built: his thighs were as perfect as a human being could be,"[12] an oddly intimate remark for a mere bed-sharer, and reminiscent of the classical Greek pederastic tradition known to the educated of their day.

Lincoln spent another four years in a narrow bed with a man named Joshua Speed who was such a dear friend that Lincoln's letters to him are signed, "Yours forever," and they remained dear friends throughout Lincoln's life. Speed himself said, "no two men were ever more intimate."[13] The poet Carl Sandburg alluded to the nature of their relationship when he wrote that Lincoln and Speed had "a streak of lavender, and spots soft as May violets."[14]

As an adult, Lincoln's relations with women and his later marriage were troubled, and he suffered debilitating depression, while his intimate friendships with men continued. One well known relationship was with a man named Captain David Derickson. The official government history of Derickson's regiment notes that Derickson "advanced so far in the president's confidence and esteem that in Mrs. Lincoln's absence he frequently spent the night at his cottage, sleeping in the same bed with him, and — it is said — making use of his Excellency's night shirt!" The affair was so well known around Washington that the wife of a Naval secretary wrote in her diary: "Tish says, Oh, there is a Bucktail soldier here devoted to the president, drives with him, and when Mrs. L is not home, sleeps with him. What stuff!"[15] I will apply here my standard disclaimer that it cannot be said with certainty that Lincoln had gay sex or anything like a gay identity, but clearly something colorful was going on during those long years of nightshirt swapping and thigh admiring.

More interesting to me, Abraham Lincoln is modern enough, and well documented enough, to begin puzzling through what these socially atypical behaviors indicate about his greatness. A man who invited another man to his bed whenever his wife left town was clearly not 100% heterosexual. From what is known of Lincoln's thinking, I proudly claim him as a queer spirit — atypical, eccentric, and different — and maybe those were precisely the differences that made Abraham Lincoln so great. It is a common trait of gay people that we are born nearer the gender divide, humanity's primary division, and experience gendered attractions outside the norm, and then must learn how to reconcile those divisions in ways most straight people never have to work through for themselves. Only through reconciliation of his own internal divides could he stand as the bridge across history's bloodiest civil war and guide his nation through to the other side. As he said at the time: "The dogmas of the quiet past are inadequate to the stormy present. The occasion is piled high with difficulty, and we must rise with the occasion. As our case is new, so we must think anew and act anew."[16]

As an aside, Lincoln was probably not the first President to love another man in the White House. In contrast to the greatness of Lincoln, his predecessor President James Buchanan is often considered one of America's least effective presidents. Buchanan was also a lifelong bachelor who spent thirteen years living with William Rufus King, another bachelor who had served as America's Vice President in an earlier administration. These two were so effeminate that the older President Andrew Jackson referred to them as "Miss Nancy" and "Aunt Fancy," while others called them "Buchanan and his better half."[17] When King went off to France for a time Buchanan grew lonely, writing: "I am now 'solitary and alone,' having no companion in the house with me. I have gone a wooing to several gentlemen, but have not succeeded with any one of them. I feel that it is not good for man to be alone, and should not be astonished to find myself married to some old maid who can nurse me when I am sick, provide good dinners for me when I am well, and not expect from me any very ardent or romantic affection."[18] I love the idea of an effeminate President and an effeminate ex-Vice President showing each other affection in the stately rooms of the White House.

One of the greatest celebrities of the nineteenth century was the openly gay Irish writer and personality Oscar Wilde. He was best known for his humorous plays that were the hits of London in the 1890s, like *The Importance of Being Earnest* and *Salome,* his novel *The Picture of Dorian Gray,* and the witty remarks that made him so quotable. I cannot resist sharing a few of my favorite Wilde quotes:

> Selfishness is not living as one wishes to live, it is asking others to live as one wishes to live.

> Arguments are to be avoided; they are always vulgar and often convincing.

> Always forgive your enemies; nothing annoys them so much.

> When the gods wish to punish us, they answer our prayers.

> What is a cynic? A man who knows the price of everything and the value of nothing.

> In this world there are only two tragedies. One is not getting what one wants, and the other is getting it.

> The only thing worse than being talked about is not being talked about.

We are all in the gutter, but some of us are looking at the stars.

While traveling to the American West he also gifted San Francisco one of its most famous quotes: "It's an odd thing, but anyone who disappears is said to be seen in San Francisco. It must be a delightful city and possess all the attractions of the next world." Wilde also became one of the first modern people famous for being gay because of the phrase he made famous: "the love that dare not speak its name."

Wilde married and had two children, but his great love was Lord Alfred Douglas, son of the Marquess of Queensberry, the man who gave boxing the Marquess of Queensberry rules. It appears the Marquess's machismo was offended by Wilde dating his son, so Queensberry called out Wilde as a "posing somdomite [sic]" in public. Wilde unwisely responded by suing Queensberry for libel, a charge that carried a penalty of two years in prison. Queensberry was arrested, the scandal was picked up by the press, and the trial became a spectacle.

In Queensberry's trial the prosecution called several male prostitutes to testify that Wilde was leading young men into degenerate homosexuality. Initially Wilde was flippant and witty. Accused of kissing a particular servant boy, Wilde replied, "Oh, dear no. He was a particularly plain boy — unfortunately ugly — I pitied him for it." When the lawyer pressed Wilde for why the boy's ugliness was relevant, Wilde grew flustered. "You sting me and insult me and try to unnerve me; and at times one says things flippantly when one ought to speak more seriously."[19] Several of the prostitutes testified they had, in fact, had sex with Wilde and he lost the case, making Wilde responsible for all of Queensberry's legal expenses, which bankrupted him.

On leaving that trial, Wilde was arrested for gross indecency, the term of the time for improper relations with other men, based on the previous trial's testimonies. In court again, the prosecutor asked Wilde: "What is 'the love that dare not speak its name'?", to which Wilde replied:

> "The love that dare not speak its name" in this century is such a great affection of an elder for a younger man as there was between David and Jonathan, such as Plato made the very basis of his philosophy, and such as you find in the sonnets of Michelangelo and Shakespeare. It is that deep spiritual affection that is as pure as it is perfect. It dictates and pervades great works of art, like those of Shakespeare and

Michelangelo, and those two letters of mine, such as they are. It is in this century misunderstood, so much misunderstood that it may be described as "the love that dare not speak its name," and on that account of it I am placed where I am now. It is beautiful, it is fine, it is the noblest form of affection. There is nothing unnatural about it. It is intellectual, and it repeatedly exists between an older and a younger man, when the older man has intellect, and the younger man has all the joy, hope and glamour of life before him. That it should be so, the world does not understand. The world mocks at it, and sometimes puts one in the pillory for it.[20]

In the end Wilde was convicted and sentenced to two years' hard labor. The judge declared that sentence "totally inadequate for a case such as this," declaring it, "the worst case I have ever tried."[21] As if Wilde's actions were worse than all the murders, rapes, and child abuse this judge had heard. After a life of comfort, the "hard labour, hard fare and a hard bed"[22] of prison destroyed Wilde's health. Although he worked for a couple of years after his release, his health never recovered, and he died of cerebral meningitis in 1900.

From prison Wilde wrote a letter to Lord Alfred Douglas called *De Profundis,* or from the depths, that reads like a manifesto of the modern gay movement. While people told him to forget who he was after prison, Wilde responded: "To regret one's own experiences is to arrest one's own development. To deny one's own experiences is to put a lie into the lips of one's own life. It is no less than a denial of the soul.[23] Wilde's arrogant honesty, heard around the world, meant that "the love that dare not speak its name" was heard with increasing clarity and volume over the next hundred years. And while there is controversy about what was actually said and when, there is a wonderful legend that Wilde's final quip came in the form of his last words as he lay dying in a shabby Paris hotel room, looked up, and uttered, "Either that wallpaper goes or I do."[24]

To name just three more of the great nineteenth century gay men: Pyotr Ilyich Tchaikovsky, the Russian composer who wrote *Swan Lake, The Nutcracker,* and the *1812 Overture;*[25] Cardinal John Henry Newman, recently sainted, for whom the Catholic Newman Centers at universities around the world are named;[26] and Lord Robert Baden-Powell, the British lieutenant-general who founded the Boy Scouts.[27] I call out these three names to note the connection with modern times as Russia, the Catholic Church, and the Boy Scouts have all excelled in their homophobia, yet each one gained so much from gay men. Someday society will understand the connections that link the truths of these men's natures with the importance of their accomplishments.

Heroes

Make visible what,
without you,
might perhaps
have never been seen.

~ *Robert Bresson*

One of the joys of more modern history is the acknowledgment that women also have lives worth recording. Early American history, like most of history, tended to leave women out. In all the histories of colonial America, for example, there is only one record of sex between women. Plymouth Colony residents Sarah White Norman and Mary Vincent Hammon were charged with "lewd behavior each with other upon a bed" in 1648.[1] Of course that does not mean lesbian relationships did not exist in colonial America; it just means they were not acknowledged. By the 1800s things were changing, a fact visible to people as distant as my Mormon ancestors out in the desolation of the Utah Territories. An 1856 diary entry of a Salt Lake City man noted that a Mormon woman "was trying to seduce a young girl,"[2] and by 1873 the church's *Women's Exponent* magazine published an essay called "Woman Lovers" that explained, "Perhaps you do not know it, but there are women who fall in love with each other."[3]

Lesbian relationships entered the mainstream American lexicon in the late 1800s via Henry James's novel *The Bostonians*, which told the story of two unmarried and financially independent women living together, an arrangement that came to be known as a Boston marriage. One of the most famous partners in a Boston marriage was Jane Addams, an immigration activist who founded Chicago's Hull House, a settlement house designed to integrate newly arrived and impoverished European immigrants with their more prosperous American neighbors. Addams went on to become the first woman awarded the Nobel Peace Prize, and Hull House is a National Historic Landmark open to visitors. Hull's closest companion was a woman named Mary Rozet Smith, with whom she shared a home in Chicago and a summer house in Maine, and who helped raise funds for Hull House.[4]

My favorite reminder of a Boston marriage is *America the Beautiful*, a song of such evocative simplicity it is often mistaken for America's national anthem. Written by Katherine Lee Bates when she was teaching English in Colorado Springs one summer, "One day some of the other teachers and I decided to go on a trip to 14,000-foot Pikes Peak. We hired a prairie wagon. Near the top we had to leave the wagon and go the rest of the way on mules. I was very tired. But when I saw the view, I felt great joy. All the wonder of America seemed displayed there, with the sea-like expanse."[5] As the song says: "Oh beautiful for spacious skies, For amber waves of grain, For purple mountain majesties, Above the fruited plain!"[6] How striking the Rockies must have looked to a woman who lived for twenty-five years in Wellesley, Massachusetts with her companion Katherine Coman, to whom she wrote: "It was never very possible to leave Wellesley [for good], because so many love-anchors held me there, and it seemed least of all possible when I had just found the long-desired way to your dearest heart... Of course I want to come to you, very much as I want to come to Heaven."[7]

With the rise of women's rights in the twentieth century, a variety of lesbian and bisexual writers emerged into the public eye like Virginia Woolf, Edna St. Vincent Millay, Elsa Gidlow, Radclyffe Hall, and novelist Sarah Orne Jewett, or "Pinney," who lived in a Boston marriage with her partner Annie Fields, or "Fuff," widow of *The Atlantic* editor James T. Fields.[8] One of the most fascinating women of that period, and famously lesbian, was Gertrude Stein, who was such a powerhouse that she literally helped create twentieth century culture.

If I were to pick the one person who best exemplifies the ability of gay people to synthesize culture into something new, it might be Stein. She grew up in Oakland, California in a wealthy Jewish family that collected art and valued education. After graduating from Radcliffe, Stein moved to Paris in 1903 and began holding Saturday salons where like-minded people gathered to entertain each other through conversation, readings, and the like surrounded by the art of her friends Gaugin, Bonnard, Renoir, Toulouse-Lautrec, Manet, and Picasso. Years later, the *New York Times* called her home the first museum of modern art.[9] In 1907, Stein met the love of her life, Alice B. Toklas, about whom she wrote the delightfully named *The Autobiography of Alice B. Toklas, by Gertrude Stein*. By integrating poetry, people, paintings, visitors, writing, and friendships, Stein was one of the people who helped to create twentieth century culture's forward lean into creative change and relentless synthesis.

While Germany's Nazis hated the Jews, they also demonized homosexuals. The creative always threaten the rigid, and few were more rigid than the Nazis. By the end of World War II, over one hundred thousand gay men were arrested, and fifty thousand convicted and sent to prison. Many hundreds were castrated or mutilated in Nazi experiments to cure them.[10] While Jews wore two overlapping gold triangles to form the Star of David, homosexuals were given pink triangles to label them deviants, a symbol the modern gay movement reclaimed many years later. Five to ten thousand gay men were sent to concentration camps where they were among the worst treated inmates.

In a horrifying postscript, the gay victims of Nazi atrocity were not liberated after the war.[11] With the fall of the fascists, homosexual prisoners were left in prison because their convictions as sexual deviants were considered just by the German and Allied governments. When finally released at the end of their sentences, these men were labeled sex offenders and denied reparations and state pensions.

Paradoxically, if there is a single individual who can claim credit for stopping the Nazis, it was a gay man named Alan Turing. A brilliant scientist, Turing was the first person to conceptualize the "thinking machine" now called a computer. During the war Turing was a key member of the secret code breaking team at England's Bletchley Park where he and his thinking machines cracked the Enigma code, allowing the Allies to intercept commands sent to German U-boats in real time, turning the course of the war. Alan Turing was described by *Time Magazine* as one of the one hundred most important people of the twentieth century, but saving the world was not enough to prove a gay life acceptable in his day. In 1952, Turing was convicted of being a homosexual by a British court under the same gross indecency statute used against Oscar Wilde. Publicly humiliated and chemically castrated by court order, his career and personal life destroyed, Alan Turing committed suicide in 1954 at the age of forty-one. It is hard to overestimate the importance of Alan Turing. He is often called the father of modern computing, and science historian George Dyson declared the entire digital world Turing's cathedral.[12]

Back in America, African Americans pursued their struggle for equal rights, and one of that movement's greatest leaders was a gay man named Bayard Rustin. While most people may not know his name, they know what he did, as it was Rustin who organized the 1963 rally where Martin Luther King gave his *I Have a Dream* speech. Raised a Quaker, it was Rustin who convinced King to get rid of guns during the Montgomery bus boycott and not respond to the horrors of white cruelty with retaliatory violence. It was Rustin who pushed the black civil rights leaders to pursue Gandhi's ideas of non-violence, pushing the movement into action but without violence, greatly increasing its moral authority. Rustin also helped found the Southern Christian Leadership Conference and was known to be such an honorable man that he would not lie about his homosexuality, even when such honesty was incredibly dangerous. One of Rustin's lovers from the 1940s said Rustin never showed any shame about his sexuality, which seems appropriate for a man who based his life on the slogan: "Oppose all injustice."[13]

For one more empowering example, it is hard to comprehend how much Gandhi's conceptualization of nonviolent revolution has contributed to peaceful change across the world. By appealing to British moral justice, Gandhi led the Indian people to overthrow centuries of imperial British domination without ever going to war. The name Mahatma was a title the people gave Gandhi, meaning great spirit, and part of Gandhi's wisdom came from his unique experiences in life, including his love for at least one other man. Back in 1908, while living in South Africa, Gandhi left his wife to live with a German architect and body builder named Hermann Kallenbach. For two years they lived together in the same house from where Gandhi wrote to Kallenbach, calling himself "Upper House" and Kallenbach "Lower House: "Your portrait (the only one) stands on my mantelpiece in my bedroom. The mantelpiece is opposite to the bed," while insisting that Kallenbach never "look lustfully upon any woman." Gandhi also wrote cryptically that Vaseline and cotton wool were a "constant reminder" to "show to you and me how completely you have taken possession of my body. This is slavery with a vengeance."[14] Later stories made Gandhi sound more sexually diverse, but faced with atypical sexual desires and the many racial and legal troubles he experienced, the highly moral Gandhi had to work out his own internal divisions. In the process he learned how to transform the world.

Creative thinkers come in every flavor. Gay people have no magical qualities unavailable to the rest of the population, but as the truth of queer lives became increasingly visible in modern times, it grew more and more obvious that many of society's most pivotal figures were gay, which should come as no surprise. Out of the fog of denial came an understanding of people like the Mahatma Gandhi, teaching the world a new and more peaceful way to overthrow injustice, and people like Bayard Rustin, who followed Gandhi's example and helped topple some of America's most intransigent prejudices. When global warfare threatened, Alan Turing subverted the dark powers and launched the digital revolution. Through it all, powerful women like Gertrude Stein forged modern life from the converging forces of the twentieth century. As gay and queer people became more and more visible, our roles as the bridges carrying humankind across the dark and into a better place grew increasingly clear, and at some point that power had to burst out into public view.

Liberation

There is a deep-seated repugnance
in the human breast
against understanding the processes
in which we are involved.
Such understanding involves
too much responsibility for our actions.

~ *Marshall McLuhan*

GAY LIBERATION GREW out of many different forces, but the story of how my native San Francisco became a gay mecca provides one colorful example of how gay people gathered, found each other, and formed a collective sense of identity. Born of the gold rush of 1849, San Francisco exploded into existence as a large, wealthy, and powerful city populated almost entirely by men. As the easily accessible gold petered out, the city's port remained notorious as the Barbary Coast, America's gateway to the Orient and home to a thriving community of debauched sailors from all over the world.

After Japan attacked Pearl Harbor, the United States entered World War II, and San Francisco became the center of America's mobilization against the Japanese empire. Almost every American soldier, sailor, and airman sent to fight in the Pacific and Far East was processed through San Francisco. This had two big effects. First, men and women from small towns across America discovered our beautiful and libertine city. Second, by throwing together small town people from all over the country, young gay men and women discovered each other. The military helped through official postings of the places military personnel were not supposed to go, so closeted young gay people knew exactly where to find others like themselves.[1] Stories of American gay men from the 1970s are filled with references to the importance of this massive war mobilization in their process of self-identifying as gay.

Servicemen in the Pacific Theater later caught in compromising situations had their official documents stamped "dishonorable discharge" and were sent back to the nearest American port, usually San Francisco.[2] With no money to continue traveling and their shame stamped in their official papers, many of these gay ex-servicemen found new homes in America's most liberal city Here they flourished and built a new kind of community social engineered by the US Military.

After the war, San Francisco was the leading edge of a counter-culture breaking out of the restrictive 1950s. I cannot imagine the thrill the night Allen Ginsberg read *Howl* to an appreciative crowd in North Beach. "I saw the best minds of my generation destroyed by madness, starving hysterical naked, dragging themselves through the negro streets at dawn looking for an angry fix."[3] People of the day were shocked by Ginsberg's blunt vernacular language describing his gay life. The result was an obscenity trial followed across the country that *Howl* eventually won. As Ginsberg later explained, "The poems get misinterpreted as promotion of homosexuality. Actually, it's more like promotion of frankness, about any subject."[4] He also described the connection he felt between being gay and his creative abilities: "Homosexuality is a condition. And because it alienated me, or set me apart from the beginning, it served as a catalyst for self examination or detailed realization of my environment, the reasons why everyone else is different and why I'm different."[5]

San Francisco certainly was different. It was here that William S. Burroughs wrote the *Naked Lunch*, which was also challenged, but under the sodomy laws.[6] As in other cities, San Francisco police routinely arrested men for the crime of being gay, yet a man named Jose Sarria performed opera at a bar called the Black Cat, in full drag. His shows often ended with the crowd holding hands and singing "God Bless Us Nelly Queens" to the tune of "God Save The Queen," spilling out into the streets as they sang. As Sarria used to say, "United we stand, divided they catch us one by one."[7] In 1961 Jose Sarria became the first openly gay person to run for public office in America as a candidate for San Francisco City Supervisor. He had a hard time, back in those fearful days, getting the twenty-five signatures needed to put his name on the ballot; but even running a campaign without publicity, he nearly won.[8] When I moved back to San Francisco in the 1990s, Sarria was hosting a counterpoint to the traditional Christmas sing-along *Messiah* called the *Dance-Along Nutcracker*, where Sarria himself, then in his seventies, danced as the Sugar Plum Fairy. The photos of him in his tutu and fairy wings, flanked by young men dressed as toy soldiers, are an utter delight. I regret to this day that I never joined in.

Organized political action for gay rights in America arrived with the formation of the Mattachine Society. Founded in Los Angeles in 1950 by Harry Hay, they took their name from unmarried men in medieval France who performed as masked jesters mocking oppression and stirring rebellion. Organizing as gay men was so dangerous in those days that it took Hay years of searching to find six gay men brave enough to meet in secret at his home with the window shades drawn. At a time when being public about homosexuality meant the loss of employment, friends, and family, it was the Mattachine Society that first mobilized to provide legal support for a gay man faced with fabricated police accusations of sexual misconduct.[9]

A few years later, a young San Francisco lesbian couple named Del Martin and Phyllis Lyon founded the Daughters of Bilitis as a social organization supporting lesbians, naming it after a fictional friend of the Greek poet Sappho. They later admitted the name was a bit of camouflage. "If anyone asked us, we could always say we belong to a poetry club."[10] Fifty years after meeting, Martin and Lyon made history as the first same-sex couple to legally marry in the state of California.

One of the Mattachine leaders who stood out in the march towards gay liberation was a gentle man with a strong moral compass named Frank Kameny. Kameny was a veteran of World War II working as a Harvard trained government astronomer in 1957 when he refused to answer questions about his sexual orientation. As homosexuals were banned from government service, he was fired. What happened next made history, because Kameny fought back, taking his case all the way to the US Supreme Court, the first equal rights claim based on sexual orientation. Kameny lost that case, but spent the rest of his life fighting for gay rights.

In 1965, Kameny led the first gay rights protest in front of the White House. There were only ten demonstrators, as most gay people of the time were too afraid to appear in public. The men dressed in white shirts, jackets, and ties, and the women wore skirts to conform to public sensibilities and prove to a skeptical world that homosexuals were equal to straight people. Though their protests were small, ten openly gay protesters was such a radical occurrence that the demonstration was covered by every major news outlet across the country.

Kameny simply refused to be ashamed of being gay. As he wrote more recently, not long before his death:

> I am a gay veteran of front-line combat in Europe in World War II. I did not fight that war to return to second-class citizenship or back-of-the-bus status (or off the bus altogether) for me and my fellow gays...
>
> We gays know that our homosexuality is a divinely inspired gift and blessing, given to us by our true God to be enjoyed to its fullest, exultantly, exuberantly and joyously.
>
> We seek not "special rights and privileges" as you term them, but precise equality of rights and privileges in what is our America, for us explicitly as gay Americans (not merely "American Americans" so to speak) fully — fully — as much as it is your America as non-gay Americans.
>
> To repeat: For us, as gay Americans, this is our America, fully as much as it is yours, and you are not going to be allowed to steal it from us, try as you may — and you are certainly trying very hard.[11]

The movement grew, but slowly, and gay people continued to lose their jobs. An employee of the Library of Congress was fired in 1962 because, as the Library's report found: "that you find members of the male sex attractive; that you have been in bed with men; and that you have enjoyed embracing them." That document is now a symbol of the incredible progress we have made, as that anti-gay report is now part of the Library of Congress's official Frank Kameny collection.[12] In 2010, Kameny stood next to Barack Obama as the President signed a bill giving equal benefits to gay federal employees. A dozen of Kameny's original protest signs are in the Smithsonian museum, and the US Park Service put Kameny's home on the National Register of Historic Places. In the 1960s Kameny coined the term Gay is Good; he believed it and worked tirelessly to prove it to a country that could not even understand what he was trying to say.

As the beatniks of the 1950s were replaced by the hippies of the 1960s, San Francisco led the worldwide revolution in changing sexual mores. Seeking the colorful freedom of hippie life, men and women who felt different and out of sync with mainstream conformity fled to the liberal haven of San Francisco. Among all those hippies were closeted gay people who felt disenfranchised from their home communities, finding a new sense of openness in the heady free-for-all of social transformation. Over time the gay hippies spilled out of the Haight-Ashbury neighborhood and over the hill into the neighboring Castro district, a neighborhood filled with neglected Victorian homes ripe for renovation. News of this transformation spread, and San Francisco became famous around the world as a magnet for gay people.

Early gay rights workers faced threats from every direction. In the 1950s and 60s it was a brave act to simply mail a gay rights newsletter, as the US Mail often labeled them obscene, illegal, and subject to punishment. Slowly, these pioneers added small success to small success. The legal framework was ready for what came next, because when change did come, it came quickly, as the tidy assumptions of the straight world blew open with the Stonewall riots of June 28, 1969.

The Stonewall Inn was a hole-in-the-wall bar on Christopher street in New York's Greenwich Village, across from a tiny wedge of a park. The bar was controlled by shady underworld types, as were most gay establishments back when homosexuality itself was illegal. Stonewall's clientele included an assortment of people society considered misfits: drag queens, dykes, gay men, and displaced young people. At 1:28 AM on that summer night of 1969, the New York City police came in to do what they routinely did — they raided the bar, lined everyone up, checked that the gender of their clothing matched the gender printed on their government IDs, threatened them with exposure, and probably extorted money. In other words, New York's Finest were doing their regular job, asserting the power of the straight majority over the deviants.

On that night, however, the cops pushed the wrong drag queens, because on that night, the drag queens fought back. Someone in the crowd shouted "Gay power!" A drag queen got shoved by a cop and she hit him back with her purse. Someone else started singing *We Shall Overcome*. Meanwhile, four policemen were wrestling a powerful woman in handcuffs who fought back and escaped, twice, swearing and shouting. Her name is not known, other than the description of bystanders that she was "a dyke — stone butch." A policeman hit her over the head with his billy club as others picked her up to throw her into a police car as she yelled, "Why don't you guys do something?" And the crowd erupted.

The Stonewall riots lasted for days, spreading across lower Manhattan. More importantly, gay expressions of affection, so long hidden, spilled out into the streets. As one participant put it, "The word is out... The fags have had it with oppression."[13]

I owe my right to full and equal rights as a citizen of the United States to a bunch of angry drag queens and a stone butch dyke, the mothers of gay liberation. We are only where we are today because of their fury and audacity. These were not the polite gays in swanky apartments sipping cocktails and telling themselves everything was OK. These were the misfits who could not pass as straight or pretend any longer. I will always honor drag queens, angry dykes, and anyone willing to let their atypicality blaze bright enough to embolden the rest of us. They certainly changed my life. Many other actions of thoughtful resistance and preparation preceded the success of Stonewall, but the world tipped over that night at the Stonewall Inn, and it has not been the same since.

One year later, a bisexual woman named Brenda Howard organized the Christopher Street Liberation Day March to commemorate the one-year anniversary of the Stonewall rebellion, a march that grew into New York's Gay Pride Parade. Howard became known as the Mother of Pride.[14] For the first time in modern history, gay people marched down the middle of the street declaring we were not just OK with who we were. We were Out, we were Proud, and we were done with the oppression. Over time the stridency of the original Gay Liberation and Freedom marches morphed into the more neutral sounding Gay Pride, and to this day pride events around the world are often held in June to commemorate that pivotal event outside a New York City gay bar.

As Frank Kameny summed up the changes: "When I got involved, going back to '61, there were five or six gay organizations in the country. At the time of Stonewall, there were 50 or 60 gay organizations. The best count by 1970, there were 1,500 gay organizations. A year after that, the best count, there were 2,500 and people stopped counting. So there was a very real change."[15]

I was born in 1960, so I missed those fundamental events of gay history, but I did catch one of the earlier gay pride marches back in the 1970s. I was a teenager, and after spending the morning at the Metropolitan Museum of Art in New York, I went out onto the street to find Fifth Avenue closed to traffic. Far to the south, a crowd was moving up the boulevard, apparently a parade of some sort. I approached a big Irish cop on the street corner and asked what was going on. He gave me a bit of an eye roll and told me it was "some homosexual thing." My mind reeled at the thought. It is almost hard for me to wrap my head around today, but I spent the rest of that incredible afternoon as a young Mormon boy wandering through a 1970s gay pride parade and the subsequent gathering in Central Park. I marveled at the astonishing variety of people there and wondered in my seventeen-year-old naiveté how much I was one of them. It took me several years to solidify that answer. At the time I was a preppy kid, clean-cut and wholesome, and I did not feel much kinship with the diverse urban crowd I saw there.

The first publicly gay person I can recall was Technical Sergeant Leonard Matlovich who appeared in his military uniform on the cover of *Time Magazine* in 1975 under the headline "I Am a Homosexual." His face is forever etched in my memory because of that act of public bravery. Matlovich received a Purple Heart for serving in Vietnam and was the first US service member to openly declare that he was gay, an action he took to fight the military's ban on homosexuals. It would be thirty-seven more years before the military removed that ban, and Matlovich died of AIDS in 1988. His tombstone in Washington, DC's Congressional Cemetery does not bear his name. Instead it stands as a monument to all gay veterans, bearing the inscription: "When I was in the military, they gave me a medal for killing two men and a discharge for loving one."[16]

While a few smaller successes preceded him, it was Harvey Milk who made national news when he won a seat on the San Francisco Board of Supervisors in 1977 as an openly gay man. Building a diverse political base from his little camera shop on Castro Street, Milk's success reached across demographic divides and even included organized labor among his supporters. Milk famously fought against the highly publicized Briggs initiative, led by Florida orange juice spokesperson Anita Bryant, that sought to ban all gay teachers from California schools. As Milk said in a victory speech in 1978, there are kids in far flung places who will hear about an elected official in San Francisco, and it will give them hope. "Without hope, not only gays, but those who are blacks, the Asians, the disabled, the seniors, the us's: without hope the us's give up. I know that you can't live on hope alone, but without it, life is not worth living. And you, and you, and you, and you have got to give them hope."[17]

Milk's success and vision angered many. Fellow city supervisor Dan White was particularly troubled by the political success of the city's gay community. White's good Christian law and order sensibilities were so offended that he went to San Francisco's ornate city hall and shot dead Mayor George Moscone and Harvey Milk. The city was left in turmoil. During White's murder trial, his defense argued White had eaten too much junk food which caused mental deterioration, a condition the press dubbed the Twinkie defense. The jury was sympathetic, and for killing two men in cold blood White's sentence was seven years in jail. With time served and good behavior he would be released in five. Hearing the verdict, the gay community exploded in what became known as the White Night riots. Thousands poured into the streets and fought the police, throwing rocks at buildings and lighting police cars on fire. When the gay riots subsided, the police rioted back, storming into the Castro neighborhood in their riot gear to beat patrons of the Elephant Walk bar and random citizens along the street. By the end of that night, sixty-one policemen and one hundred rioters and gay residents of the Castro were in the hospital. Five years later, Dan White was released. A year and a half after that, White committed suicide.

Harvey Milk believed in a brighter future for gay people. In the taped statement he made right before the assassination he believed was coming, Milk said, "I cannot prevent anyone from getting angry, or mad, or frustrated. I can only hope that they'll turn that anger and frustration and madness into something positive, so that two, three, four, five hundred will step forward, so the gay doctors will come out, the gay lawyers, the gay judges, gay bankers, gay architects ... I hope that every professional gay will say 'enough,' come forward and tell everybody, wear a sign, let the world know. Maybe that will help."[18] Milk was right of course, people coming out changed everything, but he had no way of imagining the health epidemic that finally made that happen.

There was plenty of gay history before Stonewall, but it was often hidden or camouflaged. To give just one wonderful example from an earlier period, the Harlem Renaissance of the 1920s was a powerful cultural movement. Langston Hughes, Alice Dunbar-Nelson, Claude McKay, Wallace Thurman, Alain Locke, Angelina Weld Grimké, Richard Bruce Nugent, Bessie Smith, Gertrude "Ma" Rainey, Ethel Waters, and Josephine Baker were all important members of the Harlem Renaissance, and every one of them had gay or bisexual experiences. As Ma Rainey, often called the Mother of the Blues, sang in the *Prove It On Me Blues*, "Went out last night with a crowd of my friends, They must've been women, 'cause I don't like no men."[19] Any number of male artists, including the powerful Robert Johnson, sang and recorded the *Sissy Man Blues*: "Lord, if you can't send me no woman, please send me some sissy man."[20] The acclaimed writer Langston Hughes largely hid his attraction to men, but as his biographer Arnold Rampersad wrote, "Hughes found some young men, especially dark-skinned men, appealing and sexually fascinating," specifying that, "Virile young men of very dark complexion fascinated him."[21]

Looking at these figures of such cultural importance, it is interesting to note the part non-standard sexuality and gender played in this pivotal revolution. As historian Henry Louis Gates, Jr. observed, the Harlem Renaissance "was surely as gay as it was black."[22] It makes me think — if the Italian Renaissance was super gay and the Harlem Renaissance was super gay, then many of history's great cultural rebirths were probably super gay. It appears that queer people are an integral part of cultural revolutions and progress.

Jumping forward to today, the biggest thing I notice in the modern LGBT movement is the prominent rise of gay women. Part of this is the result of AIDS, which that killed off so many gay men in their prime, giving more space on the public stage for gay women. More importantly, there are just so many magnificently successful lesbians out there, far too many to name. Some are as affable as talk show hostess Ellen DeGeneres, while others as feisty as Rosie O'Donnell, as athletic as tennis star Martina Navratilova, as savvy as financial guru Suze Orman, or as smart as news anchor Rachel Maddow. And then there was NASA astronaut Sally Ride, who was not only the first female American astronaut, but probably the first gay person to leave the earth for outer space. What I love about this list is the breadth of their diversity. It is an incredible honor to be part of a community represented by such impressive women.

Earlier in the revolution, gay people became famous just for being openly gay and honest about it in public. These days, gay people are famous for something else first, like being a talk show host or astronaut, and the fact that they are gay becomes just another side note to a larger life. Liberation meant claiming all of our inner truths as the foundation of a life of integrity, no matter the opposition, an accomplishment we celebrate with pride to this day.

TWENTY

AIDS

When you change
the way you look at things,
the things you look at change.

~ *Max Planck*

I WAS NEWLY OUT as a young gay man when AIDS appeared. It is hard
to remember now, but gay men were dying horrifying deaths for years before
we even knew what was killing us. We did not know it was a virus. We did not
know it was sexually transmitted. We did not know if we were already infected.
All that information came later. At the time the only thing we knew was that
gay men in big cities were dying in large numbers from rare and terrifying
illnesses, and the reaction from much of mainstream America was to declare
our suffering and deaths just retribution for the sin of being gay. The story of

AIDS is often told as a morality tale. People who already disliked gay people saw AIDS as vindication of their bias, a disease that validated their belief that God hated the same people they did. I also view AIDS as a morality tale, but with a profoundly different meaning.

In the early 1980s, a new set of diseases, including rarely seen ones like the skin lesions of Kaposi's sarcoma and the lung problems of pneumocystis pneumonia, appeared in young and otherwise healthy men in San Francisco, New York, and Los Angeles. No one knew the underlying cause of those illnesses, but it seemed to arise from some kind of underlying immune deficiency. By the end of 1981, 121 Americans had died of AIDS and many more were sick.[1]

While the government response to health outbreaks in the general populace, like Legionnaires disease a few years earlier, was swift and comprehensive, dying gay men were seen as justice by social conservatives. People like North Carolina Senator Jesse Helms wrote off gay people as "weak, morally sick wretches" as he blocked funding for a medical response to the disease. Together with Ronald Reagan, a president who would not even say the word AIDS until six years into the crisis, political conservatives blocked the immediate medical responses that are key to stopping epidemics.[2]

To share but one moment illuminating moment from that era, Reagan's Press Secretary Larry Speakes was asked a question about AIDS in a White House press conference in 1982. His response: "What's AIDS?" The room erupted in laughter. When the questioner clarified that a third of the people with the virus had died, Speakes responded, "I don't have it. Do you?," and the room laughed again. The official White House transcripts records thirteen rounds of laughter at the idea of gay citizens dying.[3] Speakes never did get to a serious answer, as dying gay men were little more than a punch line to these powerful men. By the time President Reagan finally spoke about the problem, over twenty thousand Americans had died, and thirty-six thousand more had the disease.[4] I remember thinking in those years how differently the government would have responded to an epidemic killing Girl Scouts.

The nature of the illness compounded the disaster. Unlike something like a fast-spreading flu, AIDS had a long incubation period between infection and illness. People got and spread HIV for years before anyone knew the virus existed. The result was an epidemic that emerged into public awareness only after it was widespread, doubling the need for quick government action, which did not come. Conservative politicians decided being anti-gay was more important than being pro-health, and the results were predictably grisly. The Vietnam War is remembered for devastating a generation when nearly sixty thousand American soldiers were killed, yet over a similar time period three hundred thousand Americans died of AIDS.

Sometimes young people ask why there are so few gay elders leading our community today. It is hard for me to respond without tearing up a bit. Most of them died. Most of the men who should be reaching the peaks of their careers and personal maturity right now; the men who would have grown into business and spiritual leaders, movie stars, musicians, designers, innovators, grandfathers, and the wise old men of our community are gone. Many of our most dynamic, active, colorful, playful, and soulful people are long gone. They never reached middle age. They never reached their elder years. They are not here to live out the rest of their lives with us. All that is left is a bit of emptiness in the hearts of those of us who remember.

Though the thunderclouds of AIDS and the anti-gay politics of those years were suffocatingly dark, one bit of sunshine came in the form of lesbian women who took up the slack. It is almost a cliché to say that women in general, and gay women in particular, were not seen and valued by the larger society. Yet as gay men lay dying it was often gay women who carried the movement forward. They took hold of the organizations, agitated for change, and cared for their gay brothers in profoundly selfless ways. They did not have to. Gay men and lesbians often have little in common, and I am ashamed when I hear how dismissive gay men can be of lesbians. These young people are forgetting that when gay men were dying there were many, many lesbians who stepped up to the challenge.

For those who did not live through the AIDS epidemic, I recommend a few movies to help access that time in a meaningful way. Larry Kramer's *The Normal Heart* tells of how it looked for those hit by the first wave of illness in New York, and the tragedy of how both the gay and straight communities responded. Farther into the epidemic, Tony Kushner's *Angels in America* puts the devastation in the context of politics and mythology, even weaving Mormons into the story. Then to see it as it really happened, watch the documentary *We Were Here*. I cannot watch any of these films without tissues clutched in my lap, as they bring back waves of grief over how we were treated. It is essential to understand what happened to ensure no such atrocity ever happens again.

Facing a tidal wave of destruction smashing through my community, my own reaction was to find ways to help. I delivered food to the home bound sick and dying, observing health and living conditions too abysmal and nauseating to share. There are things I saw in the depths of that tragedy that I have never spoken out loud. It must be like what soldiers experience on the battlefield, scenes too horrific for trivialization with mere words. I took a course on death and dying and led support circles for those suffering through terminal illness. I sat with groups of gay men who gathered to discuss their safe sex practices and work out their personal strategies for staying safe. I marched in the streets yelling till hoarse that this neglect of the dying was not OK. And of course I volunteered at events like the AIDS quilt in the hopes that someone outside of my small community was listening.

The deaths of hundreds of thousands of gay men changed society. AIDS pushed an entire generation out of the closet, and humanity's collective denial around sexuality began to end. As the writer Fran Lebowitz put it, "You could pretend to your family that you were straight, but you couldn't pretend you weren't dying."[5] AIDS brought an end to society's collective delusion. Before AIDS, sex was barely addressed in public. After AIDS, it was irresponsible not to discuss it openly and honestly. Lives were at stake.

Ignored and despised in our suffering, the gay community rallied. The mettle of a community is seen in times of crisis, and my community mobilized to help suffering strangers in a way rarely seen in the modern world. Groups like ACT-UP, the AIDS Coalition to Unleash Power, stepped into the breach and took direct action to make the public health agencies respond as if they were in the middle of an epidemic and lives were on the line. Acting from their brilliant slogan "Silence = Death," ACT-UP made noise everywhere from medical conferences to prominent cathedrals until people started to listen. More importantly, once they had the attention of the people in power, they had detailed action plans prepared for what to do next. At a time when the government and social safety net failed, gay people formed powerful groups that eventually got the action required.

I was sexually active before AIDS. I was one of those men who had anal sex before we knew the disease existed and before the use of condoms became widespread. Although I never got the virus, I am one of the people anti-gay moralists hold responsible. The HIV virus is hard to get, but one person injecting body fluids into an absorptive part of another person's body is a highly effective method of transmitting it. I did just that, both giving and receiving. Direct injection of another person's blood is the other major transmission vector for HIV, which is why intravenous drug users who share needles are major transmitters today.

While it is obviously true that gay men had sex in ways that promoted the spread of AIDS, the moral lesson was not as simple as some wanted to believe. To begin with, the idea that God displays his disapproval through disease is a bizarre moral stance. The resulting logic would mean that God hates newborns, as so many of the world's children die in their first few months. Only a highly selective eye can pick one disease as a sign from God and declare all others fate.

The fact is AIDS developed as new diseases usually do, from human interaction with animals. From what is now known, the HIV virus existed for millions of years in monkeys and apes and then crossed from primates to humans in Sub-Saharan Africa around a hundred years ago,[6] spreading slowly until the advent of air travel. In that way the emergence of AIDS resembled the more recent disease creation mechanisms seen in the Avian flu that crossed from birds to humans, the Swine flu (H1N1) that developed from pigs, and MERS, or Middle East Respiratory Syndrome, that passed from camels into humans.[7] It is nothing new for diseases to arise this way, but it is now occurring in a world where the rapid spread of diseases around the globe is an integral part of modern life. AIDS was just the first of those diseases to hit the public consciousness.

One of the newest medical crises is MRSA or Methicillin-resistant Staphylococcus aureus infections. These new antibiotics-resistant "super bugs" are spreading through preschools, hospitals, gyms, and other places where people are in close contact. More people now die of MRSA than AIDS, yet this new affliction is not seen by religious moralists as a sign of God's disapproval of the young, the infirm, or the buff.

Social conservatives always seem fixated on sex, so it must be the sexual nature of AIDS that made it such a clear sign of God's disapproval in their eyes. Following their logic that sexually transmitted diseases are the sign of God's disapproval, then all of God's followers should become lesbians, as lesbians have the fewest STDs.[8] Knowing that heterosexuals transmit many more sexual diseases than lesbians, by their illogical logic, God must hate heterosexual sex.

This heterosexist view of AIDS is confirmed by society's view of HPV, or Human Papillomavirus. HPV is the most common sexually transmitted infection in America and the primary cause of a variety of cancers, yet how many times have you heard preachers or politicians railing against heterosexuality for this scourge? How clear are the Mormons or Catholics or Evangelicals about HPV as a sign of God's disgust at vaginal sex? They do not condemn the majority of people who get HPV because most of those people are heterosexual.

People see what they believe. Believing something first, before looking at the evidence, leads the viewer to interpret information in ways that confirm their pre-existing view, a phenomenon called confirmation bias. Religious belief systems are particularly effective at instilling in believers a framework that warps the world around a tight-knit community until no contradictory information can get in. Any illness in gay people validated the bias against homosexuality in the minds of the anti-gay, yet no illness in straight people could lead them to question heterosexuality. The solution to perspective bias is the system called justice: innocent until proven guilty. Look at the evidence first, and then make the decision, not the other way around.

It took years of decimation and terror before action on the necessary scale began, and with its long incubation period the destruction of AIDS magnified exponentially. Worse still, early inaction in America slowed both research and education, and stigmatization of the illness as a gay moral problem affected how it was perceived worldwide. The result was the deaths of millions of Africans and others in the Third World via AIDS transmitted through heterosexual sex. In the name of anti-gay moralizing, Helms, Reagan, and their social conservative allies helped turn millions of impoverished children into orphans.

Everything changed when AIDS became a health issue. With the arrival of accurate information on the nature of the disease, gay men changed their sex practices and disease transmission dropped dramatically. Research developed drug management protocols that greatly prolonged the lives of those already infected.

The medical perspective arrived too late for many. One of my beloved friends lived with HIV for years until a characteristically bizarre AIDS-related illness hit him. In his case it was cancer of the abdominal wall. This gentle man, with an advanced degree in library science and a tender attitude towards all who knew him, wasted away in great pain, dying in his loving sister's care. We held his funeral in the AIDS Memorial Grove of Golden Gate Park, the children who loved him scattering his ashes at the base of a gnarled old redwood tree. AIDS anti-viral drugs arrived that same month. My sweet friend might still be with us today if society had seen AIDS as a medical problem first, accelerating action.

According to the old saying, every cloud has a silver lining, the silver lining of AIDS was the creation of a society more honest about sex. Prior to AIDS, a man like the flamboyant entertainer Liberace could claim he was not gay. In 1957 a London newspaper described Liberace as, "…the summit of sex — the pinnacle of masculine, feminine, and neuter. Everything that he, she, and it can ever want… a deadly, winking, sniggering, snuggling, chromium-plated, scent-impregnated, luminous, quivering, giggling, fruit-flavoured, mincing, ice-covered heap of mother love…"[9] Liberace sued them for libel and won, claiming he had never committed a gay sex act. He died of AIDS in 1987 after swearing his wasting was caused by a watermelon diet.[10]

The public does not buy this kind of story anymore. When an anti-gay Republican Senator was arrested in an airport bathroom for playing footsie with an undercover policeman in the next stall, no one believed his claim that his foot crossed under the bathroom partition because he had a wide stance.[11] Be it Catholic priests, evangelical ministers, or conservative Senators, the truth about homosexuality is out in public, even in the increasingly publicized sex habits of the repressed. After AIDS, pretending homosexuality away was no longer an option. It is hard to imagine how long the modern gay rights successes would have taken without the tectonic shifts created by AIDS.

Across the world, over thirty million people are living with HIV-AIDS. 97% of them live in the poorer half of the world, many of them in sub-Saharan Africa. Man of the afflicted still do not have access to care and treatment. Viewed globally, AIDS is not a gay disease, but of course it never was a gay disease. There is no such thing as a gay disease.

Over a million Americans are now living with HIV, but infection rates are dropping steadily, down a third over the last decade.[12] There are now drug cocktails that can lower the levels of HIV in an infected person's blood to the point it is undetectable, meaning there is little or no chance they are infective. There are also drugs HIV-negative people can take that ensure they remain uninfected. At this point one of the world's leading AIDS doctors, Doctor Anthony Fauci of the National Institutes of Health, says, "we have the tools to end this modern-day plague."[13] The only thing keeping the world from ending AIDS is willpower.

The story of AIDS did turn out to be a powerful morality tale. It was a tale of religious judgment blinding people to the humanity of others and the devastating cost of that blindness. Over time AIDS became a resounding tale of how truth wins out. It is tragic to note how prescient Oscar Wilde was when he wrote over a hundred years ago: "I have no doubt we shall win, but the road is long, and red with monstrous martyrdoms."[14]

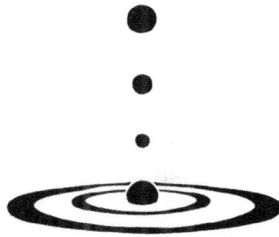

TWENTY-ONE

Now

You are a child of the universe,
no less than the trees and the stars;
you have a right to be here.
And whether or not it is clear to you,
no doubt the universe
is unfolding as it should.

~ *Desiderata*

LOOKING BACK OVER modern gay history, the exhilarating days of the sexual revolution and gay liberation were followed by a devastating epidemic and the anti-gay culture wars. By the 2000s, however, everything seemed to be moving into a more mature stasis. Society was softening and acceptance was growing. As the zeitgeist shifted, we started to think of the future, of things like marriage, families, children, and lives free from the constant attacks. Suddenly strollers appeared all over gay neighborhoods, gay pride festivals added children's play spaces, and parenting groups became part of our social matrix. Young gay people stopped caring so much about the old bars and neighborhoods because they were welcomed everywhere they went. Straight people started crowding into the traditional gay ghettos, realizing we had created some of the cities' best neighborhoods. We appeared in movies and television shows as human beings rather than buffoons or psychopathic killers. Looking around, things seemed pretty good, and for the first time in modern gay life, we began to relax and trust that everything really was going to be OK.

Into that dreamy interlude, the Mormon-lead Proposition 8 came like a punch in the face. Earlier that year, the California Supreme Court ruled for marriage equality, so couples across the state were busy celebrating their joyful weddings. Lurking in the background, though, was the group determined to play the evil villain in the gay rights story. With a gusto that surprised even those of us who knew them well, the Mormon church responded with astonishing aggression, launching an all out attack on gay marriage rights with their millions of dollars, their organizational zealotry, and a campaign filled with lies and defamation. As columnist Maureen Dowd described it in the *New York Times*, "The anti-gay-marriage proponents whipped up a moral frenzy (in California) in 2008, suggesting conjugal parity would harm children, summon the devil, tear down churches and melt civilization."[1] Proposition 8 succeeded, and marriage equality ended in California. Stunned, gay people across the country woke up the morning after that election in a state of shock, realizing the anti-gay forces were as alive as ever and coming after our rights, our families, and our lives.

Looking back on what has happened since, the Mormon leader looks less like a prophet of God and more like Japanese Admiral Isoroku Yamamoto in the movie *Tora! Tora! Tora!*. On surveying their overwhelming success at Pearl Harbor, the Admiral considered the response that would come from a wounded America and declared, "I fear all we have done is to awaken a sleeping giant and fill him with a terrible resolve."[2] The Mormons and the other backers of Prop 8 won the ballot measure, but they overplayed their hand. After witnessing their campaign and its results, something shifted in the country. From that moment on, the irrational side of the anti-gay zealots stood increasingly revealed. The result has been a series of unparalleled successes for gay rights ever since. Most notably, our fight for gay marriage has gone from win to win across America and around the world.

To describe all that is happening in the culture now is impossible, as so much is in flux, but there is one great shift worth noting. Paradoxically, the increased acceptance of gay lives has resulted in an apparent decrease in the importance of gay-straight distinctions. Whereas the old argument pitted heterosexuals against homosexuals, the newer view embraces all people as sexual. Suddenly the labels seem less important and more flexible than was ever allowed in the older ways of thinking. These new attitudes around sexuality are similar to the way young people are increasingly post-racial,[3] moving beyond the idea that these kinds of fixed characteristics indicate anything useful about a person's personality, potential, or value. As the larger collage of humanity becomes increasingly visible in our globalized world, the beauty of each individual piece remains, but the relative importance or "right-ness" of each individual fragment fades. The result is a younger generation without so much interest in pigeonholing everyone into specific boxes, even as they are busy creating an ever expanding list of colorful descriptors.

Increasingly, we live in a world that has space for us to live our lives however we choose. Being gay now means you can get married, buy a house in the quiet suburbs, raise a bunch of kids, and dream of retiring to Florida. Or you can dip yourself in glitter and ride your rainbow-stripped unicorn down the middle of your city's main street, rainbow flags streaming. You can move to the big city and live life in the fast lane, settle into a quiet small town, or travel the world and never put down roots in any one place, all without interference from the government, fear of the neighbors, or the need to hide anything about who we are. That is liberation indeed.

Part of this shift is occurring because children now have the space to grow up noticing their differing sense of gender or sexual interests at age-appropriate times. More and more, they do not have to grow into their twenties and thirties before exploring what it means to be different. They can grow up feeling what they feel when they feel it, without all the years of suppression and hiding. It is hard for someone like me to imagine what their adult world will look like, as it will be so different from all that has come before.

Sometimes it is hard to have fought so hard for something and then watch the younger generation heading forward into their new lives, largely unaware of what created this world they take for granted. The battles we fought over

AIDS and basic civil rights were often soul-crushing and bloody, but our success is most visible when people spread out picnics on the old battlefields without really understanding the tragedy that happened there.

One day I was feeling solemn, and went to visit the redwood tree where we spread my friend's ashes in the AIDS Memorial Grove. Arriving in the center of the gardens, I found a bride and groom, and their photographer, and some complicated lighting people, all gathered around taking the couple's wedding pictures amidst the beautiful blooms. I am ashamed to admit it now, but my first reaction to this scene was rage. I felt a full-bodied urge to walk up to those people and start yelling in their faces, to be that crazy person who goes off on complete strangers, screaming at them about how they do not understand. I wanted to tell them how rude it was to celebrate the youthful bloom of their heterosexuality in the midst of one of my most sacred spots, a place that honored the disease, the suffering, and the deaths of so many. I wanted them to know how unconscious they appeared in that grove that was one of the few places on the planet that honored all that my people went through because straight people were so committed to not getting it.

Then I mellowed a bit. The bride was beautiful, her dress gleaming clean and white in the brilliant sunlight. The groom was delightfully awkward, but so handsome in his crisp dark suit. They both looked so happy, so lovely, so thrilled to be themselves in that beautiful place on that beautiful day. So I decided to leave them in peace, although honestly, I am still a little angry. That is my generation's right — to remember, and to feel what it was to be there and live through all the terrible things that happened to us. At the same time, I hope their photos were beautiful and their wedding joyful, as that is their generation's right — to move on and build lives together, without feeling the burden of everything that came before.

Young kids today are growing up without the old baggage. I wish them well, and feel nothing but optimism for the possibilities. When I get a chance, I tell the current generation to pay attention and take notes, to really feel this moment we are living through, because they will be the last generation that will be able to tell their grandchildren of how things used to be and all that came before.

The time for gay equality has arrived. It is an exciting time, a time for celebration, for flowers in our hair and dancing in the streets. If there is one thing I know about what is happening now, it is that gay people are becoming part of our families, communities, churches, and societies again. And that is good news for every human being on the planet.

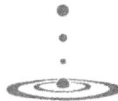

NATURE

Seeing

> Reality is that which,
> when you stop believing in it,
> doesn't go away.
>
> ~ *Philip K. Dick*

THE ABILITY TO SEE the humanity in ourselves and others, especially with complicated and highly personal topics like sexuality and gender, requires looking through all the available lenses, objective and subjective. Having discussed the nature of gay people as viewed through the subjective lenses of personal stories, archetypes, and history, the next sections take off those subjective goggles and put on the objective lenses of science in search of what truths can be gleaned from there. The best definition of science I know comes from the writer Isaac Asimov who said, "Science does not purvey absolute truth, science is a mechanism. It's a way of trying to improve your knowledge of nature, it's a system for testing your thoughts against the universe and seeing whether they match."[1]

As an example, people used to believe being gay was a choice. Social conservatives viewed variations in sexuality or gender as behaviors, and they made clear their disapproval. It was common to hear religious people declare it an act and a sin, likening it to lying, stealing, adultery, murder, and addictions, or naming it a lifestyle choice like joining a street gang or a cult. On the other side people argued sexual orientation was something intrinsic and natural, present from birth and baked into the hard wiring of our bodies in a way far beyond personal choice. From this perspective being gay was more like a nationality or race — something you were born into, with no option to un-choose or modify it. The question was how to determine which side was right, or if the answer lay in some third option that contained elements of truth from each.

The simplest way to tell if sexuality is a conscious choice in human beings is to ask. I have never met anyone, straight or gay, who said that they chose their sexual attractions. I have never heard anyone report that they sat themselves down, looked over the choice between genders, and then picked one to be their favored attraction for the rest of their lives. Some thoughtless people say things like, "Sure I chose to be straight – the first time I saw a pretty girl," but that is not a particularly compelling description of choice.

Given the absolute consistency of that answer, it is hard to understand the persistence of the notion of sexuality as a choice. It always seemed the kind of statement people made about others: "Well, my sexuality is natural and intrinsic and something I have never had to think through, but those people over there chose theirs, a fact I know because I disagree with their choice!" I no more chose to be gay than I chose to be tall, but personal testimonies from every gay person on the planet were not enough to alter those beliefs. Other approaches were needed.

A more objective test of the choice hypothesis came from looking at animal behavior. If animals practiced same-sex behaviors, then homosexuality was, by definition, natural. Animals cannot "choose" their behaviors. Animals living in the wild can only do what comes naturally. Going deeper, the discussion of animals illuminates a third solution to the gay choice question

— differentiating what parts of human sexual behavior are natural, like the animals, and where human choice begins.

Scientific studies of gay people can be complicated because every gay person experiences sexuality, gender, love, sex, and relationships differently. Defining exactly who is straight and who is gay in a scientifically rigorous way can be tough. In addition, gay people often fear this kind of data could be misused — that the discovery of a genetic marker for homosexuality would result in the abortion of gay embryos, rounding us up into camps as adults, or systematically denying us jobs, housing, and services with even more efficiency than done today. People with anti-gay beliefs also fear and block this kind of research because the results may challenge their existing beliefs, a problem best defined by the comedian Stephen Colbert who famously said, "reality has a well-known liberal bias."[2] I do not believe that science will ever explain everything about life, as humanity is more complex and interesting than that, but genetics, biology, and psychology all provide useful clues, even if incomplete conclusions.

It is not necessary to prove that homosexuality and gender variations are natural for gay lives to be valid. Even if being gay was a choice, people get to make choices, even unnatural ones. Modern culture is practically defined by unnatural choices of things like knitting, computers, race car driving, books, wheelchairs, and chili-cheese dog eating. It is only around other people's sex acts that moralists get so judgmental over what they consider natural.

As demonstrated in society's reaction to AIDS, even scientists can be blinded by confirmation bias. Naturalists working in more homophobic times could not see animal behaviors that challenged their cultural assumptions. Even if they did observe same-sex behaviors in the wild, society and its academic institutions would not let scientists publish their observations while retaining their reputation.

To illustrate the problem, picture an English biologist in the early 1900s, dressed in his khaki suit and pith helmet, observing lions in the wilds of Africa, pen and notebook in hand. Imagine him out on the plains of the Serengeti on a hot afternoon as he watches one male lion mount and penetrate another male. Because this scientist came from a class-based society that assumed the only natural sexuality was heterosexual, he applied his human filters to his observations of lions and wrote in his notebook that he had observed a domination ritual, one lion showing power over another. A more modern scientist would strive for objectivity, so she might record: "One male lion mounted the other, as the second male lifted his tail and presented his rump in a manner resembling female sexual availability. The top lion appeared to penetrate the second lion, who roared and moaned in response but did not flee or resist. The two remained in apparent coitus, the top lion thrusting, the bottom lion with back arched and rump raised, until the top lion appeared to orgasm, although this could not be confirmed. This behavior was repeated several times over the course of the day."

The first interpretation may have been right. This may have been domination ritual establishing hierarchy between lions. Or it could have been two lions enjoying a little hot dude-on-dude action on a lazy afternoon. Most likely it was some mix of uniquely lion desires and motivations that humans will never be able to discern with accuracy, at least until humans develop a way to ask lions about their interior experiences and motivations.

To be scientifically accurate, calling these animals gay is wrong. If gay is a term of self-identification, rather than a descriptor of observable activities, then it is wrong to say there are gay animals. No matter how many same-sex sexual activities are observed, it is impossible for a human observer to know an animal's inner sense of identity, attractions, or motivations. Because of this, scientists now use more clinical terms like "same-sex sexual activity" to describe what those lions were doing. I am not a scientist, and in casual speech the term gay is used to describe animals that have sex with their own gender. In this book I continue the colloquial tradition of calling animals gay if they have same-sex sex, as it is simply easier to read.

Beyond the problems of observer bias, it can be hard to see what is going on during animal sex. If two dolphins are entwined in a sexual position, their genitals underwater and moving fast through a dark ocean, a less observant scientist might assume it is a male and a female dolphin having sex, but that assumption might be wrong. Two monkeys in the trees, two birds in a nest, two snakes intertwined, all may be assumed heterosexual until the observer looks close enough to verify their assumptions. Even more challenging are the sexually monomorphic species, where the males and females look alike. If two sexually monomorphic birds, clams, or worms are having sex, it can be difficult for humans to know if it is same-sex or other-sex sexuality without detailed genetic testing to determine genders.

Even physically sexing the animal does not necessarily reveal anything about gendered behavior because the female of a species is not necessarily more ornate, submissive, smaller, or even the one who gets pregnant. In animals, as in humans, gender roles do not always correlate with physical sex.[3]

Of course all of this animal behavior is amoral, meaning outside of morality, as animals do what comes naturally and cannot make ethical choices. That fact does not stop people from applying their human judgments. One poor scientist studying Mazarine Blue butterflies in the Atlas Mountains of Morocco observed the butterflies engaging in homosexual sex and was so appalled that he published his observations in 1987 as: A *Note on the Apparent Lowering of Moral Standards in the Lepidoptera.*[4] The moral lapses of butterflies. Not exactly scientific objectivity, but a great example of trying to squeeze the real world into preexisting human judgments and beliefs.

I saw this same moral filter on display the first time I visited the Monterey Bay Aquarium, one of the world's most engaging museums. They had an amazing exhibit called *Mating Games*, filled with exhibitions of all kinds of fish sexuality and gender — male fish who raised the babies, gender-switching fish, decorator crabs that covered their shells in pretty things, and much more. There was nothing overly graphic there, as it was tastefully done, but it was a version of life on Earth far different from that taught in most Sunday Schools. My favorite part was the last wall before the exit. The aquarium had guests fill out cards describing their response to the exhibit and then posted a selection of the responses across the wall. Most were gushingly positive, but some expressed outrage, especially in a place where people brought children. I found it fascinating that people would go to a museum dedicated to life in the ocean, but leave offended if the museum actually showed ocean life, fearing their children's minds would be warped if they discovered how the world actually works. If the museum had shown mommy fish with daddy fish having baby fish I doubt these parents would have been offended, as it was the variations from the defaults they found challenging. Some people prefer to believe in a cartoon ocean filled with little mermaids and singing crabs, untainted by the realities of actual nature.

At the core of the gay debate lay a disconnect between religious views, meaning what people believed to be true about the world, and the facts, meaning what science and objective observation revealed to be true. When I think of science versus religion, I think of the wave-particle duality of light. It took scientists a long time to figure out whether light was a wave or a particle, but it turns out the answer is both. Measured at one exact time and place, light looks like a particle. Measured as a pattern over time, it appears as a wave. Both ways of measuring are equally accurate, but light cannot be seen as both a wave and a particle at the same time. Arguing science versus religion is like arguing waves versus particles. Yes it is one, and yes it is the other. Although it looks different from two different perspectives, the thing being viewed remains the same. Yes, science is an incredible tool to discover the marvels of the universe. And yes, humans need soulful explanations of life and the cosmos that reach beyond the measurable. One does not invalidate the other, just as waves do not invalidate particles. To argue relentlessly from only one perspective — that truth is in science or truth is in spirit — is to endlessly prove your own argument but miss the larger truth. Antoine de Saint-Exupéry touched on a powerful truth in *The Little Prince*, "It is only with the heart that one can see rightly; what is essential is invisible to the eye."[5] And yet as Senator Daniel Patrick Moynihan said, "Everyone is entitled to his own opinion, but not his own facts."[6] Harmony comes from seeing with both — heart and mind.

At the beginning of this chapter I shared Isaac Asimov's definition that science is a system for testing whether your thoughts matched reality. He also gave a powerful prescription for what to do when they do not match: "So the universe is not quite as you thought it was. You'd better rearrange your beliefs, then. Because you certainly can't rearrange the universe."[7]

TWENTY-THREE

Animal Sexuality

Nature is the glass reflecting God,
as by the sea reflected is the sun,
too glorious to be gazed on in his sphere.

~ Brigham Young

I AM A DIRECT DESCENDANT of the first Mormon pioneers who traveled to Utah by oxcarts and handcarts, long before the railroads. My childhood was filled with their stories, and their impact is written across the Mountain West. When my ancestors arrived in the deserts of Utah in 1847, mortally exhausted from their long migration, they dug in and prepared for winter. When spring arrived, they planted and nurtured the crops on which their survival depended, knowing new waves of hungry immigrants would soon arrive. Just as those first crops were bearing fruit, great swarms of katydid-like insects called Mormon crickets descended, eating every plant in their path. The pioneers fought back with blankets and farm tools, without success. Faced with a biblical-style plague that would have decimated the tiny colony, the settlers considered it a miracle from God when seagulls flew in from the nearby Great Salt Lake, and began devouring the crickets. For weeks the seagulls ate the crickets, threw up, ate more crickets, and threw up, until the crops, and the Mormons, were saved.[1] A generation later, the ancestors of those pioneers raised Seagull Monument in Salt Lake City's Temple Square, with two bronze gulls on top of a great granite column, and Utah crowned the seagull the state bird in lasting gratitude for this life saving miracle.

Given the mythic importance of those seagulls in the Mormon story, and the negative Mormon attitude towards all things gay, it is ironic that same-sex behavior is common in seagulls.[2] I love the resulting image — Mormon pioneers saved by the divine intervention of lesbian rescue gulls. Yet if I were to enter the church's Temple Square today wearing a t-shirt celebrating those miraculous gay birds, I would be surrounded by church security men in dark suits and earpieces and thrown off the property, as Mormons put a lot of effort into denying our obvious existence. It gives me pleasure to know that the gay realities of nature are already there on Temple Square, as their most unique monument is crowned with two rambunctious, and possibly lesbian, seagulls.

Mormon powers of denial aside, seagulls are not the only queer animals in Utah. While there are many to choose from, I note a few I knew from my time living there including bighorn sheep, domestic sheep, white-tailed deer, and mule deer.

Southern Utah is famous for its sculpted red rock, epitomized by the splendors of Zion National Park. The last time I was in Zion I saw herds of bighorn sheep grazing their way through the scrub brush and clambering up and down the slickrock canyons. Even though they live in a place called Zion, male bighorn sheep have a lot more sex with each other than with females, as heterosexual copulation only occurs on the few days a year the females are in heat. On all the other days, bighorn sheep live clustered in same-sex group-ings where they court and have sex with each other, particularly when young. After signaling interest and approaching, a male mounts another male and anally penetrates him, while the mountee arches his back to facilitate entry, in a manner resembling female bighorns. Groups of males also form huddles where they rub, nuzzle, lick, horn, and mount each other. Females play with each other in similar ways in their own groups. In addition, as many as 5% of bighorn rams are transgender. They refuse to have sex with the other males, but otherwise act like females, squatting when they pee and remaining with the female group throughout their lives.[3]

Domestic sheep are similar to their wild cousins, and 7-10% of domestic rams are exclusively gay. According to the US Sheep Experiment Station in Idaho, 35% of domestic rams are bisexual or asexual. Their research also found physical differences in the gay sheep's brains, or in the words of the government report: "Neurochemical and neuroanatomical studies suggest that male-oriented ram behavior may be a consequence of individual variations in brain sexual differentiation."[4]

Of course sheep do not have the corner on that market, as cattle, goats, pigs, and horses all sexually mount same-sex partners.[5] The barnyard is a busy place, it seems, which should be obvious to farmers. It is funny to hear the people who cannot see what is happening right in front of their eyes. Christianist activist Anita Bryant, for example, led the fight against gay rights in the 1970s saying, "even barnyard animals don't do what homosexuals do."[6] Clearly Bryant had not spent much time on a farm, as biblical shepherds watching their flocks by night knew a lot more about same-sex sexuality than she did.

For a different cultural perspective, Utah's indigenous Navajo people came from a tradition that honored their differently-gendered human children in the two spirit tradition. In a similar way, Navajo tradition considered their differently gendered sheep good luck for the whole flock, and as aids to their heterosexual sheep's reproduction. Navajo hunters even had rituals that used intersex deer and antelope to try to create more hermaphroditic sheep, rubbing the intersex animal's genitalia on the tails of their female sheep and the noses of the males.[7]

Back in Mormon Utah, people so love their guns and shooting at things that in my public school days the first day of deer hunting season was a state-wide holiday. The two most common deer in Utah are the white-tail and mule deer, and each of those species has three genders. In white-tailed deer the third gender is called velvet-horns, infertile males with simple antlers covered in a velvety skin and bodies that look more like female deer, with undeveloped testes. Third gender mule deer are called cactus bucks, as their horns resemble stubby cactus.[8]

Of course there is a lot more to America than Utah, and the continent's largest and most iconic land mammal is the American bison or buffalo; and they are very, very gay. Buffalo males mount other males more often than they mount females, especially when young. Females only mate with bulls once a year, but males may mount other males several times a day, even during rutting season when females are available.[9] There is similar behavior in European bison, and when Asian water buffalo are in heat, 15-20% of females are mounting other females.[10] It appears that American bison are not good examples for those who say homosexuality means the end of a species, as they were plentiful when European settlers arrived. It was humans that nearly wiped them out, not homosexuality.

Of course the most famously charismatic animals live in Africa. I used the example of lions before but did not specify their behaviors. Female lions roll around in a variety of sexual positions with other females, mirroring hetero-sexual activities. Males do a lot of rubbing and affectionate playing in pairs or groups of three, and sometimes one male will court another male, following the other male around for days as they play together sexually. In male African lions, as much as 8% of their sexual activity is with the same sex, while much of the female sexual activity is same-sex.[11]

To earn my Eagle Scout award I did a volunteer project with friends near the elephant pens at the local zoo. We learned the dramatic power of those beasts when an elephant picked up a friend by his arm and we had to wrestle him back. I cannot imagine being close to elephants in full sexual frenzy, and a lot of male elephant sex is homosexual. African elephant males kiss, intertwine their trunks, put their trunks in each other's mouths, and caress each other's penises with their trunks. As often as four or five times a day they engage in "erotic combat," pushing against each other with their trunks inter-twined while aroused. Females elephants do not exhibit as much same-sex behavior, although they are known to masturbate each other with their trunks. Intriguingly, elephants do not form lasting heterosexual bonds, but male elephants form long lasting same-sex companionships, often between older and younger males.[12]

Fascinating as the eroticism of elephant trunks sounds, it is the sweet flirtations of giraffes with their long necks that wins my heart. Those necks are so weird and wonderful, and they use them as part of their sexuality, "necking" by rubbing each other along their necks and bodies. At any one time, about

5% of giraffe males are necking with another male, and necking leads to sexual arousal, which is often followed by mounting and orgasm. Among male giraffes, over 90% of their sexual relations are same-sex, while fewer than 1% of female giraffe sexual interactions are same-sex.[13]

The species genetically closest to humans are the bonobos, a smaller variety of chimpanzees, and they are fully bisexual. Bonobos live in a matriarchal society, which is rare among primates, and about half of their sex is same-sex. Female bonobos are particularly sexual with each other, one female wrapping her arms and legs around another female, face to face, staring into each others eyes as they rub their genitals together, screaming and grimacing until climax. Female bonobos also have sex rump-to-rump and mount each other from behind. They have a lot of sex, averaging once every two hours, and twice that often if the relationship is new. Male bonobos fondle each other, perform oral sex, and engage in the descriptively named "penis fencing" which leads to ejaculation.[14] Intriguingly, numerous studies have found that bonobos maintain a peaceful society by using sex as an alternative to conflict, in contrast to their less sexual and more violent relatives the chimpanzees.[15] Maybe humans have something to learn from bonobos about creating a peaceful world.

In an intriguing side note, the importance of bonobo lesbian social behavior may explain the location of the human clitoris. It is an enduring enigma why human female pleasure neurons are located separately from the vagina, resulting in females who are not necessarily stimulated by penile penetration.[16] Pondering why this was true for bonobos, behavioral ecologist Marlene Zuk hypothesized that the bonobo clitoris is "frontally placed, perhaps because selection favored a position maximizing stimulation during the genital-genital rubbing common among females."[17] Human males are already wired to derive maximum pleasure from procreative sex, as an abundance of pleasure centers are located in the tip of the penis, so it may be human females have frontal clitoral pleasure centers to maximize the benefits of female-female bonding.

Among other primates, same-sex behavior is also documented in chimpanzees, gorillas, orangutans, white-handed gibbons, siamangs, langurs, leaf monkeys, proboscis monkeys, golden monkeys, Japanese macaque, Rhesus macaque, stumptail macaque, bonnet macaques, crab-eating macaques, pig-tail macaque, crested black macaque, savanna baboons, hamadryas baboons, gelada baboons, squirrel monkeys, and rufous-naped tamarins, among others.[18] Our evolutionary cousins, it seems, are quite naturally gay.

Then there are the marine mammals, where same-sex sexuality is frequent and exuberant. Studying marine mammals is important for the same reason people study monkeys, as whales maybe be as close to humans in how they function as apes.[19] For most marine mammals, group same-sex play is an essential part of their young lives. Dolphins, walruses, and whales grow up learning the basics of sex with others of the same sex, forming friendship bonds through their sex play that last throughout their lives.

While I have seen pictures of people swimming in pools with dolphins, my own close encounter came in a more unexpected place, deep in the Amazon jungle. It was my first day on the Rio Negro, a warm, inky black river running through some of the most isolated parts of the Amazon. Taking a break from the heat, our jungle boat pulled up to a sandy beach and I slipped into the dark and silky water as pink and blue freshwater dolphins swam around me. Dolphins are a good sign in the Amazon as it means there are probably no piranha around, because dolphins fear piranha for the same reasons we do. Like other dolphins, Amazon river dolphins enjoy same-sex play involving snouts, flippers, penetration of the genital slit and anus, and generally rubbing each other.

Amazon river dolphins also practice a unique sex configuration where one male dolphin swims above another, the top dolphin's erection penetrating the lower dolphin's blowhole. This blowholing, as someone called it, is the world's only known example of nasal sex.[20] Sadly, pink Amazon river dolphins are an endangered species and their numbers are dropping fast. Proponents of nose sex had better step up the preservation efforts, as they are our only known example of this delightful sexual variation.

The more famous and charismatic bottlenose dolphin, star of films and aquatic shows, is also bisexual. Males cavort, rub, muzzle, and stroke each others genitals in sexual play that can go on for hours. The genitals of both sexes are held inside a slit which closes around them for streamlining, and dolphin heterosexual sex is achieved by swimming belly to belly. Male homosexual sex is done the same way, with one partner penetrating his male partner's genital slit or anus, and either sex can probe their partner with their beaks. Female spinner dolphins add a stunningly visual position — one female positions her genital slit or vulva over the lower partner's dorsal fin, and then they swim together in a synchronized rhythm, which must be one wild ride. In addition to couples sex, dolphins also have sex in same-sex groups. Bottlenose dolphins like orgies of three or four, while spinner dolphins enjoy groups of a dozen or more, all swimming along while rubbing and being sexual with each other.

To put dolphin behavior in human terms, dolphins, like many mammals, are bisexual during mating season and revert to their long term same-sex companions for the remainder of the year.[21] As youths, the male sexual play teaches them about sex, provides opportunities to practice in preparation for later engagement with females, and facilitates bonding that continues into adulthood as they hunt, play, and pursue females and procreation together.[22]

Gray whales are similar to dolphins, but a whole lot bigger, and they commonly form homosexual orgies. Up to five males will roll around in the water together — racing, sliding, splashing, squirting water, and rubbing bellies and penises together. I cannot imagine coming across an orgy of gray whales. It must be quite a sight.

The highly social black and white orcas, or killer whales, often swim together in male-only groups, engaging in intertwined sex play as they splash, touch, and rub each other. Most impressively, when one male orca rubs another male's three foot long penis to the point of orgasm, diving deeply together in a double-helix beak-to-genital orientation, the second whale reciprocates 90% of the time.[23] That must be some kind of record for sexual reciprocity.

Male walruses spend their first four years having homosexual sex. When they reach maturity they become bisexual, mating with females during the breeding season and with males the rest of the year. Males rub their bodies against each other, embrace, and sleep together in the water.

To wrap up the aquatic mammals, consider the West Indian manatees, those big slug like animals that hold their nursing babies to their breast and may have inspired the legend of the mermaids. As much as their mythical incarnation represents a heterosexual vision, real manatees appear to like homosexual sex even more, as their gay sex lasts four to eight times as long as their heterosexual sex acts. Males gather as pairs or groups and thrust and wallow together, kissing and interacting head-to-tail or flipper-to-penis in a variety of ways, holding each other tightly. What a sweet image for such gentle creatures.[24]

The insect world offers many more examples, but my favorite is the dragonfly. Being a hot spring aficionado, nothing lights up a summer day like watching dragonflies as they skim the surface of a hot pool at eye level while I soak the day away. It is common at those times to see dragonflies copulating in flight, the upper male's legs clenching the lower female's head, his long tail curling under to meet the lower fly's body. Scientists used to assume all those copulating dragonflies were heterosexual, but more detailed research proved otherwise. Female dragonflies had distinctive dents in their heads after mating where the male had clamped on, and when scientists found the same head dents in male heads, it became clear male dragonflies were having sex with other males.[25]

Of course the most famous insect in science is the fruit fly as its thirty-day lifecycle makes it ideal for research, and scientists found they could manipulate fruit fly brains to make them bisexual, or more accurately, gender blind. By changing one gene, researchers changed the fly's brain's synapses, altering how the fly smelled the pheromones of other fruit flies. The result was male fruit flies that approached other males in the way males typically approached females. Stranger still, this effect could be turned on and off by the researchers, meaning that in fruit flies, at least, this behavior was biological, but not permanently hard-wired.[26] Studies on the serotonin levels of mice found a similar ability to change a female mouse's sexual attractions, which is interesting because serotonin is not a sex hormone.[27] More study needs to be done to understand the implications of these findings, teasing out the biological basis for sexual behavior, separating its malleable parts from more permanent orientations.

The difficulty of research on gay animals is best demonstrated in the long story of studying Laysan albatross on Oahu. The scientists who study these birds are obviously lucky because Hawaii is beautiful, but unlucky because understanding albatross sexuality proved surprisingly difficult. Every year Laysan albatross gather on Oahu to breed for half the year. For generations, scientists studying the birds admired their monogamy. When First Lady Laura Bush visited the research site, she praised the bird's lifelong commitments as moral exemplars.

But there was a problem in the egg count. Laysan albatross females only lay one egg a year, but some nests had two. Because these couples could not care for both, one of the eggs would be rolled off to the side, abandoned in neglect. Since the 1920s, scientists struggled to understand where that extra egg came from, developing theories about some birds laying two eggs or other females "egg dumping" in the wrong nest. Finally someone checked the sex of the birds and were surprised to find that many of those seemingly monogamous couples were female-female. This revelation shattered two myths at once. Not only were many of the birds lesbian rather than heterosexual, but the fact that they were impregnated meant the colony's males were not as monogamous as previously thought. In the end scientists found that thirty of the 125 nests studied were occupied by female-female couples.[28]

There are evolutionary reasons for this kind of gay coupling, as demonstrated by another set of bird couples. One quarter of Australian black swan families are headed by male-male partners who form long-lasting pairs, perform the standard courtship rituals, and have sex together. Using the combined strength of two male parents, these couples maintain a territory averaging from 1,500 to over 3,000 square feet of the best parts of a pond, while the territory of heterosexual couples averaged fifteen to sixty square feet,[29] an astonishing difference. As a friend of mine quipped, "What is it about gays and real estate?" Because they can defend larger high-quality territory, these male-male couples can keep their eggs safe and their family fed more effectively than male-female couples. They obtain eggs by bringing in a female for breeding and then chasing her off, or by stealing eggs from the nest of another couple. The two male parents then work together, splitting egg-tending duties more equitably than heterosexual couples. Their success rate is extraordinary: 80% of the male-male pairs successfully raise their chicks to adulthood, versus only 30% of heterosexual pairs.

I said it before, but it is worth repeating here. When people make the argument that homosexuality is a threat to reproduction, they forget that it can also be an enhancement to survival. The key to evolutionary success is not the number of children birthed, but the number who make it to reproductive maturity so the cycle can repeat itself. Black swans require a coupling of male and female to produce their eggs, but male-male couples are far more successful at child rearing.

The most famous same-sex bird couple lived far from the wild in New York's Central Park Zoo, where Roy and Silo became local celebrities and successfully raised a chick from an abandoned egg. The story of their life together was chronicled in the charming illustrated children's book *And Tango Makes Three*. While the travails of heterosexual penguin reproduction made great cinema in *The March of the Penguins*, there are male-male penguin couples that build nests and mate together for many seasons. Zookeepers often try to break up the same-sex couples by force or by tempting the males with additional females, but this has proven unsuccessful.

In a humorous side note that illustrates why this information seems so new, researchers in 2012 found the papers of the Scott Antarctic Expedition from over 100 years ago where they had documented same-sex behaviors in penguins, but left those details out of their official report in English, recording their penguin behavior findings in Greek so as not to traumatize the general public. As the scientist of that exhibition wrote in the judgmental language his time, male penguins formed "hooligan bands of half a dozen or more and hang about the outskirts of the knolls, whose inhabitants they annoy by their constant acts of depravity."[30] And now we have children's books that share the way penguins actually live, so the times they do change.

There are far too many stories of avian homosexuality to cover here, but I conclude with a gay favorite, the flamboyantly pink flamingos. Immortalized as plastic lawn ornaments, real pink flamingos form homosexual couples that live, eat, drink, preen, travel, sleep, have sex, and raise young together. They even form triads, or *ménage à trios*, of two males and one female.[31] Somehow pink flamingos being gay does not seem like such a big surprise.

Unfortunately, I only have space to cover a small sampling of all the gay animals in this brief overview. Left out of the discussion are the ibis, brown bear, Amazon molly, emu, caribou, field cricket, jumping spider, clubtail dragonfly, mite, marmoset, cheetah, vulture, water strider, bed bug, king penguin, gopher snake, Japanese scarab beetle, cockroach, western rattlesnake, silkworm moth, Guinea pig, mallard, house fly, Hawaiian orb-weaver spider, Houting whitefish, broad-headed skink, acanthocephalan worms, blowfly, tsetse Fly, water moccasin, Australian parasitic wasp, jewel fish, raccoon, whiptail lizard, Appalachian woodland salamander, queen butterfly, red ant, desert tortoise, box crab, domestic cats, red-tailed skink, stag beetle, green swordtail, rat, turkey, budgerigar, incirrate octopus, hamster, mite, glasswing butterfly, blister beetle, black-spotted frog, and those reproductive champions, rabbits. Long as it sounds, even that is the short list. Author Bruce Bagemihl chronicled over 450 species with documented same-sex behavior back in 1999 in his exceptionally informative book *Biological Exuberance*,[33] and that list has only grown since. I highly recommend his book as a fascinating encyclopedia on the subject. Not one of these names comes from casual observations of the "Oh, I saw two male dogs doing it at the dog park" variety. Each one comes from serious scientists who have documented their observations and published their findings in peer reviewed journals.

God made the animals male and female, but to end the story there is to miss much of the splendor and fascination of God's kingdom. The dragonflies skimming the pond interlocked in sex may not be a male and a female. That buffalo on that postcard is probably a huge homo. A good percentage of those rescue seagulls were lesbian. That is the world as God made it, all of it beautiful, strange, and resplendent, and much of it playfully, and fascinatingly, gay.

Animal Gender

All God's creatures
got a place in the choir.

~ *Bill Staines*

AS WITH ANIMAL SEXUALITY, so with animal gender. Just as we added the T to the LGB to represent human variations in gender, animal gender varies widely. The funny thing is, everyone already knows this. Every third grader learns that honey bees live in hives and is taught that it takes three kinds of bees to make a hive: the queen bee, worker bees, and drones. What no one pointed out to my third grade class is that this means bees have three genders. New bees are created like all procreative life, from the joining of two genders, the male sex cell with a female sex cell, and from that male-female reproduction come bees of three different genders.

Queens are the largest bee and the only sexually developed female, while drones are males born without stingers from unfertilized eggs, whose only role is to mate with a queen. The bee sex act occurs only once in a queen's life, as she mates with male drones during one great flight, gathering the millions of sperm she will use through the rest of her life. That makes two procreative genders in the hive: one female queen and a few hundred drone males. The bees buzzing around the garden, on the other hand, are usually neither reproductive males nor females, as most workers of the hive are asexual females. Pretty much every bee you have ever seen was a non-reproductive third gender. Something similar happens in other insect colonies, like ants, where the reproductive males and females are distinct minorities, while most of the colony consists of asexual females. Contrary to the simplistic notion that all of life is divided male and female, much of Earth's life thrives in larger systems that transcend the roots of male-female cellular reproduction. It is easy to remember how natural a third gender is by thinking of bees. Male-female sex makes the bees, but most of the bees pollinating plants and making the delicious honey are of a third gender entirely.

For a very different illustration of gender in nature, consider one of my favorite animated movies, *Finding Nemo*. Nemo was a clownfish who lived in a sea anemone with his mother and father. At the start of the film, Nemo's mother was killed, Nemo was kidnapped, and the rest of the movie was a humor-filled adventure as the father struggled to rescue his son. Sounds great, except *Finding Nemo* got clownfish gender wrong. Clownfish are gender switchers; every clownfish is born male. They do live in a single anemone in monogamous breeding pairs of one female and male, along with some juveniles, but if the breeding female died in a real clownfish anemone, the adult male would grow and change into a larger female, and one of the juveniles would become the adult male, a process called sequential hermaphroditism.[1] To make the movie accurate, Nemo's father should have transitioned into a larger female, and Nemo would have become her husband. That certainly would have made a more surprising movie for the kiddies, and I imagine Pixar had some lively meetings talking through the human-like story they wanted to tell using fish with very non-human ideas of gender and family.

Evolutionary biologist Joan Roughgarden runs through a seemingly endless list of nature's gender variations in her book *Evolution's Rainbow*, along with the interrelated issues of mating and child rearing roles. The most interesting stories, like Nemo's, come from coral reefs, source of the planet's greatest diversity. Roughgarden describes males that become females and vice versa, like the clownfish, and fish that are male and female simultaneously like the Hamlet fish, where one Hamlet fish releases an egg and another the sperm, and then they switch. Okinawa gobies change from male to female, and sometimes back again, while Great Barrier Reef gobies mature into females, but later change to male, and later back to female if needed. It is hard to imagine as a tourist snorkeling through tropical reefs, but about a quarter of all reef fish are hermaphrodites, including nearly all of the wrasses, parrot fish, and larger groupers, and many damselfish, angelfish, gobies, porgies, emperors, soapfishes, dottybaks, and moray eels.[2]

Of course it is not just bees and fish that mess with humanity's simplistic notions of gender. I already mentioned Utah's three gendered deer, while bullfrogs also have one female and two male genders, as do canary-bird fish and salmon. Sunfish, wrasses, cichlids, and tree lizards have three male genders and one female, while white throated sparrows have two male genders and two female, and the side-blotched lizard has three male genders and two female.[3] Gender in nature expands and flourishes far beyond the procreational basics of the male-female binary.

To pick an example of a variation that confounded humanity from antiquity, consider the hyena. Writing around the time of Christ, the Roman poet Ovid expressed the classical belief that hyenas were hermaphrodites that could change their gender back and forth. Later Europeans found the hyena's variation between male and female so disturbing that hyenas came to represent sexual deviance, prostitution, and witchcraft. The confusion came from the female hyenas' clitoris that is 90% the length of the male's penis and labia that are fused and filled with fat tissue so they look like a scrotum. In a mind blowing evolutionary variation, female hyenas have no vaginal opening, as they have sex and give birth through the tip of the clitoris.[4] These exceptional females, and their male counterparts, also have homosexual sex, but it is their unique genitalia and gender presentation that has confounded humanity across the millennia.

These examples go on and on. There is the Brazilian cave fly where the female has the penis, which she inserts into the male's vagina, and then sort of slurps the male's semen up into her body.[5] There is the male *octopoteuthis deletron* squid that mates with both sexes equally, squirting a sperm packet into the flesh of any other passing squid, male or female, without seeming to consider gender at all.[6] The seas slugs *siphopteron quadrispinosum* have both male and female organs and can mate with each other using both at once.[7]

As with same-sex sexual behavior, most people did not learn about these animal basics in school because so much of the information is new. An Antarctic mollusc named *Lissarca miliaris* was first described in scientific papers in 1845, but it was only recently scientists realized that they reproduce as males when they are young and then grow female organs to gestate eggs as they age.[8] It takes a lot of careful observation to suss out the gendered reproductive nuances of Antarctic bivalves, sea slugs, deepwater squid, and cave flies.

And then there are the animals that gave up sexual reproduction altogether. There is a species of whiptail lizard that lost its males somewhere along the evolutionary trail, and now only reproduces asexually, solving the problem of DNA replication mistakes by carrying a double set of genes in each female, meaning a new geographical area could be populated by a single individual without negative health consequences.[9] Isolation in zoos revealed that copperhead snakes and their poisonous cousins, the cottonmouths, can also reproduce without males,[10] so there are probably many more examples out there yet to be discovered. A freshwater clam called *corbicula* also reproduces hermaphroditically, a single clam producing both the male sperm and female eggs, but it keeps its DNA mix diverse by occasionally stealing DNA from other clam species.[11]

As for gender expression, who knows what that scientist offended by gay behavior in butterflies would have thought of bilateral gynandromorphic butterflies that are half male and half female, with the wings on one side the shape and colors of one gender, and the wings on the other side the shape and colors of the other gender.[12] This same effect has been found in other animals like lobsters, crabs, and birds, exemplifying the intertwined realities of male and female that resonate across the natural world. When people say God created male and female, they do not normally include the animals where male and female are both present, half and half, in the same body.

Noah's Ark makes a wonderful children's toy as a celebration of the charismatic animals, all paired off together. I love that simple story, but life as God actually made it includes far more exotic variations as well. To bring it all home, most Americans experience genetic gender flipping every morning over breakfast, as chicken eggs come from XX males and XY females, the opposite of human genetics. Every chicken egg you ever ate was laid by a female with XY chromosomes, so every morning is a gender-bender in America.

Beyond animal examples, it is worth noting that plants are the majority of life on the planet, and plant reproduction and gender are even more diverse. National politicians may declare gender variation unnatural, but the Japanese cherry blossoms that surround Washington, DC's Tidal Basin have both male and female flowers at the same time; the elms that line the National Mall have bisexual flowers; and the gingko trees that line many of the capital's streets are sexed male or female but sometimes produce flowers of the other sex.[13] Of course gardeners and farmers already understand this truth about tree gender because so many fruit trees self-pollinate. The sweet Meyer lemon growing in my backyard self-pollinates, as do most citrus trees along with cherry, peach, quince, pomegranate, persimmon, apricot, and many nut trees.

Joan Roughgarden summarized: "The most common body form among plants and in perhaps half of the animal kingdom is for an individual to be both male and female at the same, or at different times during its life."[14] Understanding life on Earth requires seeing both the typical and the variations. Honoring the centrality of the male and female elements in reproduction is the starting point to a fuller understanding of how gender plays out across the spectrum of life. The reality of nature makes clear that the God who made the living things on this earth rejoices in diversity and does not feel constrained by anything as simplistic as the male-female duality.

TWENTY-FIVE

Evolution

> The most important scientific revolutions
> all include, as their only common feature,
> the dethronement of human arrogance
> from one pedestal after another
> of previous convictions
> about our centrality in the cosmos.
>
> ~ *Stephen Jay Gould*

KNOWING THAT SAME-SEX SEXUALITY and gender variations are common in the animal kingdom, it is natural to ask why. Charles Darwin proposed an answer in natural selection. Often reduced to the idea of "survival of the fittest," natural selection is actually more sophisticated than that. The simplistic version of evolutionary success says that life is perpetuated by a male impregnating a female, the female giving birth, the parents possibly playing a role in bringing the child to sexual maturity, and the cycle repeating. What is missing from that story is the context, as overall survival of a species is a group effort, not necessarily dependent on each individual's survival or procreation. A queen bee can only live and reproduce successfully if she has the support of vast numbers of asexual drones. Hive survival requires individual bees working together, but does not require that each individual reproduce, as God made most bees incapable of individual reproduction. Zebras survive as a herd, with one tough adult turning to face the lion, or one older zebra falling behind as victim, as the rest of the striped mass races away. Salmon swarm upriver in great enough numbers that some will survive the feasting bears and reproduce. Sea turtle babies hatch on the beach in such plenitude that some will make it into the sea and grow old enough to return to the beach to produce again. In each case, the behavior of individuals serves the collective survival, but no single individual carries the full responsibility. Species survival is never based on individual procreation, unless they are the last breeding pair of their kind.

This same logic applies to human beings. Sending young men off to war, for example, is incredibly risky and counter productive for that individual's chance of reproduction. The individual is sacrificed at his reproductive peak for the benefit of the whole, because the destruction of that young warrior's tribe or nation would mean the end of his people's collective procreation. If humanity actually believed it essential that every human being procreate, soldiers would be encouraged to breed before departing for war. Other examples of human activities that do not support the perpetuation of one's genes range from adopting other people's children to bungee jumping. While these activities may lessen direct individual procreation, they are still considered valid variations within the human experience.

The same is true of homosexuality. At first glance it may seem like nature creating some individuals as gay might be a mistake that hinders human procreation, as gay people may be less likely to have other-sex sex that leads to children, but that is not the whole story. As in animals and discussed in more detail in later chapters, same-sex couples can be more successful at parenting than other-sex couples, and viewed from the perspective of survival of the species, homosexuality and gender variation can play essential roles in the overall reproductive success.

Same-sex sexual play by young people, for example, can be the social glue in forming bonds and alliances that last for a lifetime, like those pods of male bottlenose dolphins that played together sexually as youths and then hunted together for food and sex as adults. Reproduction is enhanced when young animals practice courting and mating skills with same-sex partners, making them more successful with other-sex partners as adults. I have heard plenty of stories of straight kids, male and female, fooling around with each other as a form of youthful sex play before they face the other sex, a period some adults look back on with fondness.

Overall reproductive success also goes up in communities with well-functioning social relations, and same-sex activities can be both the social glue that binds individuals, as well as a lubricant that reduces tensions and prevent future conflicts. This phenomenon was demonstrated earlier in female bonobos, but is visible in animals as far from humans as acorn woodpeckers, birds that also cooperate in supporting young who are not their own.[1] And of course sex can be used as a way to reconcile after a conflict, as seen in female Japanese macaques who increased their sex with each other after periods of conflict.[2] Because macaques are the monkeys known for sitting in natural hot springs during snowy winters, and I love both hot springs and reconciling sex, I hold female Japanese macaques in particularly high honor.

Of course straight sex often brings out people's competitive sides, and the same can be true of same-sex sexuality. The obvious example in animals is the way they can enforce their dominance by head-butting or marking territory, but some, like the male American buffalo, may use gay sex as another way to establish dominance in their herd. Sometimes one male can use gay sex acts to enhance his own potential, like the way male flour beetles engage in same-sex play until one male gets his sperm onto the another male's sex parts, so when the second male has sex with a female, he may impregnate her with the first male's sperm. In an even funnier example, a male can use sex to reduce his competitor's chances, as when one male dung fly sexually mounts another male in flight and then lets go and flies off when a female flies by, gaining the advantage.[3]

Yet another theory for the prevalence of homosexuality in nature comes from the idea that same-sex courting may be a simple mistake in identifying the gender of the partner, a phenomenon *Time* magazine called the "oops" theory.[4] Some male toads, for example, mount other male toads, and only release when the mounted toad lets out a distinctive call telling his paramour of his mistake. Although this phenomenon is widely observed, the roots of this fumbling behavior are poorly understood. It seems bizarre that an animal cannot tell a male from a female of its own species. Maybe they just cannot be bothered to care.

Finally, animals, like humans, sometimes choose same-sex relations when deprived of access to the other sex, a behavior dubbed the prison effect. Male damselflies kept without females, for example, will court other males.[5] And just like male human prisoners, the male damselflies revert to sex with females when they are again available.

While the relationship between homosexuality and human genetics is covered in the next chapter, there are various ways gay genes could be carried forward even as homosexual behavior lowers reproductivity. The top four are bisexuality, overdominance, antagonistic selection, and epigenetics.

Genes endure if they create multiple benefits for the carrier, which may be the case with bisexuality. A practicing bisexual may procreate with the other sex while forming the social glue bonds with same-sex companionships. The obvious example is men who like bonding with other men, intensely and for long periods of time, while still enjoying sex with women and having children. In this case their attractions to the same sex benefits the overall community while their genes are successfully carried forward into the next generation. Researchers have validated this idea by finding that people with higher levels of progesterone, sometimes called the social hormone, are more inclined to be bisexual. The lead author of a recent study on this effect, Diana Fleischman, noted that for hunter-gatherer societies: "The research suggests that having exclusively heterosexual thoughts is a disadvantage — it's better to be a little bit attracted to the opposite sex."[6]

The process of overdominance is a bit more technical, as a gene received from one parent creates one trait in a child, but the same gene received from both parents creates a different trait. The sickle cell gene is a famous human example, as a child who gets the gene from one parent is immune to malaria, a profound survival advantage, but the same gene from both parents results in crippling sickle cell disease. Likewise, an overdominant sexuality gene received from one parent might make that child more reproductive, but if received from both parents it could make the child gay and potentially less reproductive. In sexually antagonistic selection, a gene has different results in differently sexed offspring. While a particular gene may make a male child gay, that same gene may make his sisters more fertile, resulting in a net increase in family offspring. The most recently discovered factor is a process called epigenetics. Described more fully in the next chapter, epigenetics is the idea that a gene can exist across a population, but will only be expressed under particular environmental or life circumstances.

There is a good chance that all of these genetic processes, and more yet to be discovered, are at work to create human reproductive, sexuality, and gender variations. The science of genetics is still far from explaining the role of DNA in making people into the individuals they become.

Evolution occurs across the animal kingdom as individuals do their best to survive, procreate, and raise their young to maturity, so the cycle can repeat. Along the way, the successful solutions are perpetuated. There are also ways communities of animals, and humans, that work together to solve the larger problems individuals can surmount. Each individual rarely has to survive as a lonely predator in the jungle, as that is not how most of life works.

Mother Nature is astoundingly beautiful, and richly complex. She is hermaphroditic, with male, female, and intersex parts, and she is sexual, homosexual, and pansexual in ways science is only beginning to understand. To study all of this diversity in the natural world and really strive to understand how nature works is to stand in awe of the beauty and splendor of what the author Hakim Bey called "the magnificent overabundance of reality."[7]

BODIES

TWENTY-SIX

Genetics

Genetic code
is a divine writing.

~ *Toba Beta*

GROWING UP MORMON meant I was always aware of my genealogy, as Mormons are some of the world's most enthusiastic genealogists. My own family can trace my father's father's father back through England and Scotland to where medieval record keeping grows murky in the 1400s. Along with this respect for my ancestors came the traditional belief that I am the product of my familial origins, my heritage, and my genetics. The word genetics actually comes from the Greek word for origin, the same root as the word genesis, or beginnings. The study of genetics, then, is the search for the original code from which all of life is built.

After mapping the human genome in the early 2000s, it seemed that scientists would soon crack the code and decipher the instruction set undergirding human life, but that is not what happened. The role of genetics in creating life is more complicated than people imagined. As a simple example, every cell of the body has the same DNA, yet one cell becomes a nose, another a kidney, and a third a fingernail, all created from the same code. Identical twins have identical DNA, yet end up as two distinctly different people, including variations in physical characteristics, differing propensities for diseases, and often very different personalities.

As the genetic roadmap unfolded, researchers searched for a gay gene, some kind of on-off switch that regulated sexuality, and could not find one. In retrospect this was not surprising as we now know there are no singular genetic switches for any complex human trait. There is no single gay gene for the same reason there is no single gene for something as obvious as eye color.[1] The role of genetics in creating an individual is more complex than that.

While doubtful a gay gene exists, some aspects of sexuality do appear to be affected by genetics. If that linkage does exist, then homosexuality should be more likely in identical twins, as they share the same DNA. In the early 1990s, Michael Bailey and Richard Pillard studied identical twins and found strong evidence for a genetic component to male homosexuality. They found that if one identical twin brother was gay, the likelihood his twin was also gay was 52%, an astonishingly high number given that the likelihood a non-related person being gay is 5%.[2]

Searching for larger patterns, a 1993 study lead by Dean Hamer at the National Cancer Institute found that homosexuality ran in families, even when family members were raised apart. Most intriguingly, gay men had more gay relatives on their mother's side than their father's, indicating the gene for male homosexuality may be inherited from the mother. Subsequent studies confirmed the general finding,[3] while other studies confirmed the lack of this effect on the father's side.[4] A recent twins study, published in 2014 and much larger than the original, confirmed that there may be a link on the mother's side, but the data remains tantalizing but inconclusive.[5]

A new area of genetic science called epigenetics may help explain how genes create different sexual orientations without their being a deterministic "gay gene." Epigenetics, from "epi-" meaning over or above, says there is a layer of functionality that overlays our genetic code. At its simplest, epigenetics is the acknowledgment that diet, lifestyles, and other environmental factors affect how individual bodies use their DNA. An individual may have a gene for cardiovascular disease that is only expressed if the individual experiences famine, or a gene to be tall that is only expressed with an abundantly healthy diet.

Science writer Kayt Sukel describes epigenetics with a computer analogy: if genetics is our hardware, then the epigenome is the software that tells the hard wiring how to express itself, and one cannot exist without the other. It is increasingly clear the genetic code itself has very limited meaning until it is put in an environment and run as system. As Sukel says, "There is no more nature versus nurture debate. Nature and nurture are intertwined and they are really impossible to separate."[6] That explains how homosexuality can be genetic without every person with the gay-propensity gene becoming homosexual, just as every member of a family can have a cancer-propensity gene without every individual getting cancer. Genes are not deterministic because there are so many outside factors in play.

Using this new understanding of epigenetics, scientists at the US National Institute for Mathematical and Biological Synthesis believed they found a way homosexuality could be passed from parent to child — father to daughter and mother to son. Instead of passing traits through genetic markers, parents may be passing epi-marks. One parent's resistance to a hormone, for example, may be passed to their other-sex child. A mother may have an epi-mark that protects her female body from overexposure to testosterone while carrying a male child, and when passed to the embryo it feminizes his body and tends to make him gay. Similarly, a father could have an epi-mark that protects his male body from underexposure to testosterone, and when passed to a daughter it masculinizes her body and tends to make her lesbian.[7] In this scenario, an epigenetic process may be protecting one parent's health while creating a gay other-sexed child, with a net overall improvement in family health.

One of the most unexpected bits of genetic evidence for homosexuality comes from the bodies of gay men's mothers. Looking at the mother of a gay son, there is a one in four chance her body is genetically different from most other women. Human bodies are always producing new cells, and as the cells divide they tend to use the X chromosome as their blueprint. Male bodies typically use the X of their XY, while female bodies can use either one of their two Xs. In most female bodies, the dividing cells pick one or the other X randomly, so the cells in most women's bodies are 50-50 for each X. One quarter of gay men's mothers, on the other hand, have bodies that only use one of their Xs.[8] According to researcher Sven Bocklandt who made this discovery, "What's really remarkable and very novel about this is that you see something in the bodies of women that is linked to a behavioral trait in their sons. That's new, that's unheard of."[9]

Further proof that the genetic process that creates homosexual children may strengthen families came from a 2004 Italian study that found gay men's mothers, maternal aunts, and maternal grandmothers are all more reproductive than average.[10] In other words, in families where the gay-related genetic processes were present, overall reproduction went up. If the process that creates the occasional gay uncle raises the family's net reproductivity, that genetic process will prosper and be carried into future generations.[11]

Beyond even that, as researcher Andrea Camperio Ciani explains, gay men's mothers and aunts have many advantages. "They are more fertile, displaying fewer gynecological disorders or complications during pregnancy; they are more extroverted, as well as funnier, happier and more relaxed; and they have fewer family problems and social anxieties."[12] Again it may be that female relatives of gay men are more attractive as heterosexual partners, again enhancing the family's overall reproductive success.

A completely different theory says that a mild version of the gay genetic propensity may be a net plus for the straight males in a family. While the full-on expression of the trait might make a man exclusively gay, and therefore less likely to reproduce, a milder expression of those same qualities might make his brothers less aggressive and more empathetic, among other desirable qualities, and therefore better long term mates for women.[13] If the mild expression of the trait is more common than the full expression, human reproductive success goes up.

Reviewing the available research in 1998, Michael Bailey and Richard Pillard concluded that "genes account for at least half of the variance in sexual orientation."[14] Amusingly, recent research made a similar declaration about political ideology, declaring that 30-40% of what makes people conservative or liberal may be genetic.[15]

Researcher Giorgi Chaladze of Georgia took all this genetic evidence, including the fact that gay men tend to have fewer children but often come from larger families, and came up with an interesting calculation. According to his analysis, the genes that make people gay are carried by 50% of the population, male and female. The next time you hear someone condemning homosexuality, remember there is a 50-50 chance that very person is carrying and propagating the genes they are denouncing.[16]

While there is no evidence for a single gene explaining any complex human trait, there is increasing evidence that genetics and epigenetics are big parts of why I, and many others like me, are gay. At my core I live just as nature made me, regardless of the code that got me here. I am my genetic heritage, and I am so much more than my DNA.

Physiology

Today you are you,
that is truer than true.
There is no one alive
who is youer than you.

~ *Dr. Seuss*

IN THE ONGOING SEARCH for a biological component to homosexuality, the strongest known correlation is the older brother effect. The more older brothers a boy has, the higher the chance he will be gay. According to one study, each older brother increases the chances the next son will be gay by 33%. At an average homosexual orientation of 4% (assumed by the researchers), it would take nine to ten older brothers to reach a 50-50 chance of being gay. Younger brothers and any sisters have no correlation, and there is no similar effect in women.[1]

One result of the older brother effect is validation of the old idea that mothers make their sons gay. It appears that a woman who carries a series of male children and is then pregnant with yet another male, may have an immune response in her body that affects fetal development, including sexual differentiation of the child's brain. This could be a reaction of her body to all the testosterone of those male embryos, or it could be an evolutionary adaptation that ensures that if daughters fail to appear in a family, the mother's body will create a feminized boy. Either way, it appears mothers' bodies really do help create gay sons.

Searching for other correlations between objectively measurable evidence and the experience of being gay, scientists looked at the bodies of gay and straight people and noted the structural differences. Physiological differences indicate a correlation between sexuality and physical development. The earlier the differentiated body structures developed during fetal growth, the clearer the evidence that homosexuality is hard wired from the start. Among the scientifically documented variations are brain structures and asymmetry, left and right handedness, finger length, fingerprints, bone lengths, penis sizes, inner ear clicks, eye blinks, and responses to pheromones and sweat. That list may sound funny, but each of those measurements reveals something about the origins of sexuality. At the same time, none of those factors are determinant, as they are just correlations, some stronger and some weaker. It is impossible to look at people's finger lengths or listen to their inner ear clicks and determine whom they would like to date on a Friday night.

The first and most obvious place to look for differences between gay and straight bodies is in the brain. Scientists used to believe male and female brains were the same, but research in the 1970s and 80s revealed there are significant structural differences between gendered brains. It is hard to remember what big news it was back in 1991 when Dr. Simon LeVay announced he found differences between the brains of gay and straight men. Within his sample, gay men's hypothalami were half the size of straight men's, a proportion more like that of women.[2] This early study was later questioned because of the limitation of LeVay's samples, but the publicity around his discovery launched gay-straight biological research into public awareness.

Subsequent research confirmed other differences in gay and straight brains. While straight women's brains are symmetrical, with both hemispheres around the same size, straight men's brains are asymmetrical, with a larger right hemisphere. Swedish researchers using MRIs to compare straight and gay brain hemispheres found that gay men's physical structures tend to be more like heterosexual women's, and lesbians brains tend to be more like straight men's.[3]

Those same researchers also did PET scans, or positron emission tomography, to measure the blood flow to the amygdala of each hemisphere. They found that straight men and gay women had more nerve connections on the right side of the amygdala, while straight women and gay men had more neural connections on the left side. As a British scientist explained to the BBC: "In other words, the brain network which determines what sexual orientation actually "orients" towards is similar between gay men and straight women, and between gay women and straight men." Not only is this physical difference an important clue, but the amygdala itself is interesting because it is the center of emotional learning and memory consolidation, affecting behavior as part of our "fight, flight, or mate" response (a concept more easily remembered as the three Fs).

These Swedish brain studies also stand out for political reasons. Because research monies were often blocked by conservative Americans who wanted to know less about gay people, it was often gay scientists who pursued gay research, opening the results to charges of bias. These Swedish results, on the other hand, were found during research on strokes. The gay-straight results were discovered by chance.

In confirmation of the brain asymmetry studies, other researchers found that gay men's more female-like symmetrical brains are better at facial recognition than straight men's, just as women tend to be better at facial recognition than men. Another tie was found between homosexuality and handedness, as left-handed people also have more asymmetrical brains that excel at facial recognition, and gay men tend to be more left-handed.[4]

The discussion of handedness gets confusing, but one study only found a correlation between left handedness and homosexuality in gay women, while another only found it in gay men. The more older brothers a boy had, the more likely he was to be gay, but only if he was right-handed. Left-handed males were only more likely to be gay if they have no older brothers.

Right-handed males without older brothers and left-handed males with older brothers were homosexual at about the same rate.[5] There is clearly something going on between sexuality and handedness, but the meaning remains unclear.

In a study that is easier to understand, researchers set up photocopying machines at street fairs, asked participants to complete a questionnaire about their sexuality, and then photocopied their hands for later measurement. Men tend to have longer ring fingers than index fingers, while women's index fingers tend to be slightly shorter or about the same length as their ring fingers, the difference resulting from varying exposure to testosterone in the womb.[6] The researchers photocopied hands revealed that lesbians finger lengths tended towards the male patterns, indicating higher testosterone exposure in the womb, and gay men's finger lengths tended towards the female patterns, indicating lower testosterone exposure. Just to complicate things, this effect was not seen in gay men who had more than one older brother. From a seemingly random data point, like the length of index and ring fingers, comes evidence that there is a link between testosterone levels in the womb and homosexuality for both gay men and lesbians.

Everyone knows that each individual has a unique fingerprint. It is less well known that most people have more fingertip swirls on their right hands than on their left. Here again there is a gay-straight difference, as 86% of straight men have more fingertip ridges on their right hands, while only 70% of gay men do. This adds to the evidence for a role of genetics, as 90-95% of fingerprint variation is genetic and fully in place by the fourth month of embryonic development.[7] Like other body asymmetry evidence, these results correlate with the ability to perform certain cognitive tasks. Men with more right hand fingertip swirls tend to excel at the kind of tasks where men typically excel, while men with more left hand fingertip swirls tend to excel at the tasks where women typically excel. Here again, this time written on the tips of our fingers, is evidence of a genetic component to sexuality and gender that is present early in the womb, affecting how adults process, experience, and understand the world.

Beyond brains and hands, straight women and gay men tend to have shorter arm, leg, and hand bones in proportion to their stature than heterosexual men and lesbians.[8] These bones grow longer in children exposed to more androgens in the womb, so this is another piece of evidence of a role for prenatal testosterone in creating sexuality.

Penis size, the source of many jokes, gives contradictory evidence on prenatal hormone levels. More testosterone in the womb results in a larger penis, and the best available evidence says gay men's penises are larger than straight men's, based on data the Kinsey Institute collected on over five thousand male penises between 1938 and 1963, including those of over nine hundred gay men.[9] For the curious, straight men's erections averaged 5.99 inches long and 4.80 inches around, while gay men averaged 6.32 inches and 4.95 inches around. So gay men are over 5% longer and 4% thicker than straight men. So much for gay guys being "less of a man" than straight guys. While an interesting study, there are problems with the data, as penises are notoriously difficult to measure with consistency. Even though it was a large sample size, questions remain whether the Kinsey data accurately represents the population.

From the humorous to the obscure, there are tiny bones in our inner ears that make weak clicking sounds called otoacoustic emissions. Lesbian's inner ears emitted less frequent and weaker sounds and were one third as sensitive as straight women's ears, indicating physical structures that resemble the inner ears of men. Because these delicate structures are highly affected by testosterone, they are yet one more indication for the effect on lesbians of high testosterone levels in the womb. Gay men's inner ears were no different from straight men's.[10] The study's author declared this a major finding: "Their auditory centers have been masculinized, and the presumption is that so have the sites in the brain that direct sexual preference."[11]

From ears to eyes, everyone blinks when startled. Eye blink researchers startle their subjects with a loud noise, then rate the response on the prepulse inhibition (PPI) scale, which has to be an amusing test to watch. Lesbians have a strong blink response, closer to that of straight men. Gay men's responses are weaker than straight men's, but not so dramatically.[12] As one of the study's authors explains, "The startle response is pre-conscious and cannot be learned. It is mediated by an ancient region of the brain called the limbic system which also controls sexual behavior. This is very strong evidence that female sexual orientation at least may be 'hard-wired' in this region."

Next is the nose, as the sense of smell is another part of our bodies that is hard-wired. Without knowing what they were smelling, lesbians and straight men were attracted to the smell of female sex hormones, while gay men and straight women were attracted to the scents of men. Likewise, people attracted to women were irritated when they smelled male androgen, and people attracted to men were irritated by the smell of estrogen. Brain scans taken during the sniffing tests showed that the responses in the participants' brains followed the same patterns as sexual response. This was another test where researcher bias played no part, as they were studying the brain for smells that could trigger epilepsy when they stumbled on these results around sexuality.[13]

In another smell scenario, volunteers sniffed samples of underarm sweat from males and females, straight and gay. Straight men and lesbians responded positively to women's sweat, and straight women were attracted to straight men's sweat. The sweat of gay men stood out as the most different, as it generated the strongest positive attraction from gay men, and the least attraction, and even repulsion, from the other groups.[14] The study's authors concluded that gay men produce unique odors, and that gay men also perceive sweat odors differently.

To finish the discussion of body parts, it is worth mentioning one that went wrong. A well publicized study reported that gay men's hair tends to swirl around the crown of their head one way, while straight men's hair tends to swirl the other direction. The technical term is hair whorl, and researchers looked at gay and straight men's whorls and noted their clockwise and counterclockwise orientation.[15] The results have since been questioned as scientists are not sure hair whorls are a valid feature to count. As one researcher said after analyzing the report: "It's hard to determine which way the hair whorls in people with long or curly hair, and the data do not fit the simple genetic model perfectly. So you should not use hair whorl direction to demonstrate basic genetics."[16] As a man who is bald on top, I am all for rejecting a test were someone like me does not count.

To summarize all this evidence from the body: there is clearly a genetic component in gay men, an epigenetic component in both gay men and women, and a genetic difference in the mothers of gay men. Male homosexuality also correlates with the number of older brothers, indicating that some tuning of male sexuality may occur in the mother's womb. Gay men tend to have more symmetrical brains, more feminine finger length patterns, more fingertip swirls on their left hands, and shorter proportional bone lengths, all of which points to gay men having less exposure to testosterone in the womb and somewhat feminized bodies. Gay men's larger penis sizes either contradicts that conclusion or are the result of faulty data. In addition, an innate attraction to both male pheromones and gay male sweat indicates a strong biological root to gay men's sexual attractions.

As for gay women, current evidence has not found a genetic component to female homosexuality, but the unfolding understanding of epigenetics may change that. Lesbians do have more asymmetrical brains, masculine finger length patterns, longer proportional bone lengths, and weaker inner ear sounds, all pointing to increased exposure to testosterone in the womb and somewhat masculinized bodies. Correlations between lesbian attractions and strong eye blink responses indicate a hard-wired limbic system response, and attraction to female pheromones and sweat indicates an innate biological component to female-female attraction.

These findings of a somewhat lesser biological role in creating female sexuality fit with Lisa Diamond's observations on female sexual fluidity. While men appear to be more hard-wired for attraction to one sex or the other, women may be more generally wired to be sexual, and therefore subject to a greater possibility of experiences that can be fluid over time. Women may experience varying attractions based on particular circumstances or an individual's characteristics, while other aspects of their sexuality remain fixed. The exact nature of this experience of being human can be a hard thing to nail down with certainty.

Many gay people have mixed reactions when hearing about this research. It can be comforting to have hard science back up our experience that our attractions to the same sex are deep, intrinsic, hard-wired, and immutable. On the other hand, many gay men are insecure about their masculinity, and cringe at evidence that their bodies and brain wiring may be physically feminized and more like women. Some lesbians, meanwhile, feel disappointed that there is not the same level of genetic evidence for female homosexuality. In the end I am not sure these details matter, because once it is clear being gay is not a choice, the size of the evidence pile, or the details of what is in that pile, are not as important as the big picture. We are who we are, no matter the details of what got us here. I do not really understand interstellar physics either, yet I manage to live comfortably in the solar system I call home.

It is worth pausing for a moment, after all this evidence from science, and consider the implications. The claim made by gay people that our sexuality and gender variations are as unchangeable as our height or eye colors turns out to be quite literally true. What that means is that countries like Uganda, Egypt, and Russia are persecuting, imprisoning, and killing their children for an in-born trait, and religions like the Mormons, Baptists, and Catholics that condemn homosexuality are getting God's creations wrong and demonizing a choice that was never made. Society got gay people wrong, and attitudes must now change to fit the truths revealed.

The evidence is in. It is written in our genetic code. It is displayed across our bodies. It is visible throughout the animal kingdom and all of life. It is time for people of integrity to hear the truth loud and clear. The debate over choice is over, and it is time for humanity to move towards a more integrated view of normalcy and variations across the behavioral spectrum. While science is not yet able to fully explain what makes some people gay and some people straight, all available evidence confirms that same-sex attraction and gender variations are not a choice. It is the way God made us as we came blinking and crying out of our mothers' wombs and into the tumult of our distinctively queer lives.

MINDS

Psychology

You're only given
a little spark of madness.
You mustn't lose it.

~ *Robin Williams*

BACK WHEN I WAS a young gay man being scrutinized by my disapproving Mormon elders, the dominant theory said that male homosexuality was a mental disorder created by distant fathers and over-protective mothers. This theory prevailed until someone pointed out that it got causality backwards. It is natural for a father to feel distant from a son who does not enjoy sharing men's activities, and equally natural for a mother to feel protective of a sensitive son she can bond with over shared feminine interests. It was a sign of how society got the psychology of sexuality so horribly wrong that these completely natural parenting instincts were labeled detrimental.

Every child is different, and good parenting means teaching sons and daughters how to relate to the masculine and feminine energies in themselves and others. Of course this process will vary by child as the parent tailors their child-rearing to fit the child's inborn sexual or gendered nature, just as reading is taught differently to the dyslexic and sports differently to the naturally athletic. A father can teach both his girly girl and tomboy daughters how to relate to men and the masculine, but the lessons will vary for each child, just as mothers can teach both their macho and effeminate sons how to relate to women and the feminine. It is the nature of life to grow slowly into who we are and then figure out how to live as that person. Guiding children through that process is among the most important tasks parents perform, right after keeping them safe and ensuring they eat their vegetables.

Part of keeping children safe used to include keeping them away from anyone gay. Some of this came from the misplaced belief that gay people were child molesters. More absurdly, many adults also feared that homosexuality was contagious. Bizarre as it sounds today, there were people who believed homosexuals "recruited" innocent young people into the gay "lifestyle" from which their victims could never escape. By merely seeing a gay person on television or experiencing a gay schoolteacher, the child's heterosexuality could be threatened. I always found this laughable. If mere awareness of gay people could turn a straight child gay, then heterosexuality must be remarkably frail indeed. Every gay person I know was tested in a crucible of heterosexual fire, so we never fret that exposure to heterosexuality will change us. This same argument was used against two lesbian mothers as parents, saying that role modeling and exposure would turn their children gay. Not only has that theory been proven false,[1] but it overlooks the fact that most gay children came from straight parents.

I often wondered if these fearful straight people were speaking some personal truth — that they needed to be constantly vigilant against gay people because their own sexuality was more fragile and tenuous than they wanted to admit. That is the only explanation that makes sense to me, as no one living their authentic sexuality would go around fearing exposure to others might change it.

The world's experts have looked deeply for psychological origins for homosexuality, and came up empty. As the United Kingdom's Royal College of Psychiatrists summarized, "Despite almost a century of psychoanalytic and psychological speculation, there is no substantive evidence to support the suggestion that the nature of parenting or early childhood experiences play any role in the formation of a person's fundamental heterosexual or homosexual orientation. It would appear that sexual orientation is biological in nature, determined by a complex interplay of genetic factors and the early uterine environment. Sexual orientation is therefore not a choice."[2]

In a joint statement to the US Supreme Court, the American Psychological Association, the American Medical Association, the American Academy of Pediatrics, the American Psychiatric Association, the American Psychoanalytic Association, the American Association for Marriage and Family Therapy, and the National Association of Social Workers, among others, signed a joint statement declaring:

> Scientific evidence strongly supports the conclusion that homosexuality is a normal expression of human sexuality; that most gay, lesbian, and bisexual adults do not experience their sexual orientation as a choice; that gay and lesbian people form stable, committed relationships that are equivalent to heterosexual relationships in essential respects; and that same-sex couples are no less fit than heterosexual parents to raise children and their children are no less psychologically healthy and well-adjusted than children of heterosexual couples.[3]

I used to think these official declarations were more political than scientific, the expressions of empathetic therapist types rather than the legitimate findings of clear-eyed scientists, until I read about the early research. In the 1950s, a psychologist named Dr. Evelyn Hooker lived in Los Angeles and had a number of gay friends, including her neighbor, the openly gay author Christopher Isherwood. Noticing that her gay friends seemed as well adjusted as anyone else, she devised a way to test her theory by having gay and straight men take three standardized psychological tests, removing the individuals' names, and then having the anonymized results reviewed by a panel of experts. The experts used their best training to try and sort the gay respondents from the straight, and failed.

It was common at the time for psychologists, and the public, to view gay people as sick. By looking at people through that predetermined lens, every problem in a gay person appeared as a symptom of the underlying sexual disorder. When that negative filter was taken away by anonymizing the test results, gay men tested as emotionally healthy as anyone else.[4] To this day the results remain the same. Gay people test normally on standardized tests for the big five personality traits: openness to experience, conscientiousness, extraversion, agreeableness, and neuroticism. The only standardized tests where we stand out is on the masculinity-femininity test, which is understandable, as differing around gender is part of the definition of who we are.[5]

No professional psychological association today considers homosexuality a mental illness. The only organizations that continue to make those kinds of anti-gay claims are the organizations that exist solely for that purpose, like those tobacco company experts who swore cigarettes were good for you. The most prominent example is NARTH, the National Association for Research & Therapy of Homosexuality, which has a history of dodgy science and shady leaders, many of them Mormon. Professional anti-gay organizations like NARTH issued pseudo-scientific studies on a regular basis, claiming their inability to publish properly peer-reviewed studies in actual scientific journals was the result of a liberal bias in academia and the media. One of the great turning points in the gay rights movement came when even that claim was proven false.

The evidence arrived, or more accurately, did not arrive, in the court battles after the Proposition 8 debacle. No court would overturn the popular will of the voters unless there were powerful reasons to do so, but two of America's most prominent lawyers, Ted Olson, who was famously conservative, and David Boies, who was famously liberal, joined together to challenge Prop 8 in Federal court. Together they claimed that Prop 8 was not passed as a rational step to protect children and heterosexual marriages, arguing that it succeeded because of an irrational prejudice against gay people and a desire to punish a despised minority. To the shock of everyone on my side, with this most critical of decisions in the balance, the legions of "experts" in the professional anti-gay crowd were complete no shows. When the stakes were high and lies could lead to prison, the anti-gay were nowhere to be found. Not one of the professional anti-gay campaigners was willing to testify in Federal court. Not one of the pseudo-scientists of NARTH, or the professors of the anti-gay

Christian colleges, or any of the political anti-gay organizations were willing to present their evidence in a forum where it could be challenged by rational analysis. As Boies later summarized, "All of that is Junk Science. It's easy to come on TV and lie, but to sit in a witness chair and present your opinions, and have them challenged and be cross examined is a lonely place. It's a lonely place to lie under oath."[6]

Actually that is not quite the whole story. Two witnesses, Kenneth Miller and David Blankenhorn, did attempt to testify for Proposition 8. Miller was there to testify that gay people were not a despised minority, as we had plenty of political clout, but his actual testimony ended up supporting our side. Blankenhorn, founder and president of the Institute for American Values, gave his testimony in support of Prop 8 but ended up admitting under cross examination that "adopting same-sex marriage would be likely to improve the well-being of gay and lesbian households and their children."[7]

Some gay people appear completely normal, while many of us are totally nutty, and others are just really creative and non-conforming. But of course I can say all those same things about straight people. Being gay did make me different, which is something I celebrate, but it did not make me sick or mentally ill. If I am a sick or damaged person in some way, I believe that is the direct result of the torture and abuse I experienced for being gay. Otherwise my homosexuality and my sense of gender just made me into a regular human being with little gay sparkles, expressing a pretty standard set of strengths and weaknesses, just like everybody else.

Cures

The most confused we ever get
is when we try to convince our heads
of something our hearts know is a lie.

~ *Karen Marie Moning*

SOME GAY PEOPLE do not want to be gay. They learn from their religions or cultures that homosexuality is a bad thing; they look at gay role models in the media and society; and they decide they would rather be something else, different from who they are. In short, they want to be cured. During the centuries of anti-gay persecution, the incentive to change sexual orientation could not have been stronger. Yet even under threat of torture and death, people's sexuality remained — intact and unchangeable.

At the same time, people are always free to choose their behaviors. While our attractions and passions may be deeply ingrained, how we act on those feelings is a matter of choice. Put straight men in prison without women, for example, and they often choose sex and intimacy with same-sex partners. Being forced to make choices that go against their primary orientation does not change their sexuality. It just makes them a straight person having sex with another straight person because their natural and preferred options were taken away. In much the same way, societies can deny a gay person the option to connect with people of the same-sex. Denied their preferred human contact, that person may choose an other-sex partner instead. In fact it was pretty common for gay people to marry an other-sex partner, have children, and live within the traditional family structure, but that does not make them heterosexual. It makes them a gay person choosing a relationship with someone of the other sex, while their sexual orientation remains unchanged.

A dear friend of mine is a gay man who followed his religion's moral guidance and chose to marry a straight woman. My buddy is handsome and athletic, with a tender heart and a creative spirit. Back in his college years he was openly gay and became friends with a wonderful woman. Their friendship grew and deepened, and following the guidance of their Christian faith, they married, had several beautiful daughters, built a life together, and still live in a marriage enriched by an authentic and abiding love for each other after nearly thirty years.

Pausing there my friend's story sounds like a triumph of traditional values over homosexuality. But going deeper, they have a very hard time with sex. He is rarely able to maintain his erection through the act, even as he pictures the type of men he is attracted to in an attempt to keep himself aroused. He once told me that their best sex occurred when he took a Viagra, fell asleep; and then his wife woke him for sex while he was only half awake. His lack of success at becoming heterosexual was not for lack of trying. For decades he devoted himself to prayer, Bible study, hard work, and the desire for change, to no effect.

Devotedly monogamous through the first half of his marriage, he increasingly felt that the full-body aches he routinely experienced arose from a loneliness rooted in his desire for the touch and affections of a man. After much soul searching, he reached the point where he could no longer ignore the callings of his heart. Committed to his wife and the well-being of his children, he made the decision to stay in his marriage, and he finds sexual release and more fulfilling forms of intimacy with men on the side. My friend's wife knows some of this, and she often weeps over the lack of physical attention she receives from her husband. Through it all, though, she says that her faith carries her through, finding solace in the belief that true love comes from God, and she therefore does not require that kind of physical love and attention from her husband.

The example of my friend and his wife illustrates a flaw in the logic of those who believe gay people can be cured if they just act straight — the avalanche of pain a gay spouse can create for their partner. As the Mormon author Carol Lynn Pearson, whose own gay husband died of AIDS, said, "Enough women have been sacrificed on that altar."[1] My friend now says that as much as he loves his wife and daughters, and as devoted he is to never leaving them, he regrets the choice he made back in those college years. He tells me he would never recommend that path to a young gay person today.

Wanting to be cured, and firmly believing that God meant for them to live as straight, many gay people tried to change their sexuality. The biggest organization of ex-gays, meaning gay people who claimed they were cured of their homosexuality, was called Exodus International. Based in the Evangelical community, Exodus supported gay people in rejecting the "gay lifestyle," curing themselves of their sexual orientation through self control and prayer centered on a homosexuality-rejecting Christian life. In June of 2013, the Exodus Board of Directors voted unanimously to shut the organization down, and its longtime head issued a formal apology to the gay community for the harm he had caused.

Organizations like Exodus failed because their claims of success were a lie. There is no evidence of anyone ever "cured" of same-sex attractions. Only one serious study ever claimed evidence for a cure, and in 2012 the author of that study, Dr. Robert Spitzer, recanted. The original study was of only nine men, the only supposedly successful examples Spitzer could find even after decades of reparative therapy affecting countless thousands of people. Soon after publishing he realized that even those few self-reported claims of success were probably not the whole truth. As Spitzer himself put it, "I believe I owe the gay community an apology."[2] The best these programs can do is suppress an individual's overall sex drive. They cannot change the direction of it. Now even the most famous reparative therapy counselor, Dr. Joseph Nicolosi, says,

"I have never said I could cure someone completely from homosexuality. All my books make it quite clear that homosexual attractions will persist to some degree throughout a person's lifetime."[3]

At five years of age, a boy named Kraig began showing signs of effeminacy, so his parents took him to another prominent therapist named Dr. George Alan Rekers, who then built a career based on the claim he cured the child of his homosexuality. A recent search turned up Kraig's true fate. His actual name was Kirk Murphy, and according to Murphy's family, Rekers's "therapy" left Murphy traumatized for life, ultimately killing himself at the age of thirty-eight.[4] Meanwhile, his supposed success with "Kraig" made Rekers one of the few nationally recognized anti-gay experts, an officer of NARTH, and a professional witness in court trials against gay rights. The state of Florida, for example, paid Rekers $120,000 to appear in court defending the state's ban on gay adoptions, and his written research appeared in support of gay marriage bans in California's Proposition 8 trial. Rekers' career as an anti-gay expert ended in 2010 when he was photographed at Miami airport returning from a European vacation with the young male prostitute he found on a website called rentboy.com and hired to "carry his bags" and give daily sexual massages.

The American Psychiatric Association reviewed over eighty-three different studies on reparative studies going back to the 1960s and concluded that change therapy was more likely to be harmful than helpful. According to the APA:

> The potential risks of 'reparative therapy' are great and include depression, anxiety, and self-destructive behavior, since therapist alignment with societal prejudices against homosexuality may reinforce self-hatred already experienced by the patient. Many patients who have undergone 'reparative therapy' relate that they were inaccurately told that homosexuals are lonely, unhappy individuals who never achieve acceptance or satisfaction. The possibility that the person might achieve happiness and satisfying interpersonal relationships as a gay man or lesbian are not presented, nor are alternative approaches to dealing with the effects of societal stigmatization discussed.[5]

Panel leader Julia Glassgold framed the issue nicely: "Both sides have to educate themselves better. The religious psychotherapists have to open up their eyes to the potential positive aspects of being gay or lesbian. Secular therapists have to recognize that some people will choose their faith over their sexuality."[6]

A fellow ex-Mormon gay man named Steve Lee wrote online about his experiences with gay cures. As a participant in the Mormon equivalent of Exodus, Lee spent over twelve years attending weekly meetings where he and other gay men learned manly activities like how to fix their cars in the hopes that gaining more masculine abilities would help cure them of their attractions towards men. As Lee put it, what they ended up with was a group of gay guys who knew how to fix cars. Because the Mormon gay cure program used the addiction model, however, participants were taught that any gay thought was a relapse, and their inability to become un-gay was framed as a personal moral failure. As Lee puts it now: "It's a disgusting way to live your life."[8]

There are no good statistics on the gay cure industry because its leaders never allowed outsiders to view their techniques or review their case documentation. The reason for this extreme secrecy from an industry happy to take people's money arose from the results that are known — cures: zero, casualties: countless. As Lee reported from his Mormon gay cure group, at least a third of the men committed suicide.

I have known many gay people who tried to deny that they were gay, and they always remind me of something I saw once on the other side of the world. I was traveling through India in the height of summer, driving across a hot desert highway when the traffic slowed to a crawl. Little by little we inched forward until reaching the source of the congestion: entertainers performing in the middle of the road, busking for money. At the center of the show was a large and tortured bear being poked with a stick to keep him up on his hind legs, dancing for the entertainment of travelers. Seeing the weary torment in that bear's eyes, his paws cracked raw on the hot black asphalt, I thought of the high Himalayas from where he was probably stolen and the hellish life he now leads, forever tormented for the satisfaction of others. I turned my eyes away as a wave of nausea rolled over me. I think of that bear every time I see gay people claiming they are cured of homosexuality. They have that same look of torment and submission in their eyes as they contort themselves into whatever dance will please those around them and make the painful poking stop. A straight friend of mine calls this the "if we hurt them enough they won't be gay" solution. Which is, in fact, no solution at all.

There is a simple reason gay cures do not work. It is impossible to un-choose what was never chosen, or cure what was never broken. Homosexuality cannot be cured because there is no cure for this condition called life.

Homophobia

> Who sees all beings in his own self,
> and his own self in all beings,
> loses all fear.
>
> ~ *The Upanishads*

GIVEN THE POWER of homophobia, and the damage it has done across history, it is important to understand what motivates people to become homophobic. The answer may sound strange and counter-intuitive at first, but the root of the problem appears to be the homophobe's own same-sex attractions.

To test for sexual attraction, men were hooked up to machines that measured fluctuations in their genitalia while being shown erotic pictures of men and women. Predictably enough, straight men were aroused by pictures of women, but the surprise was that homophobic straight men were also turned on by pictures of men. Of the participants who told researchers they were repulsed when viewing erotic images of other men, 80% were physically aroused by them.[1] Picture that physiological response the next time you hear an anti-gay sermon. Most disturbingly, these homophobic men were so unaware of their own body's responses that they did not believe the researchers when told. As the US National Institutes of Health clarified: "Homophobia is apparently associated with homosexual arousal that the homophobic individual is either unaware of or denies."[2] So homophobes are gay, or have significant gay attractions, but there is no way for them to know that because their denial of their own body's responses is so complete.

Fortunately, healthy people never have to experience this kind of attraction-repulsion because they can choose honesty instead. Given that everyone has at least some awareness of the beauty and sexiness of their own gender, most people learn to be comfortable with their little bisexual moments, no matter how fleeting. Those who hate those occasional feelings in themselves create a pattern called reaction formation — hating in others the thing they cannot stand in themselves. Believing they have to keep their discomforts hidden, homophobes go overboard to prove they could not possibly be gay. This is the overcompensation of teenage boys who puff out their chests and declare loudly and often how much they hate the fags, for fear anyone might discern this might not be the whole story. It is also the clergyman who grows red faced over the story of Sodom and the once-a-year Gay Pride celebrations, or the politicians who put anti-gay rhetoric at the center of their agendas. This reaction is an understandable, if unattractive, phase in adolescence, but it is pretty inexcusable in adults.

Acknowledging that homophobes have sexuality issues is not to say that the redneck farmer declaring how much he hates the fags is secretly wishing he could move to Provincetown and open an art gallery. But it probably does mean that he knows which farm hand looks best in tight jeans. The question for the rest of us, then, is how to help him find relief given that his internal fears cannot be directly addressed, as he cannot acknowledge they exist. The answer lies in creating a culture of authenticity. Give him the space to feel what he feels without the negative voices, and he can relax and let his version of maleness be OK. In my experience, comfortably masculine men are indifferent to other men's sex lives, not reactive. The cure for homophobia is to let people be who they are: both the parts that fit the idealized patterns and the squiggly bits that vary from the norms. In my ideal world no one would have to live behind a mask of normalcy, as our little variations would also be celebrated.

Even among the tolerant, the idea of gay sex can bring repulsion because of the tendency to focus on gay men and anal sex. Of course that leaves out women's sexuality altogether, which is always a loss. More directly, that disgust is misplaced because far more straight people have anal sex than gay people, a subject for a later chapter. Even among gay men, not everyone likes anal sex. One recent American study found that 75% of gay men had oral sex during their most recent sexual encounter, while only 34% had anal sex.[3] A major British study found a third of gay men had never had anal sex.[4]

At its core, this repulsion over other people's sexual habits comes from reducing everything about a person down to a singular sex act. During a debate on gay marriage, a New Hampshire state representative made clear her opposition came from her disgust: "We're talking about taking the penis of one man and putting it in the rectum of another man and wriggling it around in excrement."[5] Hygienic inaccuracy aside, imagine opposing straight marriage because it is a man putting his penis inside a woman and wriggling it around in her vaginal juices. Reducing relationships to mere sex acts makes the vulgar rise to the top, obfuscating any emotional depth or meaning behind the act.

Traditional societies considered it offensive for a man to be the passive sexual partner to another man, because that would be a man lowering himself to the status of a woman. That is why the most patriarchal religions like Mormons, Catholics, and Muslims are the most homophobic. Their belief systems insist the male must maintain dominance over the female. The most pungent definition of homophobia says that it is a man's fear that another man will treat him the way he treats women.

So much of this discussion of homophobia centers on male homosexuality, the question arises why female homosexuality appears to be so much less threatening. One obvious reason is that straight men tend to eroticize all things female. The male gaze transforms lesbians into lust interests for men, denying women their own lives outside the male dominated world. It may also be that males and "masculinity," are more fragile, as male gender norms are often more rigid and therefore more easily violated.[6]

As to why homophobia was persistent across the ages, when homosexuality and gender variation were so clearly normal and natural, I can think of three useful explanations. The first is regret. Many people live in miserable culture-conforming relationships. Note how many men routinely disparage women or refer to their wives with phrases like "the old ball and chain." When I hear these sentiments, I hear expressions of bitterness about their fate. I do not automatically think the speaker is gay, but a bit more space around gender roles might help these people find a more authentic path to love and happiness. The second reason is rooted in misogyny. Patriarchies dismiss the feminine as less important, declaring it subservient to male authority. They degrade women and female roles or put women "on a pedestal," transforming them into symbols for men rather than self-empowered individuals. This same disrespect for the feminine is then applied to gay men who dare to openly embody both masculine and feminine energies. The third reason centers on the persistent human tendency to reject the different. The blind, deaf, or physically handicapped were viewed as inferior human beings, rather than as equally valid people with differing abilities. It seems no coincidence that progress in the public awareness and acceptance of gay people has paralleled improvements around disabled people's rights, as both represent humanity learning to incorporate its rather natural variations.

This human tendency to demonize the Other, dividing the world into Us and Them, is often enforced through the tyranny of small differences like skin color or religious practices. The Us group is then declared good, righteous, hard working, and normal, while the Them group is portrayed as opposing the goodness of Us, and therefore sick, perverse, threatening, evil, and bent on destroying civilization. A quick scan of the political landscape reveals how common this kind of thinking remains. Popular Thems in my lifetime included blacks, Jews, immigrants, Catholics, women, the handicapped, Muslims, Mormons, and many others. White America projected its fears onto black people for generations, and Christian conservatives turned homosexuals into the primary demons of their culture wars in the 1980s. When gay people became the culture's Thems, all of American culture's negative fears were projected onto us, without any regard for our true strengths or weaknesses.

Most often, homophobia occurs as something small and easy to dismiss — the tiny insults, slights, and indignities that pervade the culture. One example of this phenomenon is embedded in the phrase "that's so gay," used to mean the worst thing possible. When I was young, Polack jokes were the standard joke format, even for kids in Utah who had never met anyone Polish. As a result of all those Polack jokes, I actually grew up thinking Poles were, in fact, a little stupid, as they only existed as a punchline in my world. The jokes ended when Lech Walesa and the Solidarity movement initiated the demise of the Soviet Union. Suddenly, Poles became heroic and stopped being funny, and I have not heard a Polack joke since. The routine use of disparaging words like "faggot" are the same. Any individual usage may just be dumb or rude, but the cumulative effect of using it to mean the negative can be deeply harmful.

The group that may benefit most directly from a decline in homophobia might be straight men. Of all Americans, straight white men have the fewest friends, to the point that most modern American men have no confidants at all,[7] a fact directly attributable to their fear of appearing gay.[8] A decrease in homophobia would allow men to relax into deeper authenticity and more peaceful connection with each other. Under the current paradigm, heterosexuality is infinitely fragile, vulnerable to slipping away in one wrong look, one wrong kiss, or one night playing with the wrong team. Paradoxically, relaxing homophobia may create stronger heterosexuality, as men will be able to support each other in more traditional ways, without all the fear.

In conclusion, I offer a simple standard to determine if peace and harmony towards gay people has been achieved. We will know homophobia has been conquered when it is safe for everyone to express their genuine affections and sense of gender on any public street without fear of scorn or attack. When that magical sense of freedom and safety arrives, we will know that we are all free. Until that time arrives, there is work to do.

The cure for homophobia is to recognize the fear of self being expressed in the homophobic individual, and creating a society where they feel safe to be real with all the truths in themselves and others. Validating the homophobe's persecution of gay people results in ongoing harm to the perpetrator. It is time for that to end, for the benefit of all.

Healing

> It is by going down into the abyss
> that you recover the treasures of life.
> Where you stumble,
> there lies your treasure.
>
> ~ *Joseph Campbell*

THE DAY AFTER I finished high school I got on a bus and left for a month-long trek on America's most extreme survival program. Now called the Boulder Outdoor Survival School, it is based in Boulder, Utah, a town so geographically isolated it was the last place in America to have its mail delivered by burro. The first segment of our trip was called Impact, where we walked for three days and three nights through the sculpted deserts of southern Utah with no food and only what pungent desert water we could find. Impact forced our bodies to adjust to the scorching heat of day and the shivering cold of night. Over subsequent weeks we hiked the mountain ranges, flat-topped mesas, and winding canyons of that region. Some days we walked as much as fifty miles, learning lessons about living off the land and personal fortitude along the way. I started off the trip slim and lost thirty pounds in twenty-eight days, but in a lifetime of adventures, that time away from telephones, electricity, and civilization remains one of the best things I have ever done.

The last part of the trip was called Solo. One by one, participants were dropped off along the bends of the Escalante River, a shallow river winding through red rock canyons. There we lived alone for five days, without anyone else nearby. For five days I slept in my single blanket, tended my little fire, and bathed in the warmth of the summer river. Throughout my Solo I had no other company than the wind in the cottonwood trees, the water rippling over the rocks, the rustling of birds and insects, and the sound of my own thoughts. There I discovered, on the red sand banks of one of America's most isolated rivers, something I had never known for sure before that moment. Away from the constant judgments and criticisms that formed the background of my Mormon life, I discovered that I was a good person. I found myself to be good company, interesting and entertaining. Most importantly, I discovered that I was profoundly comfortable with all that quiet. For the first time in my young life, with no other voices telling me otherwise, I got to spend several days in a row feeling that I might be OK.

By the time we grow into independent adulthood, most gay people have run a gauntlet of criticism, teasing, and bullying from our peers. We absorbed negative messages about ourselves from the highest pulpits and from the culture at large. We lost friends and family for speaking our truths. While much of this book addresses the reasons we should be proud of who we are, I want to pause for a moment and consider the pain all that wounding brings and the profound necessity for healing in most gay lives.

There are times I walk through a gay neighborhood and I am stunned at what beautiful, creative, diverse, and shining people we are. Sometimes it feels like a truism that many of the best people are gay. There are other times, however, when my perspective shifts and we look more like the straggling survivors from some faraway war — bloodied, bandaged, crippled, and leaning on each other for support. The damage done by a society that does not know how to raise its gay children is made visible by symptoms like depression, suicide, and low self esteem along with the usual coping mechanisms like drugs, sex, food, pornography, money, and alcohol. More subtly, some of us get caught in a poverty mentality, never believing we are good enough to be truly comfortable. Others overcompensate with a perfectionism as we attempt to immunize ourselves from criticism by having the ideal bodies, homes, clothes, and lives. The pain we carry manifests in the magazine-perfect home designed to prove our worth, the party drugs repeated over and over long after the festivities end, or in the piles of bodies from our ongoing sexual conquests. Each of these can be an attempt to comfort ourselves, salve the pain, and armor ourselves against future shame. There are so many things we would rather do than feel the hurt.

Wounded by the majority straight world, we turn to other gay people for help. Sometimes this is a move grounded in deep wisdom, as we often share life experiences and paths to healing. At other times, we retain a belief that the reflection of society's mirror was accurate, and there really is something fundamentally wrong with us at our core. Then without realizing it, we surround ourselves with friends and relationships that reflect back that self-hate, providing external confirmation that we are broken beyond repair. Or we can just go superficial, giving up on anything deeper and choosing pretty exteriors as our gloss over the muck we feel inside. It is astonishing how many gay men I meet who say they never want to be in a relationship, which makes sense given how hard it can be to stay in touch with our deeper wounded selves and find more lasting human connections. Better to have the ripped body and the status symbol clothes than let anyone see our weeping souls.

The denial path never really worked for me, although I certainly tried. Over time I learned the only way out of the pain was through it, or as I visualized this paradigm: the exit lies behind the dragon. At some point the pain in my life became so great I had no alternative but to turn and face the things that scared me most, heading straight towards what hurt, no matter the dragon's fire.

Signs that something was wrong began in my twenties. Although I had a partner and a life filled with friends and activities, I felt as if the foundation underneath was unstable. By my early thirties my life collapsed. For a while I could not hold a job, and my body kept expressing the underlying hurt that my head could not understand. I grew so used to extreme body aches that I walked around with a burst appendix for three days, thinking that level of pain was normal. It took me a month in a hospital under heavy sedation to recover. Then the constrictions on speaking my truth swelled up in my throat as a malignant thyroid tumor the size of a golf ball, a cancer with a terrifyingly high mortality rate. Over and over, my previously robust body shouted out the pain in my heart until I started to listen.

I sought help. I saw therapists and specialists. I joined support groups. I let my career stagnate as I tried to keep myself alive. Even now, decades after the worst of it, my belly swells up in some weird form of anguish as I write this, and my head swims in a sort of foggy denial. Slowly, far more slowly than I would have liked, I built a more solid foundation underneath me, much of my clarity coming from people who could mirror me accurately. I learned to be angry, an emotion I had always internalized as depression and began to let out and express. I learned to inventory my body, starting with my toes and working up, feeling each part of me without judgment or needing to fix anything, just to be in touch with my physical self.

Every gay person needs to heal those old wounds because society did not care for us correctly. As with everyone, the path to healing starts with ourselves, following the airline rule to "put your own oxygen mask on first before assisting others." Once we stand on solid ground, true healing requires reaching out to help others, in pursuit of the simple goal of becoming a whole person fully engaged with the world.

Many gay people are extraordinary, with amazing talents, fascinating personalities, and soulful spirits, but there is a phenomenon I notice in myself and others I think of as uneven development. While we may be exceptional in many ways, we can also be childish in others — some parts of us wise beyond our years, while other parts remain oddly stunted. I found a useful explanation of this phenomenon in the writings of the philosopher Ken Wilber who suggested thinking of a child born with one hundred units of potential.[11] As that child grows it reaches some stage of development that is insurmountable or something tragic happens, and a piece of the child's potential gets split off. Maybe ten units of potential are dissociated, and the child arrives at the next moral stage with ninety units of potential intact. Meanwhile that 10% gets locked away somewhere, unconscious and stuck. Worse, those ten units never grow up, so they continue operating at the age level where they got split off, trying to assert control from there. As the child grows the process repeats, and more and more bits get dissociated, left behind at challenging stages of development. That young person grows into an adult operating at something like 60% capacity, while the other forty units are running around like immature gremlins causing mayhem and demanding to be fed. But eventually life demands our fullest possible resources, so as an adult we need to go back and reintegrate those disassociated bits, or we will be unable to grow further. What could not be handled at six, or twelve, or sixteen years of age is now manageable, even if difficult and rancid from neglect. As an adult we loop back, process the old stuff, integrate whatever got split off, and grow into a fully functioning person operating at 100% capability.

This need may be somewhat true for everyone, but it is systemic for those of us denied an organic path to adulthood. Pretty much every gay person I have ever met needs an extra dose of healing. It is the legacy of the world we grew up in. Over time things can get better, but it requires a lot of work if we are to leave the world of arrested development and tread the uphill path towards the light. Over time the ground grows more solid; relationships become richer; and the reactive states calm, as the world around us transforms into a kinder feeling place. Best of all, at some point all that pain transforms into wisdom, because, as the historian Charles Austin Beard once wrote, "When it is dark enough, you can see the stars."[22]

LIFE

THIRTY-TWO

Love and Sex

In America,
sex is an obsession,
in other parts of the world
it's a fact.

~ *Marlene Dietrich*

I HAVE HAD SEX, and I have experienced love. I have experienced the high energy love where we climbed craggy wilderness mountains together far beyond organized trails until we reached the summit of a cascading waterfall, stripped off our clothes, and embraced each other as we raised our arms to the sun, yelping our shared exhilaration and joy in being so alive with each other. And I have experienced quietly connected love, where we held each other through times of tragedy, pain, and sorrow beyond human expression, riding the whole roller coaster of emotions all the way up, and all the way down, moving together in companionship, solidarity, and healing. I have experienced sex so wild and rough it was like great sweaty gorillas in heat, the basest animal spirits of our bodies and our most unbridled passions rising up and out with such ferocity we could not contain them so we let them explode and play out over and between each other again and again and again for what seemed like forever. And I have experienced sexual love so calming, harmonious, and connected that it felt as if the entire spinning universe slowed, and the progression of time paused, and our interwoven bodies seemed to float on a sea of tranquility that was not me, and was not him, but was some barely mortal experience of the greater love that underpins existence itself. All of these are love and sex, intertwining and playing out in a myriad of different ways. To discuss such complex issues, I think it is best to start with personal stories, as that is the only way I can convey what is ultimately ineffable and indescribable about the concepts of gay love and gay sex.

One of my greatest experiences of love began in my dreams. I was living in Washington, DC when I read a book on a Jungian practice called active imagination, which is essentially daydreaming with a journal in hand to capture what happens along the way and keep the mind from wandering.[1] As I read that book I grew inspired, so I stopped along one of the Potomac River's grassy banks overlooking the capital, closed my eyes, and imagined walking through a long dark tunnel until I emerged into a bright and overgrown garden. There, in my dream, I saw a little white pavilion. I walked over to it, sat down on a bench inside, and was soon joined by an extremely handsome man who came in and sat down next to me, wearing nothing but soccer shorts. Brown, lean, and athletic, I learned from our conversation that this dream figure was named Romero and he was a Brazilian soccer player. For years thereafter I filled my journals with the discussions I had with this dream element of my unconscious, my spirit guide Romero.

Years later I moved back to my native San Francisco, and one sunny day I was riding my bicycle through Golden Gate Park when I almost ran over a dark and foreign looking pedestrian. As he walked off I noticed his muscular swagger and the thick V of his back and thought, "Damn, that is a really beautiful man," at the exact moment he looked back towards me. Our eyes met, and I circled my bike around to introduce myself. He smiled and told me his name was Romero, and he was from Brazil, and he was on his way to a soccer match. I felt as if I had been struck by lightning. I had never once considered that my dream Romero could be a real person, but there he was standing in front of me. While real Romero looked visually a bit different from dream Romero, their voices, their attitudes, and even the cadence of their speaking styles were exactly the same. When I told real Romero the story of dream Romero a couple of days later, he told me that the moment we met he felt as if he had known me for a very long time, although he had no recollections of our dream conversations. We spent a few fortunate days together before he went back to Brazil, and we stayed in touch by phoning and faxing over the next many months. After a return reconnaissance trip where he came to visit for a couple of weeks, Romero moved to the United States to live with me, and our relationship lasted for six wonderful years.

This story of my life with Romero was a story of deeply committed love, but it was not a story of sex. For reasons unknown to either one of us, he was simply not into sex. At all. Just did not care for it. We both felt strongly about monogamy, so for six years I was in a deeply loving and committed relationship without sex. We slept well together, intertwined and holding each other through the night. We enjoyed each other's presence, supported each other through life's trials, and grew through our lives together; but nothing I could do or say unlocked his sex drive. Our relationship had the normal variety of good and bad points, but it was ultimately the lack of sexual intimacy that was too much for me. After six years of monogamous but sexless commitment, I came to the point where I had to move on, and Romero returned to Brazil. I have no regrets from the years Romero and I spent together. I learned more about the nature of love in those six years than any other time of my life, and decades after meeting we remain the dearest of friends. Our initial sense of connection and love that so shocked us that first day persists, more than twenty years later. All I have to do is pick up the phone and call Romero, and I am connected to a man with whom I feel spiritually intertwined in ways I have never experienced with anyone else in my life. But as handsome as his face is, and as sexy as his body is, and as lovely as his soul is, our relationship and our connections were never about sex.

Contrary to the popular image, not all gay relationships are about sex, just as not all straight relationships are about sex. One of my gay male friends is in a sexless relationship of nine years, and another in a sexless relationship of twelve years, yet they both remain deeply committed to their partners, no different from my straight friends in committed but sexless companionships. Sometimes love sustains itself without any sexual connection at all.

Of course the converse can also be true, as sex can come without love. To tell just one story of many, in my first few days after moving to Washington, DC for graduate school I drove to a dance club in the gay neighborhood, parking my car on a side road next to a forested park. As I was locking my car a cute guy walked by, flirted, and turned into the woods. I followed him just past the streetlight's illumination to where he had stopped, leaning up against a tree. I walked up to him and reached out to touch and connect. We groped, and within minutes our trousers were down while he was hugging the tree as I penetrated him from behind. This was before we really knew about AIDS, back when all of the sexually transmitted diseases were thought to be curable, so our encounter was easy, spontaneous, and profoundly carnal. We finished, zipped back up, exchanged pleasantries as we walked back to the busier streets, and went our separate ways. The encounter left me feeling like a sexy adventurer, the virile conqueror who could score whenever I wanted to, a man who could embody and express the raw heat of the moment with a complete stranger. Only later did I discover I had parked next to a place the locals called the P Street Beach, a notorious gay cruising spot. All day and all night, men circulated through the park's dark trees looking for sex, a cultural phenomenon largely lost to history now that sexual connections have moved to the internet and mobile phones. My great conquest as a newly out gay man turned out to be just one more introduction to the easy availability of gay male sex.

Between these two stories runs a life of monogamy, of sex within commitments, of sex without commitments, of love with sex, of love without sex, and of sex without much thought at all. I love and cherish deep and lasting commitments, so I always chose that path when it is available, but that does not negate my love of casual intimacy. I love the smile from the lady at the bakery counter that lights up my day, the knowing exchange with a bedraggled parent managing restless kids on the bus, or the sense of solidarity I can feel with another gay person at a cafe. As an amiable extravert I tend to get smiles and hellos from complete strangers throughout my day, and I am deeply grateful for those moments. Those fleeting connections are among my favorite experiences in life, and from there to physical intimacy is not always such a great step.

Sex can be so common for gay men that we jokingly call it the gay handshake. The powerful drive to meet for sex can lead us into lifelong friendships and profoundly human adventures. Through the desire for sexual connection I have experienced some of the finest Manhattan apartments, tidiest Indonesian apartments, grandest Parisian homes, and simplest huts in the Mexican jungle. Each of those stories represents a beautiful human being who blessed my life in a way I could never have experienced any other way. Most of these encounters centered on conversations, intimacy, and a social interactions in English, while others took place outside of shared verbal vocabularies. Each one involved opening up to another human being in profound ways unthinkable in a bar, a classroom, or a church picnic.

The idea that all casual sex is always unhealthy is absurd. Some of it is, certainly. Casual sex can become an addiction of ever diminishing returns just like anything else in life. Wine is great when savored and problematic if constantly indulged, a truism about food, Bible study, and jogging as well. Too much casual sex can leave people numb, checked out of their deeper selves as they continually play in the shallows. And yet, sometimes a casual sexual connection can be among the most powerful experiences two human beings can share. Kindness exchanged between strangers is a beautiful thing, and sex is not some weird act that exists outside of that basic human truth.

In a world where gay men often felt unloved and unwelcome in our cultures and families, we learned to find the missing warmth of human kindness in each other. Harry Hay described working on a tramp steamer off the California coast at fourteen when he met his first gay man, a sailor named Matt, who was ten years his senior. What went on between the two of them I do not know, but Hay talks of Matt introducing him to their shared brotherhood of gay men, telling Hay that if he ever felt lost in a strange land, not knowing anyone or how to speak the language, he would see a pair of shining eyes looking his way, and "All of a sudden your eyes lock into that pair of eyes, and...you're home and you're safe."[2] I have certainly found that kind of gay brotherhood connection, sometimes sexual, most often not, to be the source of warm and profound connections that have blessed and enriched my life and travels.

Straight people often wonder about this ability gay men have to connect through the eyes. While gaydar is an ability to recognize a gay person through some kind of special vibe, the eye thing is simpler. Most straight men look away when another man looks them in the eyes. Ever vigilant against other men as potential threats, looking into another man's eyes without flinching can be perceived as a hostile act in the straight male world. One of the magical powers gay men possess is the ability to look into another man's eyes with openness and without fear. If a man connects with my eyes without the reflexive fear most straight men carry, then there is a good chance he is one of the brotherhood, someone who "plays for our team," as we like to say. I regret to report this easy sorting of men based on their eye-contact fears is becoming less and less true as straight men lose their homophobia and regain the self-assurance to actually connect with other men beyond the discussion of sports. Slowly, slowly, I notice more young straight men willing to look into my eyes, unguarded and present, confident they can connect without losing their masculine dignity or starting a fight.

In my relationship with Romero I found love without sex, and in the trees of the P Street Beach I found sex without love, but in most of my relationships we shared both love and sex together. As with straight people, gay people sometimes find people we love, sometimes find people we have sex with, and sometimes, when the stars align, we find both with the same person. I am grateful to every man who has shared his life with me in committed ways that included all the juicy goodness of life, the pleasures of play and depth interwoven together, along with the growth through difficulties that comes as part of sharing a life with another human being.

Knowing gay people can be as deep or as superficial as anyone else, what is it exactly that gay people do for sex? It is ironic that we are so often accused of being overly sexual by people who are not at all sure what we do during their imagined hedonistic frenzies. The relentless negative obsession with anal sex is a particularly stunning example, as it overlooks all the gay men who do not like that act and nearly every lesbian. Hard as it is to believe in the age of the internet, there are people who do not understand how gay people have sex.

To explain it as tastefully as I can, I would start with lesbians. For some, the logistics of female-female sex seems baffling, but I think the problem is more conceptual than mechanical. Some people simply cannot imagine sex without a penis at the center. While I certainly love penis-centered sex myself, I am willing to bet most women can think of a few other things they might enjoy from a skillful and loving partner patient enough to let sensuality take primacy over sexuality. Add up every possible non-penis centered sexual and sensual acts, and that is lesbian sex.

For those whose minds are too penis-centric to imagine how that can be real sex, I offer the metaphor of vegetarianism. Some people, particularly those of the Midwestern persuasion, think dinner is a big slab of meat in the middle of a plate. There may be vegetables on the side, but any real meal centers on the meat. Meanwhile, on the other side of the globe, nearly a billion Hindus enjoy some of the world's most extravagantly rich and flavorful cuisines without any meat at all, as vegetarianism is part of their religion. Good Indian food is a healthy explosion of spices, flavors, and textures, all created without meat or meat flavoring. At its finest, vegetarianism provides such a vast array of experiences, flavors, and nutrition that the meat is never missed. As with vegetarians, so with lesbians. There may not be a penis at the center, but by moving the activities straight couples dismiss as foreplay to the center of the show, and giving each of those activities all the time and attention they deserve, lesbians can have sex that is spicy, fulfilling, creative, and frankly, really hot. They can even add dildos and other sex toys if they want to, but a lesbian friend once clarified that gay women do not use dildos as a penis substitute, but rather as a tool to pleasure the female body, devoid of any associations with the male.

As a result, lesbian sex is often richly varying. Hands and tongues play large roles. Oral sex and 69ing are popular. Dildos can be strapped onto the groin or thigh with a harness for one or both to penetrate vaginas and anuses. Two women can also lay face to face, rubbing, caressing, and masturbating each other, while exchanging long, slow, meaningful kisses. As with every other human couple, the best lesbian sex is about the chemistry the two people share more than it is about specific acts.

Sadly, lesbian sex is often degraded by the attitudes of straight men. Straight men love the idea of two hot women, which is fine, but reducing lesbian lives to a male fixation perpetuates the idea that women exist for male pleasure, or that female sex requires a male element. Disappointing as it may be for some male egos to hear, two women can love, commit, and enjoy each other outside of anything related to men.

Gay men do most of the same things lesbians do, although like all men we tend to put the penis on center stage. In our case we have two to play with, doubling the possibilities. In gay male pornography there was a nearly uniform progression to the stories. The couple meets in some hilariously contrived way involving parcel delivery or pool cleaning, and soon one man is performing oral sex on the other. They may then switch or 69 before they move to anal sex and the build up to the big finish. Kissing, licking, and looking deeply into each others eyes are optional and unfortunately rare in the externalized view of sex shown in pornography, but in general that is my experience in real life as well. We tend to follow that same progression from kissing to oral to anal to finish, with the caveat that many people leave out some of those stages, anal sex in particular, while others digress into the same kinds of intimate variations many straight people enjoy, like role playing, S&M, sensual cuddling, or whatever. Like lesbian sex, gay male sex tends to be spicy and varied, with fulsome attention given to the activities many straight people may dismiss as foreplay.

Because of this tendency to dismiss all the varying ways people have sex, it can seem like all gay sex is anal sex, and many find that image repellent. Slowly, that perception is changing as a fuller picture of gay lives comes into focus and the number of straight people trying anal sex increases. Something like 40% of straight Americans have had anal sex, while around 70% of gay males have, but there are almost twenty times more straight people than gay, so that means over seventy million straight adults have had anal sex versus around two and a half million gay men.[3] It is time to stop simplistically equating gay men with anal sex.

To be honest, butt sex can be great, and many gay men thoroughly enjoy it. It is a profoundly intimate act that can feel amazing for both partners. Much of our nervous system is in our gastrointestinal tract, which is why that is the part of the body that is most activated when there are strong nervous or excited feelings, those feelings we get "in the gut." My gastroenterologist tells me this is because our guts have far more nerves than any other system in the body, even more than the skin. Both kissing and anal sex stimulate those abundant nerves, which is why they can be so pleasurable. There is a good reason social conservatives are threatened by their imagined pleasures of gay sex, because it is highly pleasurable. Most importantly for me, as a man, I find it an indescribably bonding feeling to be penetrated by another man. When the chemistry is right, being penetrated creates a powerful feeling of connection and mind blowing stimulation. The experience of having another man inside my body also helps me understand female sexuality a bit better, as I know both the sense of vulnerability and the feelings of connection it can bring.

After disgust at gay sex, the biggest criticism of gay sexuality centers on promiscuity, and I can report that those reports are true. Some gay men really are profoundly promiscuous, but of course that is not the whole story. America's largest online dating site, OkCupid, observed their customers' online behavior and found that gay people have almost exactly the same number of sexual partners as straight people. According to OkCupid's data, 45% of gay people and 44% of straight people had five or fewer sexual partners a year, while 98% of gay people and 99% of straight people had twenty or less. Based on OkCupid's calculations, the promiscuous 2% minority of their gay members had 23% of the gay sex.[4] While OkCupid's data is not the whole picture, the general description sounds about right to me. A small percentage of people, gay and straight, male and female, are particularly promiscuous, but that is not the majority. A recent study found that over two million gay American men had not had any sex in the last five years.[5] Some of us have a lot of sex, some of us have none, and many of us have some but not a lot, making us, you know, just like other human beings.

As to why some gay men are so promiscuous, I do not think it is because we are gay. I think it is because we are men. Most men like sex — adventurous, conquest-oriented sex in particular. All kinds of men can be highly promiscuous when given the chance; think of straight men let loose in Las Vegas. In American culture, men are supposed to be the gas pedal, always go-go-go for sex, while women tend to be the brake pedal, holding back, taking other considerations into account, and generally slowing things down. Both may like sex equally, but the responsibilities for initiation and moderation are gender sorted, possibly because so many of the negative outcomes of straight sex can fall harder on women than men. Among gay men, this dynamic can result in two men with gas pedals and no one on the brake. That can be part of what is fun about gay male sex — the sheer velocity of it — as if it is another extreme sport sought out for the adrenalized thrills. My straight male friends respond to stories about the easy availability of sex in my world with far more jealousy than disgust. Gay men are living the male dream, it seems, although that also means we need an extra layer of self-restraint to maintain healthy moderation.

The female-female corollary is two women with brake pedals and no one to push on the gas. With neither woman initiating, even as both love sex and want a more sexual relationship, the result is the widely noted phenomenon of lesbian bed death, the idea that women together have less sex. Throwing a wrench in that notion, a recent study suggests that this may be viewing lesbian relationships through a male frame. Whereas women together do have less frequent sex, the sexual sessions they have tend to last much longer than male-female sex, resulting in higher female sexual satisfaction than most straight women experience with their male partners.[6]

Another reason gay people show higher numbers of sexual contacts loops back to the previous discussion of what is considered sex. If straight people included all acts of foreplay as sex in the way most gay people do, the total count of straight sexual partners would go up considerably. Think of the number of straight people who do not consider oral sex "real sex," while that is very much real sex for most gay people.

Now that so much of dating has moved online, hookup culture has devolved into something as bland and ubiquitous as fast food. In big cities it is now almost as easy to meet someone for sex over the internet as it is to order a pizza: I want this and this, a slathering of this other thing, and absolutely hold the that. If my desires correspond with what you want, then score! Highly efficient, but often lacking in the elements of truly fulfilling interactions. It is like having an itch you cannot scratch, and then finding there are people online who are really into scratching itches. There is nothing wrong with the two getting together, but it means meeting people who are really into itches, and not necessarily interested in you.

Modern culture suffers from the scourge of overabundance. While human bodies are wired to crave scarce essentials like salt, sugars, and fats, modern capitalism has made these elements cheap and abundant. Poor health and decreased survival are the result. The same is true of sex. Human bodies are wired for sex to bond and perpetuate the species, but modern culture and technologies makes sex abundant and effortless. I have heard it said that a young man today can see more naked women in five minutes than previous generations could see in a lifetime. The overabundance of staged, idealistic, and genetically freakish imagery can smother people's ability to make enjoyable contacts with real life flesh and blood partners. Fortunately, society is becoming more aware of these problems. Society may be reaching a post-decadent phase where ever increasing luxury and pleasure stops yielding the expected benefits, and people actively choose to live with less. The result can be seen in the younger generations that are more tolerant of premarital sex and gay relations, yet have less sex than their parent's generations.[7] Seeing the fuller picture seems to result in healthier choices.

One question persists: "So, which one of you is the man, and which one is the woman?" For those who understand gay sexuality the answer is obvious: None of the above. Straight people can default to cultural gender roles where she cooks and he mows the lawn while same-sex couples have to discuss and negotiate our roles with each other. The result rarely sorts into tidy "man" and "woman" roles. With two people of the same gender, everything has to be discussed and negotiated, from chores to sex acts. Being gay means we have to fully communicate our likes and dislikes with our partners, making us role models for everyone who honors equitable relations.

And then there is romance. When Tony Bennett sings *I Left my Heart in San Francisco,* he is singing one of the world's great love songs. He is also singing the words of a gay male couple, George Cory and Douglas Cross, World War II veterans who met in San Francisco. They were living together in Brooklyn when they wrote that touching song, so nostalgic for the love they found together in my beautiful city.[8]

Gay people know love — love gained and lost, beautiful and bumpy, everlasting and gone too soon. We know sex as meaningful, and we know sex as crass. We held our lovers as they died, and we stayed with each other over long and healthy lives. We lived alone and only embraced a few treasured people, and we hugged and kissed with abandon. We raised our own children and the children of others as lasting parental pairs, as single parents, and in every other combination. We had quick sex while standing up and slow sex in unmade beds. We loved well and badly in hotels, homes, and the backseats of cars. Homosexuals are, in other words, human-sexuals, doing the dance of life in our passionate, idiosyncratic, and bumbling ways, just as every human being has stumbled through love, sex, intimacy, and relationships since the beginning of time.

Gender

> When we try to pick out anything by itself,
> we find it hitched
> to everything else in the universe.
>
> ~ *John Muir*

LIKE MOST PEOPLE, I like to be seen for who I am. When I was younger, my sister in Utah often told her friends she had a gay brother in San Francisco, and was asked if I was the effeminate kind of gay. Her response was no, that I was more the lumberjack kind, which made sense as I stand six feet three inches tall, weigh well over 200 pounds, and sport a full beard under my balding head. Beyond my physical size, I am consistently told I make an impact when I walk into a room, and I am widely perceived to be masculine. Even in my very gay city, women flirt with me more frequently than men, and on learning that I am gay most straight people tell me they never would have guessed.

At the same time, people who know me well know I have a strong feminine side. I giggle freely at jokes and have a whooping boisterous laugh a straight friend calls "the gay siren." I tend to find myself overwhelmed with soft and tender feelings. I cry at movies, touching news stories, and when love overwhelms me. Sometimes all those emotions get the better of me, and I swirl in my own stormy sea of emotions. I ride those waves up as well, growing ecstatic at hikes and sunsets, dancing without inhibition across both my kitchen and club dance floors. I give warm embracing hugs that lead people to say I am like a big friendly bear. And yes, my hands can be highly expressive, as I feel no need to stiffen my wrists. As a straight male friend once told me: "Preston, sometimes you are like a dude, and sometimes you are like a chick."

I bring up these various traits to help paint a picture of where I fit on the male-female, masculine-feminine scales. I consider myself solidly male, yet balanced by a strong feminine side. Psychotherapist Carl Jung believed that every human being contains a balance of masculine and feminine energies, and that is how I view gender in everyone. It looks to me like most people are born clearly rooted in one gender, and then balanced by elements of the other. The old view held that genitals alone determined sex, but a more modern view understands gender as an interactive composite of genitalia, hormones, chromosomes, and personal inclinations.

Saying that gender has many facets does not negate the importance of two different sexes in the creation of life. At the cellular level, all sexual reproduction begins with one male reproductive cell combining with one female reproductive cell to create a new child cell, the fundamental reproductive process for most complex life on the planet. The exceptions are a few examples of asexual reproduction where a mother can produce a child without male input, but in over one and a half million species studied, a third sex cell has never been discovered.[1] Yet saying the male-female dichotomy is essential to the beginning of life is not to say that division defines all the rest of life, because as soon as those two cells get together, the simplicity of the male-female divide comes to an end.

When a child is born the parents are asked the primary question of newborns: "Is it a boy or girl?" Although the answer is straightforward for many children, for some it is not so clear. An astonishing 2% of the population is born with bodies outside the standard male-female duality, with genitalia that is not just male or female, or genetically beyond the female XX and male XY.[2] People born with bodies in-between the genders are called intersex, a physical condition unrelated to self-identity, social expression, or sexuality. Intersex conditions are the pure biology of innocent newborns. God or Mother Nature makes one or two out of every hundred human bodies in a way that does not fit neatly into the gender binary.

For reasons that baffle me, this is not common knowledge. The world was shocked when the gender of a track star from South Africa was questioned. Caster Semenya identified as female and won races around the world, yet her deep voice and muscular physique led to questions about her sex. Subsequent tests revealed a complex answer. Semenya had no uterus or ovaries, and internal testes that produce three times the normal testosterone for a woman.[3] Because every body produces both testosterone and estrogen, the question of Semenya's gender was one of degrees.

Because sports are typically segregated by gender, the International Olympic Committee has long struggled with gender definitions. The Nazis had a man named Hermann Ratjen compete as a woman named Dora Ratjen in the Los Angeles 1932 Games. In the Berlin 1936 Games, defending world champion Stella Walsh ran for Poland and lost the one-hundred meter final to Helen Stephens of the United States. Walsh then accused Stephens of being a man. The International Olympic Committee did a physical exam of Stephens and declared her a woman. In a surprising twist, Walsh was later murdered, and an autopsy found she had ambiguous genitalia and both XX and XY chromosomes.[4]

Another blurring of the male-female line occurs when children are born genetically male, but their bodies are insensitive to male androgens, so they develop external female genitalia with undescended testes. For the London 2012 Games, the IOC attempted to define gender centered on hormone levels and body androgen receptivity, so women with a Y chromosome and androgen insensitivity could compete, while women with a "male range" of androgen could not. A British endocrinologist tested testosterone levels in 650 Olympic athletes and found that 5% of the women tested in the male range, and 6% of the men tested in the female range.[5] So neither genetics or hormones are clear determiners of sex.

Intersex is not a social movement. It is a variation in human physiology that has always existed. In colonial America there are records of a man, or woman, named Thomas, or Thomasine, Hall. Hall presented as a woman, but neighbors claimed she was a man; and she was dragged into court in 1629 on accusations of cross dressing and fornication with a servant woman. According to the recorded testimony, Hall was raised as a girl in England, but at twenty she cut her hair, dressed as a man, and joined the army. On returning from military service, she returned to life as a woman. Then she immigrated to the Americas as a man, where she once again lived as a woman. Forced inspections of her private parts left some people saying she was male, while others described more ambiguous genitalia. Hall herself claimed that she had a male appendage she did not use as well as a hole, in her words. The court finally ruled that Hall's self definition was correct, that she was both male and female. In compliance with the rules of her society that said a person's outward gender expression had to match their gender-determining genitalia, the court ordered her to dress accordingly, partly in male clothes and partly in female.[6]

In modern times it became common to surgically alter intersex children at birth to make their genitals conform to societal norms as either a boy or a girl, no in-betweens allowed. Sadly, this often resulted in babies raised as girls, even as their souls felt more like boys. It is heartbreaking to hear stories of teenage girls who never felt like they fit their assigned gender, who later found out they were born with a penis deemed inferior and removed at birth. The more modern perspective lets children grow up as nature made them, leaving questions of surgical alterations for a time when they are old enough to choose for themselves.

Every human being is initially intersex, as all embryos have the cells for both male and female sex organs. Embryos then begin developing as female. To continue developing in the female direction, the male genitalia cells are discarded. To grow from a female embryo into a male is more complicated. The male Y chromosome triggers development of the embryo's testes, which then produce androgens. Those androgens suppress further development of the female organs while stimulating cells for the male organs. Given that every human embryo started as intersex, then developed as female, before some transitioned to male, it is easy to see how intermixing occurs.

I think it would benefit humanity if every man understood that he was originally female. The evidence is there every time he takes off his shirt. Those male nipples are the remnants of his once-developing female plumbing that nature retained even after they were functionally superfluous.[7] Even more evidence runs along that supposedly gender-determining male genitalia. There is a dark line that runs down the underside of the penis, up and over the scrotum, and all the way to the anus. Called the perineal raphe, this is where his, formerly her, vaginal lips came together to form the male genitals.[8] No wonder so many men are insecure about their masculinity. Their male bodies were formed by literally suppressing their inner female, and only later transforming into a male.

Understanding that physical sex is not strictly binary helps explain why gender, encompassing the more emotional and personal aspects of living as a particular sex, can be even more complex. The old binary said men are masculine and women are feminine, but a moment's reflection reveals this is not the whole picture. While the masculine-feminine binary has some validity as a generalization, it fails in the specifics. Consider exactly which gender is emotional, competitive, strong, soft, rebellious, passive, graceful, or driven. The more one tries to define exactly what traits define each gender, the more the whole thing falls apart. The cultural definition of a real man in Oxford, England is significantly different from the definition used in Amarillo, Texas, and the cultural definitions for women vary even more between Los Angeles, Tokyo, and Tehran. The concept of proper male and female roles in my parent's generation look unthinkable to young people today. This is why people who study gender often call it a social construct, as conceptualizations of gender vary so much around the world and over time.

This book is infused with discussions of gender, and in many ways the T in LGBT stands in for all these gender variations. More specifically, however, the T stands for transgender people, a word derived from the Latin *trans-* meaning "on the other side of." In contrast, people whose gender identity matches their physical sex are called cisgender, from *cis-* meaning "on this side of." Because so much of the their experience is internal, it is important to respect transgender reports of their own experience. Fortunately for the rest of us, most trans people are pretty articulate on these issues, as they have spent their lives thinking them through. Some are guarded, understandably enough, but many are really funny. One friend of mine was born a woman and grew up attracted to women, so considered himself lesbian. At some point he realized his deepest truth was that he felt male, so he had the top surgery, as he calls it, removing his breasts, and started taking testosterone. He now lives as a ruggedly handsome, bearded, and masculine man who dates both men and women. He jokes that he has been the L, the G, the B, and the T.

It used to be common to hear transgender people use the phrase "a woman trapped in a man's body." While true for some, I increasingly hear more nuanced descriptions. Former US Navy SEAL Kristen Beck lived as a married man with a wife and child while doing thirteen combat tours, earning a Bronze Star and a Purple Heart. At the same time, she felt since childhood that she was female, and after leaving the military she transitioned to life as a woman. As Beck explained on CNN: "I fought for 20 years for life, liberty and the pursuit of happiness. I want some happiness." When I hear a story like Beck's, I know she has something important to teach the rest of us about gender. As she describes herself: "I'm not a gay man, I'm not a drag queen, I am not maybe total dude, and I'm not total feminine, I'm not totally female. I think I'm living more in that gray world."[9]

Bruce Jenner won the Olympic decathlon in 1976, becoming the country's ultimate icon of wholesome athleticism. In 2015, Jenner came out as transgender, changing her name to Caitlyn. In a touching public interview, she looked back on those glory days standing victorious on the Olympic winner's platform. As commentators declared Jenner the greatest athlete in the world, she reported that the thing she felt most strongly was fear, because she had a whole different female story running inside. Trying to find words for where she is today, Jenner said: "So here I am, stuck. And I hate 'girl stuck in a guy's body.' I hate that terminology. I'm me. I'm a person. And this is who I am. I'm not stuck in anybody's body! My brain is much more female than it is male. It's hard for people to understand that. But that's what my soul is."[10] Jenner later said her experience of coming out as trans was even better than winning Olympic gold.[11] Jenner's wealth, celebrity, and conservative political views made her a poor representative of the larger trans community, but her coming out helped spark the conversation society needed to have.

For a powerful view into the lives of two highly successful transgender people, I recommend Lilly and Lana Wachowski. They lead very private lives, striving to avoid celebrity, which makes their public statements all the more powerful. Working together as the Wachowski Brothers, they made their hit movie *The Matrix* which explored human perceptions of reality. Before the release of their film *Cloud Atlas*, Lana came out as trans. I recommend finding her 2012 speech to HRC, the Human Rights Campaign, online. The sheer humanness of her sharing is powerful, and her reluctance is part of the authenticity. As she quotes from a character in *Cloud Atlas*: "If I had remained invisible, the truth would have stayed hidden. I couldn't allow that."[12]

More recently, Lana's brother also came out as transgender. As Lilly Wachowski wrote in a public letter:

> To be transgender is something largely understood as existing within the dogmatic terminus of male or female. And to "transition" imparts a sense of immediacy, a before and after from one terminus to another. But the reality, my reality is that I've been transitioning and will continue to transition all of my life, through the infinite that exists between male and female as it does in the infinite between the binary of zero and one. We need to elevate the dialogue beyond the simplicity of binary. Binary is a false idol.[13]

In everyday life, it is easy enough to let trans people live their lives in peace. The rest of us only have two trans-related issues to deal with: pronouns and the awkward social spaces of public bathrooms.

The question of pronouns, addressing someone as he, she, they, or any other option, has a simple solution — call people what they want to be called. If you do not know which pronoun to use, ask. More intimate questions about genitalia, surgeries, or previous names and identities are no more appropriate of trans people than they are of anyone else.

The bathroom question is equally simple if everybody follows what I consider the Golden Rule of Toilets: you go where you feel most comfortable, and let everyone else do the same. Birth certificates, drivers licenses, and a doctor's opinions about where you fit within the gender binary at the time of yor birth are all far too complicated to get into when someone just needs a place to poop at the mall.

Sadly, after gay marriage won across America, social conservatives felt stung by their defeat, so they found a smaller group to bully: transgender people. Across the American South, where anti-everyone-different-than-me laws are a perennial favorite, they proposed requiring transgender people to use the bathroom that fit their official documents. The result was absurd. Cops were called on cisgender women using the ladies room while wearing clothes that did not fit someone else's idea of how a woman should look. The man with a beard and a swagger, who could bench press 300 pounds, had to use the ladies room because a doctor declared him female at birth. The woman with big hair and revealing neckline had to use the men's room because she was born with a penis. Talk about traumatizing the children.

This controversy seemed irrelevant to men's rooms. Men using the stalls have all the privacy they need, and men at the urinals should not be looking at their neighbor's genitals regardless of attire — jeans, suit and tie, miniskirt, or Pokemon costume. In all cases, eyes up. Any transman in the room is probably using a stall anyway, so who cares. Go in, do your business, remember to wash your hands, and leave without bothering anyone. Simple.

Women's spaces are a bit different, as there are legitimate concerns for the safety of women and children. That is why there are laws banning loitering, disorderly conduct, voyeurism, indecent exposure, assault, and rape, all equally applicable regardless of the perpetrator's gender. If someone is being creepy in a bathroom, report them, but not because you disapprove of their outfit. As for a woman encountering a transwoman in a bathroom, you should politely ignore each other. If you do choose to engage, the proper procedure is to nod politely, compliment her dress, ask where she bought those shoes, wash your hands and leave.

Anti-trans bathroom laws did not make anyone safer as no transgender person has ever attacked anyone in a bathroom in America, and no cisgender man has ever pretended to be transgender to attack women.[14] Stopping the very real dangers of male attacks on women and children is a legitimate goal, but hurting a misunderstood group to stop a crime that does not exist is just bigotry. Besides, predatory men are not made more dangerous if they put on a dress. As someone who cares for everyone's safety, transgender people are in far more danger of assault from intolerant cisgender people than vice versa. Remember, if your fear of perverts leads you to focus on the genitals of strangers in a public bathroom, then the pervert in that bathroom is you.

School locker rooms are more complicated because they are shared spaces where children take off their clothes in front of each other. Middle school gym showers were a traumatic experience for many of us long before trans became an issue. It is part of the school's mandate to accommodate the needs of the students under their care, however, so none of this is really new. Alterations for the handicapped are becoming ubiquitous, without being particularly controversial, and I think schools can figure this oneas well if they try.

The discussions around gender can seem overwhelming as it destabilizes so many ingrained assumptions, but I find simplicity in the ways gender manifests in children. This is very different from sexuality, where a child may give signs at a young age but fully solidifies around adolescence or later. Gender, on the other hand, is often visible in children's earliest behaviors. Even the youngest child chooses what toys they like, what games they want to play, and even which clothes they prefer, often in gender typical or atypical ways. Parents who see these variations can ally themselves in support of each child's unique personality, long before the child can speak for themselves.

To clarify the discussion of sex and gender, we commonly refer to three different spectrums: Biological sex is our body and genetics, ranging from male to female with intersex in between. Gender identity is how we self identify, how we feel on the inside or how we see ourselves, ranging from male to female with transgender or non-binary in between. Gender expression is how we show ourselves to the world, ranging from masculine to feminine with androgynous in between. Of course there are also people who feel they do not fit into these simplistic spectrums, preferring labels like gender fluid, genderqueer, or some other newly coined term. Words will always struggle to describe the human condition.

Drag is something different. Drag queens are men who dress up as women, and drag kings are women who dress up as men. In both cases, drag is an external expression of some aspect of that person's personality presented for fun, entertainment, or as a more persistent persona. Drag can look like mockery, as if men in dresses are mimicking women, but that misses the deeper point. What most drag performers are mocking or celebrating is the transgressive aspect of their own personalities. I love watching men unleash the woman within, and feel kind of jealous I do not seem to have such a colorful one to share. Transvestites, on the other hand, are typically straight men who wear the other gender's clothes for pleasure or titillation in ways that have nothing to do with attractions.

Adding sexuality back into the gender discussion can seem like another layer of complexity, but again the rule is simple: knowing someone's gender tells you nothing about who they are attracted to. As a thought experiment, consider someone who was labeled female at birth but now lives as a man.

What sexuality does that make him? What gender is he attracted to? The answer is — you have no idea. If you want to know, you have to ask, just as with anyone else. Gender labels tell you nothing about a person's sexual preference.

In my understanding of gender, I think of yin and yang, the symbol representing the interrelationship of elements like light-dark, damp-dry, expanding-contracting, and masculine-feminine. Each of the fish shapes contains a dot of the other color, just as every man has a dot of the feminine, and every woman a dot of the masculine. In Chinese philosophy these elements were not opposites but complements, one blending into the other, creating a spinning motion that generates the life and energy of the universe. Thinking in this non-dualistic way moves beyond fears that the rise of one side means a loss to the other. Life has polarities, with energies running between them, ebbing and flowing in a progressive and endless dance, and gender is just another of life's polarities.

On the spectrum running between female and male, most women fit in the big bell curve on the feminine end of the spectrum, and most men in the bell on the masculine side. Social conservatives who worry about the destruction of gender differences can relax as those differences are not going away. At the same time, each gender's curve has a line that skews out from the base and crosses over and overlaps the other gender's side, representing all the people who intermix gender traits. My queer understanding of gender is not an assault on the essential natures of males and females. It is the acknowledgment that while most of humanity falls inside the typical bell curves, there are also many delightful people who transcend that binary. Yes, the binary exists as a generalization, and like all generalizations, that is not the whole story.

Gender matters. My sexual attractions are defined by my preference for males and masculine energy, so my body, mind, and spirit are all sorting humanity around this concept of gender. I also live closer to the border of the sexes than most people, so a bit of crossing back and forth seems natural to me. I love the gender binary. I love men, I love women, and I love the differences between them. I also love people outside the gender binary. I love both masculine and feminine men, and feminine and masculine women. I love the beauty androgyny brings into the mix. I love all the ways our bodies vary. And I especially love that some people are born into one category and then lead lives that bend and weave through everyone else's norms. As the famously beautiful and gender-confronting actress Katherine Hepburn once observed, "If you obey all the rules, you miss all the fun."[15]

THIRTY-FOUR

Authenticity

O body swayed to music,
O brightening glance,
How can we know
the dancer from the dance?

~ *William Butler Yeats*

IF THERE IS ANY ONE THING that makes me most proud of my people, it is the act of coming out. Coming out in public and revealing that we are the very thing society routinely ridicules and reviles is an incredible stand for integrity. Of course individual gay lives can be as fake or dishonest as anyone else's, but every out gay person has experienced, dramatically, at least once in their life, the act of choosing authenticity over comfort. The basis for this integrity comes from a sad bit of wisdom oft repeated in the gay community: It is better to be hated for who you are, than loved for who you are not.

Living the authentic life requires radical honesty. It can be painful to see ourselves with clarity, and the resistance from others committed to their false constructs and beliefs can be ferocious. People committed to rigid ortho-doxies are forever threatened by the fluidity of life. They believe they already hold life's answers, so any deviation or variation is perceived as a threat. The self discovery process, on the other hand, is ongoing — peeling away layers of superficiality in search of deeper roots. Going through this process results in a special kind of wisdom, the kind that only comes from embracing the fullness of truth, and experiencing the consequences. As the Indian philoso-pher Krishnamurti said, "Without understanding yourself, you have no basis for thought; without self-knowledge, what you think is not true."

The phrase "coming out" originated with debutantes and their parties where young ladies came out of childhood and entered the world of adults. Gay people used to view coming out in a similar way. They "came out" of straight society and "debuted" into their new life with their gay peers. That earlier meaning shifted after the gay liberation of the 1960's. The more modern phrase "coming out of the closet" evokes the feeling of leaving a hidden life of dark oppression and moving into freedom and light.[1] To the newly out I note that while authenticity and honesty are important, being out does not mean that you have to tell everyone. Being out means not caring who knows. The freedom lies in letting go of trying to control what other people see in you, and just be you.

Coming out is also a profoundly political act because of the effect it has on others. An old friend of mine, the therapist and activist Rob Eichberg, called coming out an act of love, because it is an action that gives other people the chance to connect with our true selves. A few years back, when a majority of gay people still lived in the closet, Eichberg said, "Most people think they don't know anyone gay or lesbian, and in fact everybody does. It is imperative that we come out and let people know who we are and disabuse them of their fears and stereotypes."[2] Based on that belief, Eichberg helped found National Coming Out Day, which is celebrated around the world. I still have the original National Coming Out Day t-shirt Eichberg gave me, with graffiti artist Keith Haring's joyful logo on the front showing a colorful figure stepping out of a closet door.

Of course being honest is not always rewarded, and coming out can be a huge act of bravery. Across the world, gay people are imprisoned and killed for being who we are. One group in particular should avoid coming out. Young people dependent on harshly anti-gay parents for food and shelter should wait until they can live independently before speaking their truths. Religiously conservative parents, in particular, have a history of throwing away their gay children. As a young person it can be tempting to share all the thoughts and feelings that are bubbling inside of you, but in this case it might be better to lie. If this describes your situation, trust that your internal sense of self is probably accurate, find support and comradery where you can, but postpone telling those truths out loud to people who can hurt you. We want you to make it through your childhood safe, healthy, and thriving.

For everybody else, straight, gay, in between, or whatever, time to come out. It is time to end the hiding and make a society-wide commitment to being real. Every single individual needs to be seen and loved, and that requires authentic lives lived with transparency. As Oscar Wilde famously said, "To realize one's nature perfectly — that is what each of us is here for."[3]

A long term palliative care nurse recently wrote of the lessons she learned from the dying, and number one was: "I wish I'd had the courage to live a life true to myself, not the life others expected of me."[4] Living the authentic life is a daunting, sometimes terrifying, and always rewarding journey that ennobles every individual brave enough to walk the path.

SOCIETY

Ethics

Does it really matter
what these affectionate people do —
so long as they don't do it in the streets
and frighten the horses!

~ *Beatrice Campbell*

SEX AND PROCREATION are central to the human experience. With the advent of birth control in a pill, however, the sex act became separated from child bearing. Traditional societies controlled female behavior because the entire family was responsible for children born of unwanted pregnancies and uncertain paternity. As women gained control over their reproduction, sexual ethics shifted from communal to more individual. Society now considers individuals responsible for their own choices around sex partners, birth control, and procreation, along with the consequences of those choices.

Modern sexual ethics for the individual are pretty simple: all ethical sex is consensual. Sex acts committed without the consent of the other person are wrong. This makes sex with the mentally ill, the mentally handicapped, or people under the influence of drugs or alcohol into something illegal or immoral. "But she was drunk" is no longer considered consent. Even the traditional idea that a woman had to submit to her husband is now considered wrong if the wife says no.

The most inflammatory example of sexual consent issues involve children. From the perspective of ethics, sex with children is wrong because a prepubescent child cannot give consent to adult sex. Children, by definition, have not yet developed physically, mentally, or emotionally, so they cannot make informed decisions about adult sexuality. That is why all sex with children is statutory rape. Whether pedophilia is a mental illness or an inborn sexuality, it will remain forever taboo because the other party can never give informed consent. There will never be an effective pedophile liberation movement, and pedophiles will never find the kind of love they seek from a child. To guarantee that this remains true, the rest of us stand guard in front of the world's children with torches and pitchforks to stop them if they try. Straight men around the world continue to choose child brides, demonstrating that attractions to the young run strong. In a more modern morality, the needs of the child have equal consideration, so the adult's desires may not be satisfied at the expense of the child's. Those who equate gay rights with pedophilia miss this important point, as gay rights center on two adults consenting to share with each other, an entirely different equation.

It is worth mentioning that sometimes a child is sexually curious and flirtatious with adults. In this case the adult has an opportunity to show love back in age and relationship appropriate ways. A ten year old hinting at sex with an adult needs to be loved, and maybe given a kiss on the forehead and a warm hug. Precocious and curious children need loving adults who see their emotional truths, understand their developmental age, and are able to guide them back into appropriate adult-child relations while teaching proper boundaries. A child acting out sexually with an adult is signaling a deeper need for emotional connection, not an actual need for sexual connection. It is the responsibility of the adult to know the difference.

This idea of consent applies equally to sex with animals. Animals cannot give consent to human sex, which is why bestiality is considered wrong. For some reason, this is a difficult concept for many social conservatives who routinely link the right to be gay with the right to have sex with whomever and whatever we want. Dr. Daniel Heimbach, Professor of Christian Ethics at Southeastern Baptist Theological Seminary, for example, declared, "If marriage is radically redefined as being just a way of affirming private feelings of loving attraction, then equality will require allowing people who love dogs to marry dogs, and people who love ice cream to marry ice cream."[1] Sigh. This from a professor of ethics. If Heimbach cannot discern the differences between his love for a woman and his love of ice cream and dogs, then his problems go far deeper than ethics.

Unbridled from wider societal parameters, some fear that sexual ethics will devolve into the simplistic ethos that says, "If it feels good, do it." I actually think that is a pretty useful aphorism, but only if the whole person is included. My personal sexual ethics are grounded in all of me — body, mind, and soul — working together. There are parts of me that think acting without inhibition from my rawest animal passions and having all the sex I want whenever I want it sounds like a great idea. My mind thinks that sounds hot, if maybe a little complicated. My body thinks it sounds fun and pleasurable, but also exhausting, possibly depleting, and potentially hazardous. Meanwhile my heart, the most innocent and soulful part of me, hears the idea of limitless sex without boundaries or deeper connection with endless numbers of people and just wants to curl up in the corner and cry. Sensing whether something truly "feels good" requires all of my senses, not just my carnal ones. As people across the rich world are realizing, pleasure is not the same as happiness. Happiness tends to be a by-product of activities with a deeper sense of meaning and purpose, while pleasure is more fleeting. So "if it feels good, do it" is only a valid criterion if it encompasses the totality of my being over time, and not just the satisfaction of a momentary impulse.

If most sexual decisions are now personal, the question becomes what sexual activities should be subject to public scrutiny. The answer is, nearly always: none. What two consenting adults do together is their own business. As advice columnist Judith Martin put it: "Miss Manners has come to believe that the basic political division in this country is not between liberals and conservatives but between those who believe that they should have a say in the love lives of strangers and those who do not."[2]

Of course individual ethics are not everything, as humans are social animals and we all need to function together. Cohesive societies arise from communal ethics and collective actions based on shared values. Those who viewed the family as the center of their moral universe often perceived gay people as a threat, as we seemed to undermine their favored model of a dominant father, nurturing mother, and faithful children, held together by church and community.[3] From that perspective, anyone who lived outside that idealized social structure was labeled threating, and to some extent they were right. Queer people do threaten that kind of narrow rigidity. But in the real world gay people are also contributing members of our families, so we are yet another facet of the natural and moral order. Families are bigger, richer, and more interesting than those simplistic views allowed. Call me crazy, but I believe a truly moral family structure includes all of the family.

Traditionalists are also right when they say children need good parents, but again make the mistake of holding too narrow view of what that means. The idea that marriage is one man, one woman, and kids leaves out all the messiness of life that encompasses the infertile, violent spouses, affairs, separate bedrooms, long business trips, second marriages, children out of wedlock, extended families, orphans, old people marrying, widowers, unmarried aunts, and the many other variations that occur in actual families. It is not that man-woman-children families are wrong, but they are not the only thing that is right.

Anti-gay beliefs become tangled when the same people who believe so strongly in less government intrusion everywhere else wanted more of it in our bedrooms. It was weird to watch as their sex obsessions overtook their core values. I have never understood the thought and energy Mormon leaders, for example, put into gay sex. They seem to spend a lot of time worrying about what my friends and I do on dates, in our relationships, and in our bedrooms, while not one person I know spends any time thinking about Mormon sex. Even trying to shift my mind to imagine what all those pious Mormons are doing in their beds at night to create all those children makes me cringe, yet they spend a disturbing amount of time fixated on what I do in mine. I really wish social conservatives could keep their minds in their own bedrooms and leave the rest of us alone.

Not only is this obsession with other people's sex lives creepy, but the relentlessly voyeuristic quality of this perspective creates its own perception problem. One of the definitions of pornography says it as a separation of the sex act from the emotions, and traditional moralists focus relentlessly on the sexual act. By stripping away our larger humanity, they turn our lives into pornographic cartoons, bereft of soulfulness or authentic emotion. And then, having generated a construct where they cannot perceive any depth or meaning in our lives, they condemned our existence as shallow and a moral outrage. By invoking these desaturated mental images from pulpits and political podiums, and replaying those mental images over and over in their heads, social conservatives seem to get some kind of satisfaction from the disgust and repulsion they feel with each repetition. That is harder to do, if not impossible, when sexual ethics includes the entirety of a person's humanity — hearts, souls, lives, and loves, along with the genitals.

These shallow views of sex and their resultant moral stances become dangerous and ridiculous when they are codified into law. When I was first living as an out gay man in the 1980s, a majority of Americans supported laws making homosexuality illegal. If I left my home in Washington, DC and walked across a Potomac river bridge into neighboring Virginia, I entered a state where it was illegal for a bartender to serve me a drink. It was illegal in Virginia to sell alcohol to a homosexual, just as it was illegal for two people of the same sex to dance together. I remember hearing at the time that sex in Virginia was only legal if you were a man and a woman, who were married, in a bed, and the man was on top. Anything else was illegal. Kissing your spouse's privates was illegal. Sex between a husband and wife on their sofa was illegal. Sexual relations with the person you loved and were committed to but had not married was illegal. Having your wife on top during sex was illegal. To add to that silliness, the laws of Virginia said the lights had to be off and you could not tickle your wife while making love to her. That is the kind of legal nonsense that resulted when people could not control their obsessions over other people's sex lives.

Pivotal to those old sex laws was the idea that the use of the sex organs for any purpose outside of procreation was a "crime against nature," which is a pretty silly concept. Imagine that logic applied to any other body part, as if it was a crime against God to use lips to blow trumpets, feet to skate ice, or hands to wave a flag. Part of the definition of being human, as opposed to animals, is the ability to use human bodies to do "unnatural" things. Unless of course the body part is the genitalia. Sadly, this is not a moral view lost to history. In 2013 the Attorney General of Virginia was still trying to use the state's "Crimes Against Nature" statute to prosecute its citizens, in defiance of the US Supreme Court ruling those laws unconstitutional.[4] To refute the idea that gay sexuality is a crime against nature, I defer to how the writer Samuel Johnson, back in the 1700s, responded to an erudite scientific lecture on the nonexistence of matter. "I refute it thus," he said, kicking a stone with his foot.[5] Likewise, I simply point to the prevalence of homosexuality in the natural world, and let nature have the last word on what is natural.

Most of those intrusive old laws are gone now, falling to the knowledge that gay people exist and deserve equal rights, and to the understanding that almost everybody has sex, although not necessarily in ways approved of by the Virginia state legislature. Gaps remain. In many American states today I could be fired from my job or ejected from my home for simply being a gay or trans-gender human being. But slowly, inexorably, justice triumphs. Of course there will always be those who resist change, like those old racists who still believe white people are superior to brown and black, but the rest of society moves on, leaving them behind.

As for what humanity should do with those who cannot accept this modern understanding of morality, I defer to the Golden Rule. I was taught as a child that the gospel of Jesus Christ centered on one simple rule: do unto others as you would have done unto you. Jesus illustrated the application of this concept with the story of the Good Samaritan, where a man was beaten by robbers, stripped of his clothes, and left to die by the side of the road. People who outwardly claimed to be highly religious passed him by, but a Samaritan, one of the most despised ethnicities in that society, stopped to help the man. The Samaritan man dressed the victim's wounds, took him into his home, and nurtured him back to health.[6] If there is a single story that informs my morality of what needs to happen next between the long-ostracized gay community and the stolidly anti-gay, it is the story of the Good Samaritan. If I was as morally lost and out of touch with the world that God created as so many sex-obsessed conservatives appear to be, I would want someone, even someone from a deeply despised group, to love me, nurse my wounds, and guide me back to the solid ground of reality. I believe the gay community can help. This is a difficult task, as social conservatives can be mean and prickly people, but with enough love over time, we can help them lift their self-imposed blinders and guide them back into fellowship with the rest of the human family.

I like following rules. Most of my culture's ethical rules make sense to me, and I like the sense of collective social order they create. Complex civilizations thrive when the great dance we do with each other is based on a shared set of fundamental values. At the same time, the old rules can be insufficient. Sometimes I have to live my individual life the best I can, assessing the morality of my actions as I go — respectful of the old ways, but moving into new uncharted realms when their guidance falls short.

The old arguments on the ethics of homosexuality got the question wrong. The salient question was not whether homosexuality was moral or immoral. The more useful question was whether someone's inborn sexuality, and acting from that God-given orientation, created any moral question at all. Based on what is now known, the answer is no. While sexual actions do have an ethical component, a person's intrinsic sexuality and gender exist outside questions of morality. Slowly and unsteadily, society will learn what that means, and come to understand more fully the role of sexuality and gender in the human experience.

Military

The worst things in my life
never happened.

~ *Mark Twain*

THE BEST FRAME for understanding the politics of gay rights played out in the battle over gays in the military. Seen from the anti-gay perspective, a minority of sexual miscreants were hell bent on destroying troop cohesion and undermining military discipline. According to this perspective, the ultimate goal of my community was to destroy America by rendering her defenseless before her enemies. The smears against gay people got so ugly that a poll by the *Military Times* reported that 24% of active duty service members, or half a million troops, said they would leave military service or consider leaving if the ban on homosexuals were lifted.[1] In 2010, over a thousand retired military leaders from all branches of service signed a document that said removing the ban "would undermine recruiting and retention ... and eventually break the All-Volunteer Force."[2] Social conservatives in the Senate delayed repeal for decades, expressing their belief that the open inclusion of gay people in the military would result in the destruction of the United States.

That fight looked very different from the gay community's perspective. While being condemned as soft, weak, sick, and perverse, large numbers of gay men and women were already serving in the military out of a desire to protect their nation. While being denigrated as unable to commit, we were fighting to join what the author Fran Lebowitz called, "the two most confining institutions on the planet, marriage and the military."[3]

The policy that allowed gay people to serve in the military, but required that we lie about it, a policy known as Don't Ask, Don't Tell, was repealed in September of 2011, and then — not much happened. It was kind of surreal. One of the defining battles of a generation ended, and the next day it was business as usual. Gays in the military got vast press before the ban was lifted, expressing all the fears of what was to come. After inclusion: silence. No effect on military readiness. No collapse of morale. No mass defections of soldiers. No invasion by terrorists or communists or religious extremists taking advantage of our nation's sudden plunge into moral depravity. America's defense went on, unaltered by the change.

On the day after repeal, the anti-gay chorus who had screamed and fought and legislated for so long to keep us out of military service slunk back into their corners and began plotting which group to hate next. One year later, an outside study of the military found no negative effect whatsoever.[4] Now that more years have gone by it is clear nothing bad happened.

On the first day after the repeal of Don't Ask, Don't Tell, the *Marine Corps Times* magazine had a cover that declared in big bold letters: "We're Gay, Get Over It."[5] On that same day, representatives of the United States Marine Corps walked into the gay community center in Tulsa, Oklahoma, set up a table, and started recruiting. According to the *New York Times* account: "With the law now changed, the Marines appear determined to prove that they will be better than the Army, Navy, Air Force and Coast Guard in recruiting gay, lesbian and bisexual service members."[6]

The world needs all kinds of people to succeed. It needs men who sit on the floor and read stories to kindergartners and men who are the sharp point of the spear in battle. It needs women who thrive as nest builders for their loving families and women who fight across the globe to keep their nation free. Gay people are now an essential, open, and honest part of keeping America strong at home and in war. History proves that our gifts strengthen institutions that know how to include us, from the Sacred Band of Thebes and the armies of Alexander the Great to the Navy SEALs and the United States Marines.

The fear that allowing gay people to serve openly in the military would harm America's defense was 100% fiction, a reality that only existed in the fevered imaginings of the anti-gay. Every one of their slurs and panics was based on false fears that never came to pass. If that grand list of one thousand retired officers had any of the integrity they claimed for themselves they would issue a clean-up declaration apologizing to every single LGBT American for their irresponsible slander.

Lesbian, gay, bisexual, and transgender people are fully responsible citizens of the nations in which we live. We fight for our own rights, and we fight for the right to defend the nations in which we live. Today we serve openly in the Armed Forces of the United States of America, standing proud and strong in our nation's defense, alongside every other citizen of our blessed land.

Children

You are the newest spark
of an ancient people

~ *Maria Cora*[1]

A FRIEND OF MINE told me a funny story about the effect same-sex parents can have on young children. She and her husband live in San Francisco where their children attend private schools, and her youngest daughter's kindergarten class was rocked by the arrival of a new student with two mommies. As the teachers introduced the child's parents to the other students, the classroom erupted in distress. As my doctor explained the problem, children of that age revere their mothers beyond all other creatures on Earth, so her daughter and her classmates were inconsolable over the unfairness that one of their classmates got two mothers while the rest of them only had one.

It is common for gay men and lesbians to have children, but in a debate more focused on sex, sins, and adult relationships, the children of gay parents were overlooked. These young people also deserve families that are respected and have legal stability. While the anti-gay claimed their stance was based on protecting children, some of the major breakthroughs in gay rights came when the courts started assessing what was best for all children, including the children of gay parents.

The truth is that children of gay parents do very well. Studies consistently show that children tend to do best with two parents, but that concept gets twisted into beliefs that children need a mother and a father, which is not what the data shows. Children do better, on average, with two adults caring for them, but that is true regardless of the gender or sexuality of the parents. Most studies that show "children do better with two parents" are actually proving that family stability benefits children, regardless parental sexuality or gender.[2] Based on the available evidence, citizens who seek the best interests of children should strive to reduce divorce and single parenting, as gay marriage seems to create no problem for the kids.

The idea that two adults parenting together can often do a better job than one parent working alone seems like a no-brainer to me. I think three or more adults would be even better, like the traditional family structures where the grandparents were involved, because parenting is such hard work. I have the utmost respect for parents who go it alone, but it also seems like common sense to say children benefit from a team effort.

Every study to date shows that gay people make great parents, at least as good as straight people, and often better. While this claim may sound extreme, it was a fact repeatedly conceded in the federal trials over gay marriage. In a way, this should be no surprise. Because of the extra effort required for gay couples to have children, we are by definition engaged and committed parents. Gay couples do not get pregnant by accident. That is a problem only heterosexual couples experience. Because of the added complications, pretty much every child of a gay couple was deeply wanted. The rare exceptions noted in studies come from children of previously failed gay-straight marriages where the mis-pairing of sexualities created the familial complications and disorder.

According to the most recent data, the children of same-sex parents develop a normal sense of gender identity and gender roles,[3] are not more sexually active,[4] and are no more likely to be gay than children of heterosexuals.[5] These effects are equally true for both gay male[6] and lesbian[7] parents. In the biggest American study to date, Stanford University used census data to track school progress for children of same-sex couples, and found no difference from children raised by male-female couples.[8] A large study in Australia found that children raised by gay parents were healthier, happier, and had a higher sense of family cohesion than children raised by straight parents.[9] The ideas that "a child needs a mother and father," and "marriage is for the children," were rationalizations to justify barring gay people from equal rights, and not conclusions backed by data.

The effects of gay parenting can be seen in the parents as well. Brain studies find that mothers become highly responsive to their infants' needs on a primal level, while caregiving fathers watch their children more cognitively, actively interpreting the infants' actions to understand their needs. Gay men who parent, on the other hand, show brains that are wired in both ways, with the primal attentiveness seen in mothers along with the cognitive engagement seen in fathers, with rather obvious benefits for their children.[10] On a lighter note, another study clarified how little gay parenting differs from straight parenting, as researchers found that gay parents have less sex than other gay couples because child rearing wears them out, as it does everyone else.[11]

The American Sociological Association summed up the available evidence on gay parenting in a brief for the US Supreme Court: "The results of our review are clear. There is no evidence that children with parents in stable same-sex or opposite-sex relationships differ in terms of well-being. Indeed, the greater stability offered by marriage for same-sex as well as opposite-sex parents may be an asset for child well-being."[12]

Of course, being heterosexual does not assure good parenting. The astonishing number of deadbeat dads in America demonstrates how many straight parents fail to support their children. I have friends with every variation of horrifying family story: fathers who left at birth, sexually abusive mothers and fathers, mothers who abandoned their children, violent stepparents, parents who threw their gay children out of their homes, parents who lied about the child's parentage, parents who pimped their children out to pedophiles, ritually sadistic fathers, clinically insane mothers, and on, and on, and on.

Each of those families created a beautiful adult whom I call my friend, and every one of those horrifying parents was heterosexual. Yet two loving women were considered unacceptable parents for no reason other than their gender. To say that two men or two women who love and care for their children are unacceptable, while two alcoholics, two teenagers, or two manic depressives are fully backed by church and state is illogical.

Some anti-gay people even oppose gay parents adopting otherwise unwanted children, believing that no home, no parents, no loving adults, no support, and no commitment are better for a child than two fathers or two mothers. A Mexican pop singer declared it better for a child to die of starvation in the streets than be adopted by a gay couple.[13] I can hardly imagine a more powerful example of the triumph of blind prejudice over the interests of a child.

Children know from their earliest consciousness that two people of the same sex can love each other, because a boy can love his dad and a girl can love her mom. An internet commenter shared her experience of discussing homosexuality with her young children, age three and four, initiated by the presence of her brother, their gay uncle.

> Child: Why does Uncle Bob go everywhere with Pete?
> Me: Because they're in love, just like Mummy and Daddy are.
> Child: Oh. Can I have a biscuit?

As the contributor noted sarcastically: "We're all scarred for life. Scarred, I tell you."[14]

People seem confused about the issue of discussing homosexuality around children because they think it requires discussing sex with minors, which is nonsense. This perception can only occur to people who picture sex when they speak of love. Discussing gay male couples with children should not include descriptions of anal sex any more than discussions of straight relationships require descriptions of vaginal sex. Telling children that gay people exist does not mean discussing gay sex acts with first graders. It does mean teaching children that Heather may have two mommies, little Harold can like boys instead of girls, and sometimes Alexandra goes by Alex and only plays with pink girly toys to blow them up. To give my own example, I might tell a young niece or nephew: "I love my partner very much, we enjoy living together, and we are the bestest of friends." If they want to know more they can ask, and I would answer in equally age appropriate ways.

Children need to hear stories that explain life and give them hope in a sometimes scary and baffling world. They need to hear happy stories of a handsome man who appears in a young woman's life like a knight on a white horse, and varying stories where she can reject the knight and choose her own princess, and empowering stories where she can be queen of the realm and rule without defining her life by a man. That is the thing about magical stories of mythical times; they can describe the diversity of life through metaphor and imaginary worlds where frogs are princes and ogres are love. What a wonderful thing for a child to discover that every one of their various aspects are beautiful, adorable, and worthy of love.

Some parents fear that telling children of other possibilities will lead them astray, confusing their young minds about rightful male-female relationships, but again there is no evidence that happens. Kids are way smarter than that. Better to tell them stories that prepare them for life, both the mainstream versions they are likely to slipstream into, and the life-affirming and often humorous variations they will encounter as they get older.

Things get more complicated as children age, but not by much. California schools, for example, have long banned teachers from valuing one family structure over another. All children deserve to have their home lives respected regardless of the adults they live with — heterosexual parents, single parents, aunts, uncles, grandparents, gay parents, or foster parents. The law in California only requires that schools "teach respect for marriage and committed relationships,"[15] which seems perfectly reasonable to me.

If social conservatives really want to protect the children, they should start with their own, as they throw away an astonishing number of their own kids. The US Department of Health and Human Services estimates that as many as 40% of the homeless and runaway youth in America are LGBT.[16] Abandoned and explicitly told by their parents that they are not loved, these unskilled youth have few options but to prostitute their bodies to adults who are attracted to children. Even more disturbing, if that is possible, the numbers of these rejected children may be on the rise. As the rest of the world moves towards gay acceptance, conservative parents seem to be increasing the rejection of their own children, tossing ever greater numbers out onto the streets.[17]

As usual, the Mormon church leads the way. In 2015 they declared from their highest pulpit: "We want our voice to be heard against all of the counterfeit and alternative lifestyles that try to replace the family organization that God Himself established."[18] The church then announced that Jesus told their prophet to declare anyone in a gay relationship an apostate, subject to excommunication. Doubling down, they then declared it "the mind of the Lord and the will of the Lord" that even the straight children of gay parents should be banned from the church until they turn eighteen, move out of their family home, and formally denounce their parent's relationship. The Mormon leadership called their decrees acts of compassion. I call it child abuse. Two months after that announcement, the church admitted knowledge of more than thirty children who committed suicide as the direct result of the new policies.[19] Given that Mormon parents rarely discuss their gay children in public, the real death toll had to be many times that number.

The Mormons claim fifteen million members, about a third of them children. If 5% of those children are gay, then the Mormons are currently condemning, persecuting, and rejecting more than a quarter of a million of their own children. Now. Today. As a matter of official policy. Multiply that effect times the billions of followers of much larger anti-gay religions around the world and across history, and the mind-boggling scale of the damage done in God's name becomes clear.

I experienced sexual abuse as a child, and I experienced religious abuse, and the religious abuse was a thousand times worse. My sexual abuse was a crime of passion, while my religious abuse was premeditated — cold, calculated, and perpetrated by adults with sacred authority over my life. I have met countless women and men who were sexually abused as children, but many of the most haunted adults I know were abused by their churches. As in other insular patriarchies, Mormon sexual abuse of children is a huge problem, a fact systematically covered up by church authorities,[20] but at least those victims survive. How unimaginably worse to torture children to the point they suicide themselves to be free.

Disturbed by the church's latest actions, I asked my Mormon family for their thoughts. Their response was to scream at me, in a public restaurant, for daring to ask. They then shunned me, telling me they would not be in relationship with anyone who criticized their church. For me, these attitudes represent the trap conservative Christians keep falling into. By putting their faith and beliefs ahead of actual human beings who are reaching out to connect, they do more damage than good to families and society.

Jesus warned: "Beware of false prophets, which come to you in sheep's clothing, but inwardly they are ravening wolves. Ye shall know them by their fruits. ...Every good tree bringeth forth good fruit; but a corrupt tree bringeth forth evil fruit."[21] Harsh to say, but if the fruits hanging from the tree of your beliefs include the bodies of dead children, then by Jesus's standards your prophets are false and your tree is poisoned. The fact that my family follows these leaders, while raging at me for objecting, fills me with shame for my heritage. The next generations of queer children need allies, and if their conservative parents will not change the system that harms them, then it falls on people like me to defend them.

Of course it is not just the Mormons. Merely living someplace conservative can be devastating to young lives. According to studies conducted by the state of Oregon: "Gay, lesbian and bisexual teens living in counties with the lowest social index scores [i.e., most conservative] were 20 percent more likely to have attempted suicide than gays in counties with the highest index scores. Overall, about 25 percent of gay teens in low-scoring counties had attempted suicide, versus 20 percent of gay teens in high-scoring counties." The more Republican and conservative the area, the stronger the effect, even for straight kids.[22]

The gay community long understood this problem, but it finally gained national attention in 2010 when an eighteen-year-old freshman at Rutgers University named Tyler Clementi jumped off a bridge. His dorm mate had secretly recorded and broadcast Clementi having sex with another young man, and it appears the exposure was too much for him.[23] The Suicide Prevention Resource Center estimates that 30-40% of LGBT youth have attempted suicide,[24] while the overall rate of suicide in the world is about 1.5% of all deaths.[25]

Into the madness stepped columnist Dan Savage and his husband Terry Miller, proposing a novel solution. Gay children across the nation were suffering in their schools and small towns, unaware that a larger and more accepting world awaited if they could just make it through high school alive. So Savage and Miller posted a video on the internet with a simple message: It Gets Better. Starting with their own stories, Savage and Miller told of being rejected at home and bullied at school, and surviving to find a world of friends, an accepting community, and eventually each other, as they formed a family and adopted their son. Their message of hope caught fire, as expanding numbers of gay adults used the internet to sidestep hostile families and communities that were teaching gay children they were not loved. In no time at all, thousands of people were uploading It Gets Better messages to queer youth, sharing their personal stories of heartbreak and triumph. Soon progressive companies like Gap, Apple, and Google were uploading supportive videos from their corporate websites. Hollywood celebrities joined in along with professional sports teams, municipal police departments, and even the president of the United States. The message to young gay kids was simple: life does not become perfect on coming out, but the wider options and communal support available to adults are infinitely better than what is available to most teenagers. As an adult you get to live in your own world, and leave behind the people who are toxic to your health and well being.

If you are a young gay person who believes suicide may be the only exit from the situation your church, schools, peers, or family have put you in, I have a message for you: they are wrong. There is nothing faulty about your differences. There are people who will celebrate you. Over time you may come to realize that some of these unique parts of yourself may be among your finest traits. Suicide is not the answer. If you feel overwhelmed, find help and more positive perspectives. Visit the Trevor Project at www.thetrevor-project.org. They have information, resources specifically for you, and people to talk to. You will quickly find that the gay community really does cares about you, and we strive to take care of our own, no matter how you identify or what you are feeling. Not everyone will be there for you, of course, but we have a good idea of what you are going through, and we will do our best to help.

If you know a young person who is struggling with issues of sexuality or gender, the solution is simple. Tell them you love them just the way they are. Tell them you see the light in them. Let them know you see their dark and troubled parts too, and you love all of them — the whole beautiful young person, without reservation. Tell them your love is not based on what they do or do not do, but who they are. Reassure them that as they grow older the parts of themselves that feel in such conflict now will grow more harmonious and less troubling. Remind them that every human being experiences some of these feelings of alienation and anger during adolescence, and it is not just about being gay. Reassure them it is age appropriate to feel these things now, and there is a brighter future out they cannot see from their current perspective. Extra points for sincere, lingering, and embracing hugs. Touch can be one of our most powerful tools when used with sensitivity and respect.

Every single child alive today deserves the best parental love and support possible, along with the best schools, churches, and other programs that society can muster. But most important are the parents. Every child deserves parents and other adults that love the hell out of them, stand by them, and are willing to make huge sacrifices so that they can live the best lives they can. Those are the key ingredients of good parenting, no matter what the parents look like.

My greatest wish for modern children is an end to the idea that "family" is a coded term for anti-gay. Real families embrace all of their daughters, sons, and differently gendered children. My "radical gay agenda" is for "family" to start meaning family again.

Marriage

No government has the right
to tell its citizens
when or whom to love.
The only queer people
are those who don't love anyone.

~ *Rita Mae Brown*

FOR MOST OF HISTORY, traditional marriage centered on one man. In many cultures, including those in the Bible, the man owned his females. He "husbanded" his daughters, wives, concubines, and female slaves like he husbanded his sheep, goats, and cattle. To assure the paternity of his children, he restricted the movements of his women. He kept them indoors, limited their contact with other men, and covered them in obscuring clothes. These traditional marriages were often based on business or social needs, arranged by the parents, with the bride and groom meeting at the altar. The marriage ceremony, then, was the celebration of a man taking possession of a woman, or women, in front of the community, so everyone understood that he was the father of any subsequent children. The modern marriage ceremony retains the vestiges of this tradition when the father walks the bride down the aisle and presents her to her new husband. That moment represents the exchange of the father's ownership of his daughter, "giving her away" to her new owner, her husband.

Marriage in the traditional world was rarely a sacred rite. Jesus's first miracle was performed at a wedding, but he was not there to officiate a sacred union between a man and a woman. The miracle Jesus chose to launch his ministry was turning water into wine,[1] an act in support of the party that formalized the marriage. The scriptures make no mention of Christ offici- ating over the kind of religious ceremony modern Christians would consider essential. As with the Greeks, the Romans, and most other ancient cultures, traditional Christian marriage remained a civil celebration for most of history. As the medieval theologian Thomas Aquinas put it, marriage existed by mutual consent of the couple, sealed by the act of intercourse.[2] Marriage first became a religious sacrament in the Catholic church around the 1200s, but that was a radical change rejected by many Christians. The Pilgrims who founded English-speaking America 500 years later, for example, were still rejecting the Catholic idea of marriage as a religious act, believing it should remain a strictly civil function.[3] Anti-gay Christians who claim religious marriage is a timeless tradition do not know their history.

Even when the idea of religious marriage did spread, the purpose of traditional marriages remained the same — serving the needs of the extended family, business interests, political alliances, and communal cohesion. Love was an afterthought. It took many more centuries before people accepted the idea that people could marry for love. The story of Romeo and Juliet falling in love was told as a tragedy, after all. It was only around two hundred years ago that Western societies solidified on the idea that two young adults could use love and romance as their guide to connection, and even now not everyone is on board with that change. As the head of the Catholic League, Bill Donohue declared recently, "Christians have an obligation, particularly Catholics to follow natural law. The whole purpose of marriage is to have a family. It's not about making people happy. It's not about love."[4] I doubt many young couples marrying these days would agree with this notion that marriage is a burden to be borne rather than a joining to be celebrated, but that was the traditional view.

Over time, straight people changed marriage, and modern marriage became what it is today, a voluntary commitment between equal partners. Looking at modern marriage laws, gay people realized those same legal structures applied equally well to our relationships. In June of 2015, the Supreme Court of the United States agreed, and America now has equal marriage for everyone, regardless of the gender of the partners.

The first country to have equal marriage rights was the Netherlands in 2000. Massachusetts became the first American state with same-sex marriage in 2004, and over the years other American states joined in. Other nations like Brazil and Mexico followed a similar state-by state process. Meanwhile countries across the world gained marriage equality: Belgium, Spain, Canada, South Africa, Norway, Sweden, Portugal, Iceland, Argentina, Denmark, Uruguay, New Zealand, Brazil, France, England and Wales, Scotland, Luxembourg, Finland, Slovenia, Greenland, and delightfully, the Pitcairn Islands. All of these original victories came through legislatures and courts. Then in 2012 the American states of Maine, Maryland, and Washington became the first jurisdictions in the world to pass gay marriage by popular vote. On May 23, 2015, the Republic of Ireland became the first country in the world to pass national same-sex marriage rights by popular referendum.

Contrary to predictions, gay marriage victories were accompanied by a notable lack of fire, brimstone, earthquakes, or floods. The Irish actor Colin Farrell put it best when he described the day equal marriage won in his country: "It was really funny because one of the arguments when the vote went through was that the church came out and said, 'You know, this was a dark day for Ireland,' and all you could see was literally rainbows everywhere, posters of rainbows, T-shirts of rainbows, men and women hugging, men and men hugging, women and women hugging, and yet cut to, 'This is a dark day in the history of [Ireland].' A dark day in the history of a country is internal civil conflict and war and bloodshed...It was a great day."[5] Apparently God was celebrating Ireland's vote as well, as that day saw a great double rainbow over Dublin.

My Mormon ancestors practiced a different form of marriage. They were polygamous, as described in the Bible. I can drive around Salt Lake City today and see the homes where my progenitors lived with their various wives. The city's largest park was the grounds of the Utah Territorial Penitentiary where my great-great grandfather was imprisoned for having multiple wives. Ironically, polygamy was often used as an argument against my gay marriage rights. The slippery slope argument said that if two people could choose to marry regardless of their gender, how could the state say no to three people who wanted to marry? The answer illuminates an essential piece of why gay marriage won. Modern polygamous marriage may be a good idea or a terrible one, but that decision has nothing to do with gay marriage because implementing polygamy would require new laws. It is not as simple as adding lines to the marriage form for Spouses #2 and #3. Imagine the difficulty polygamy adds to determining who is the legal next of kin empowered to make life or death decisions in a hospital emergency, splitting child custody in a messy divorce, dividing family assets between multiple partners with different lengths of commitment, determining who is responsible for the debts of other partners, or clarifying who can represent the various children at school. Polygamy exists in a wide variety of cultures around the world, so obviously these issues could be worked out, but they would require a whole new set of legal structures specifically crafted for multiple partners. Gay marriage, on the other hand, only requires two adults saying, "Yes." No changes in the marriage laws were needed other than allowing me to marry Sam without caring if my spouse's full name was Samuel or Samantha.

Gay people wanted legal marriage for the same reason straight people wanted marriage. We fall in love and have romances. We commit our lives to each other. We have children and property. We get sick and grow old together. We die and leave inheritances. And sometimes we divorce and need help with our dissolutions. Part of the drive for marriage equality arose from the fact that marriage itself is a fairly unique legal status that cannot be duplicated by two people signing a contract. On the federal level alone, the Congressional Budget Office counted 1,138 statutory provisions "in which marital status is a factor in determining or receiving 'benefits, rights, and privileges'," covering the couple's shared assets, debts and liabilities, death and property transfers, rules of divorce, and many other issues.[6] There was no way to duplicate all that with a contract between two people. Of course the corollary is also true, as many gay people do not want to marry for the same reasons many straight people do not want to marry, as it is not something they want or need in their lives or relationships.

For all the excitement that came with gay marriage victories, I thought the gay marriage debate was ridiculous. If I could have taken a big sword and cut through the nonsense, I would have made secular marriage a legal agreement registered with the secular government and backed by the secular courts, and given sacred marriage back to the religious organizations where sacred functions belong. According to my understanding of America's Constitution, the government does not issue sacred documents through government clerks. Government in my country is secular, by definition. Sacred marriage, on the other hand, is a religious function, and religions should be able to set their own guidelines, standards, rituals, and sacred covenants without government interference. Just as an American's baptismal statuses should not affect their taxes, entering into sacred marriage should not affect their secular rights and responsibilities. Freedom of religion is interrelated with freedom from religion, and by some accident of history, marriage slipped through our church-state separation barrier.

Separating church from state on the issue of marriage would allow Catholic priests to go their entire lives without ever blessing a gay marriage. Mormons could go back to banning blacks from their sacred temple marriages and Southern Baptists could re-ban mixed-race marriages. Actually, they can all do that now because religious freedom stands strong as ever. If these churches really believe their beliefs are eternal and everlasting, then there is nothing in America to stop them from acting on them within their own faith community. In the false choice between legality and religion, the question was not whether conservative Christians disapproved of gay people marrying. The question was whether disapproving Christians could use the power of the government to control what everyone else did.

The only problems reported after the implementation of equal marriage in America came from social conservatives who were horrified they could no longer discriminate in their traditional ways, claiming that mutual respect for everyone in secular society was a form of religious persecution. As the author Salman Rushdie, a man who knows a thing or two about discrimination, noted, "It is a classic trope of the religious bigot that while they are denying people their rights, they claim that their rights are being denied. While they are persecuting people, they claim to be persecuted. While they are behaving colossally offensive, they claim to be the offended party. It's an upside-down world."[7]

Strangely enough, the worst of this supposed persecution centered on Christian bakers who declared it their core religious belief to never sell a cake to be eaten at a gay wedding. After selling baked goods to every conceivable sinner through all of human history, it was gay couples committing their lives to each other that crossed their ethical line. As commentator Jonathan Rauch said, "As far as I know, during the divorce revolution it never occurred to, say, Catholic bakers to tell remarrying customers, 'Your so-called second marriage is a lie, so take your business elsewhere.' That would have seemed not so much principled as bizarre."[8]

In the early years of the fight for legalized gay marriage, it was often portrayed as an attack on decent society by decadent and militant gay activists. It is almost comical how far off that was. The truly militant wing of the gay crowd tends to reject the concept of marriage for its conformist connotations. Meanwhile, the big gay political organizations were steadfast against the marriage fight becoming a political hot potato, believing it would fail and drag down the rest of the movement. Gay marriage did not win because of those people. Gay marriage won because very average and rather un-political gay couples and families existed and wanted the same legal rights as straight people. Regular, everyday couples went to their local county clerks and asked to be married, and when the clerks said no, they sued. Over time, some of those couples started to win. The big gay organizations and radical activists only jumped in long after these smaller contests were on a winning streak.

When societal support for gay marriage did arrive, it came with shocking rapidity for one simple reason. As people got married, all those rather average couples appeared on their local news, and the demonic image of gay people began to fade. Suddenly "gay marriage" was two elderly women who have been together for fifty years, or two middle-aged farmers in overalls and beards, or two young lesbians holding squirmy kids all bright eyed with excitement. It is hard to hate people when you really see them, and suddenly gay people just looked so… normal.

After more than a decade of gay marriage in America, starting with the state of Massachusetts, the results are in: Massachusetts has the lowest divorce rate in America. The states with the highest divorce rates are in the Bible

Belt where opposition to gay marriage remains strongest.[9] It may be true that modern marriages are in trouble, and family and social structures are certainly changing, but it is ridiculous to say that gay people have much to do with it. As *The Atlantic* magazine's James Fallows put it, to "the idea that same-sex marriage is a 'threat' to the stability of marriage as a whole: Come on! I defy anyone to demonstrate that it cracks the top 100 list of forces eroding the institution of marriage."[10] Even the conservative commentator Lou Dobbs said, "The defense of marriage is sort of a peculiar construction. When the primary — according to everything I've been able to study — the primary reason for divorce is financial. [...] We have a disaster in this country. And, I mean, it could be argued, it seems to me, at least — and forgive me for saying this way — that you're blaming homosexuals for an institution that's under assault from just about everyone BUT gays!"[11] For those who still believe gay marriage destroys anything about straight marriage, remember this simple formula: If homosexuality can affect your marriage, then one of you is gay.

My favorite summation of the gay marriage arguments came from radio host Peter Sagal:

> I can refute this fear of same-sex marriage by pointing at the three same-sex couples who live on my block, raising kids, keeping up their houses, showing up at t-ball games, just like us, causing no harm and doing much good. I can refute it by pointing at the two most stable, longest-lasting, most loving couples I know, both raising children in wonderful homes: Bill and Christopher, and Malia and Margot. I can refute it by noting that even though we are practically surrounded by sodomites, my marriage is doing fine, and those marriages among our friends and neighbors that have ended... well, let's just say if you had wanted to help them, you would have not so much worried about gay marriage, and instead banned attractive secretaries.[12]

According to the US National Institutes of Health, legally sanctioned gay relationships are more egalitarian, experience significantly less conflict, and are generally happier than straight marriages. Gay couples also tend to confide more in each other, are more intimate, show each other more affection, and have more sex.[13] So according the government of the United States, the effect of legalized gay relationships is a world filled with more intimate, honest, egalitarian, sexy, affectionate, and happy couples, a net win by my count.

People living from the deepest parts of their hearts and souls can never create a tear in the social fabric, as their actions bless everyone. I am for marriage, and I am for people not marrying. I am for couples, and I am for single people. I am for people marrying whom they love regardless of the other person's race, religion, ethnicity, disabilities, social class, or gender. I am for families with lots of children, or a few children, or without any children at all. I am for relationships forming, and I am sometimes, reluctantly, for relationships ending. I support old-fashioned marriages, new-fashioned relationships, and people living outside of formal relationships altogether. The modern world can be hard on interpersonal connections, and each individual needs to work together to create a world where everyone experiences more love, more commitment, and more joyful sharing with each other as we walk the curving paths of life, families, love, marriage, and relationships.

Religion

The Lord respects me when I work,
but he loves me when I sing.

~ Shaker saying

AMERICA IS PREDOMINANTLY Christian, and throughout my lifetime the dominant Christian voices have been fiercely, relentlessly, and rudely anti-gay. While there were countless examples, the most extreme was the Westboro Baptist church, widely known as the "God Hates Fags" church, and I am not being crass by calling them that. That is what their signs say, and the church's website is www.godhatesfags.com. This is a Christian church, or should I say, a "Christian" church, that put hatred of gay people at the core of their beliefs. These are the people who hauled out their protest signs at military funerals and other events around the country to pronounce their belief that God hates homosexuals, and because there are gay people in America, God hates America and wills its destruction.

I met the Westboro people once, by accident. I was walking down Embassy Row in Washington, DC when I passed a group carrying slick signs that said things like "AntiChrist Obama" and "God Hates You" and even weirder things like the Italian flag labeled "Fag Flag." The people there were so clearly enjoying themselves and their signs were so colorful and wacky that I assumed they were performance artists mocking the Westboro types. Precocious fellow that I am, I walked up and said hello and told them their signs looked great and asked the woman about her "God Hates You" sign. She told me that God despises all of humanity because we all fail in his eyes; he regrets his mistake of creating humankind; and he curses the existence of every human being. I looked at her in confusion and said I thought the Old Testament God looked over creation and declared it good. She hissed a response about how that was before the creation of Man and now he despises his creations. As she talked her eyes grew fiery, and I began to feel some kind of abyss of hate opening in front of her. Resisting the tug of vertigo into the malevolent vortex she was opening, I realized who these people really were and left. Interesting folk, those professional anti-gays.

More tolerant Christians who believe the Westboro types do not represent mainstream Christianity are fooling themselves. When Americans were asked what phrase best represents Christianity, 91% of non-Christians and 80% of young churchgoers answered "anti-homosexual."[1] The sex obsessions of America's dominant religion hurt gay people, but we moved past the animosity and thrived. Christianity, on the other hand, appears to be collapsing under its sex obsessions, transforming its anti-gay focus into an existential crisis. At least 59% of church-going Christian children now leave the faith when they become adults, with a third of them citing the church's teachings on gay sex as a leading cause.[2] These kids were not suddenly brainwashed by crazy liberals who lured them away from righteousness. They grew up in a generation that actually knew gay friends and family. By knowing real, live, gay people, they experienced first-hand the errors of the anti-gay propaganda. No sane person would stay with a religion that preaches such patently false doctrines, so they left. At this point most Americans view gay people far more favorably than they view Evangelical Christians.[3]

For those of us outside the Christian faith, that anti-gay hate always seemed a bit suspect. Anti-gay religious leaders were often a tad obsessive in their evocation of hot sweaty men dancing in short shorts at gay pride parades. These preachers routinely took the most exceptional moments of the gay celebrations and portrayed them as normal, which would be like judging heterosexuality based on Spring Break in Florida or Bourbon Street at Mardi Gras. The most famous example of this anti-gay distortion effect came from the President of the National Association of Evangelicals, Ted Haggard, who led thirty million Americans into frenzied homo-hatred while having his own crystal methamphetamine-fueled weekends with a male prostitute on the side.[4] On a more global scale, Catholic priests preached anti-gay sermons from their pulpits while molesting and raping altar boys on the sly. Their church continues to actively withhold the records of this abuse whenever possible, protecting the perpetrators over the victims.

Child abuse aside, the Catholic church is filled with closeted gay men, or men who chose celibacy over working through their adult sexuality, who then preach and campaign against gay people. The most recent high profile example, of so many to choose from, was Cardinal Keith O'Brien. He was the archbishop of Scotland and led the fight against gay rights in the United Kingdom for decades. Then it was revealed he had relationships with multiple men, including some that lasted for years.[5] This kind of religious leader, Protestant and Catholic alike, used anti-gay hate the way schoolyard bullies do, deflecting attention from themselves by pointing out the more effeminate boy for ridicule.

I have tried to avoid telling too many anti-gay stories, as it is easy to be overwhelmed by the negativity, but to understand how anti-gay Christian hate manifests in the modern world, consider a few examples from just one year in one state. In North Carolina recently, Pastor Sean Harris told his congregation that if a son was being girlish his father should record him acting female and upload the video to YouTube so the world could mock him. If a son dropped a limp wrist his father should break it and punch him until he acts male, adding that daughters should be forced to look, act, walk, talk, and smell like a girl. To the weak he added, "You say can I take charge like that as a parent? Yeah, you can. You are authorized. I just gave you a special dispensation this morning to do that."[6] Another North Carolina pastor proposed rounding up all the homosexuals and putting us behind electric fences until we died off, apparently believing we were self-replicating and that would end the problem. When the gay community protested, over a thousand supporters gathered in the streets to cheer him on.[7] In a North Carolina church where a gay teen was bullied into suicide, they had a four year old boy up in the front of the congregation singing *Ain't No Homos Gonna Make It To Heaven* as the assembled erupted in raucous applause and approval.[8] As if in response to this anti-gay religious fervor, another North Carolina Christian killed both his four year old son and the boy's mother because he believed his son was acting gay and she was tolerating it.[9]

Christians who consider gay bashing a core value claim that secular America is blocking the full expression of their religious beliefs, so they took their anti-gay hate message on the road. Evangelical American missionaries actively promote "Kill the Gays" laws in places like Uganda, Nigeria, Ethiopia, South America, and Russia.[10] News of unfolding atrocities seem to arrive daily. Somehow mainstream Christians stand by and let these nutjobs represent their faith's beliefs to an increasingly incredulous moral majority standing outside their faith, aghast.

Revolted by the daily news feeds of religion-based anti-gay hate, I found some comfort reading of one man's awakening. A Mormon Bishop named Kevin Kloosterman told the story of watching the television show *Queer Eye for the Straight Guy,* where gay men used their queer superpowers to help a straight guy dress, cook, and primp his house to create a beautiful evening where he could propose marriage to his girlfriend. Many gay people disliked the show as it seemed to confirm stereotypes of gay men as effeminate, but I loved the selfless service and creativity these men offered. I particularly enjoyed the scene at the end of each episode as men gathered around to watch how the evening went and celebrate the straight guy's success. Watching *Queer Eye* one night, Kloosterman heard the most flamboyant of the men, Carson Kressley, say in support of a straight man proposing to his girlfriend: "We are very pro traditional marriage." As Kloosterman reports, up to that point he believed that his life and beliefs were under attack by the radical gay agenda. "That belief was dismantled at that moment, and I realized that these good men had no desire to hurt me, my marriage, or my family. On the contrary, if they were in my home, I could only see them supporting me, my traditional marriage, and my family."[11]

I was gobsmacked when I read this. I cannot count how many times I have heard about people who believed the goal of my life was to undermine heterosexuality, destroy straight marriage, and bring down civilization. I always thought those were the beliefs of a lunatic fringe, not of anybody reasonable. It is hard for me to wrap my head around the idea of people in the heartland thinking I date, fall in love, have my heart broken, find committed partners, and make sacrifices as part of some plot to hurt straight people and their families. Such is the power of people's belief systems that they can warp my everyday life into something so threatening to theirs.

I have genuine compassion for simple-minded people who cling to easy answers as pacifiers against life's complex realities, but denial of the diversity so visible in the world God created cannot be humanity's final answer. Back in the sixteenth century, a monk named Giordano Bruno was frustrated when the religious people of his day could not believe that the earth existed inside a larger universe, responding, "Your God is too small!"[12] People today who fear the magnitude of God's creations need to find themselves a bigger God.

After generations, if not millennia, of Christians obsessing over gay people, sanity arrived from the most unexpected direction: the Vatican. Long seen as a bastion of anti-gay conservatism, everything changed with the arrival of Pope Francis. When asked about gay priests, Francis responded, "Who am I to judge?"[13] I think I felt the foundations of the Christian world shake a bit in that moment. To many, the Vatican was judgment central and the Pope the high priest of anti-gay condemnations, yet Francis clarified that the church had become too obsessed, to use his word, with its doctrines on abortion, contraception, and homosexuality.[14] He was not liberalizing the church or announcing a change in doctrine. He was simply naming a misplacement of emphasis, something some of us noted a long time ago. In a later interview the Pope responded to church leaders resisting change, declaring: "God is not afraid of new things."[15]

Rather than representing a threat, the existence of gay people offers Christians a golden opportunity, as we are the canaries in the Christian coal mine. If we sing and thrive in your churches and communities, you know the air is healthy. When we go quiet and disappear, you must grab your children and run, because the air has grown noxious and could soon turn fatal. The way a religion treats its gay children is a powerful reflection of that church's ability to embrace human variation in general, and humanity's sexuality in particular.

People of spirit need to recognize that being out and gay is an act of spiritual integrity. It is a fearless striving to align our outer lives with the inner truths of our souls, in defiance of the shallowness and superficiality of popular culture and even many religions. Gay people are not straight people gone astray. We are individuals living the life God gave us with as much integrity as we can muster. Walking boldly into the face of persecution in the name of truth is an act Christians used to admire, and as gay people, we too have our martyrs.

I am not a Christian. I find it a religion of wisdom, historical importance, and resounding values, but in my age and times it has brought more sorrow than good to far too many around me, and I find it has little application to my modern life. As a person who respects the faith, the Christian rupture has been painful to watch, as the credibility of the churches drains away in the face of modern questions mainstream Christians refuse to address in meaningful ways. It is time to stop listening to people who hold their old answers so tightly they cannot hear the new questions.

For those who retain their Christian faith, I wish for you the kind of healthy religion that arises from engagement with all of reality instead of retreating into insecure victimhood and the bizarre denial of evidence. I wish the same for all religious and a-religious people alike — modern answers to modern questions that grow from the rich roots of humanity's intellectual and spiritual traditions towards the radiant sunlight of the breaking day. As Pope Francis said, the people of Jesus's times struggled with similar issues: "The scholars of the law also forgot that the people of God are a people on a journey, and when you journey, you always find new things, things you never knew before."[16] For mainstream Christianity to contribute to the great effort of building humanity's future, it needs to work through its issues around sex, sensuality, sexuality, and gender and come out the other side with a more integrated and refined ability to address all of who we are, without the denial and hostility around the difficult bits.

Scriptures

Always the beautiful answer
who asks a more beautiful question.

~ *E.E. Cummings*

GIVEN HOW CENTRAL anti-gay beliefs became in Christianity, it is worth reviewing what Jesus Christ said about homosexuality: nothing. Not one single word. In his entire ministry he never brought it up. Living under the Romans, who widely and openly practiced same-sex love, Jesus had no comment. Christ was not only not anti-gay, he was not particularly pro-family, as he repeatedly clarified there were higher causes for people to attend to — harsh words for those who have made their beliefs around "family" into their modern idol to worship.

Outside of Jesus's silence, what did the rest of the Bible say about same-sex love and gay relationships? Again, nothing. Absolutely nothing. Some people claim their hate for gay people comes from the Bible, but there is no discussion of anything like modern gay love anywhere in that book, pro or con.

What is in the Bible is a colorful set of stories and a few scriptures about gay sex acts. Along with the threatened rape in the story of Sodom, there are the love stories of David and Jonathan and Ruth and Naomi, and the shamanic tales of Joseph and his special powers with the dream world. More doctrinally, there are only a few biblical scriptures that condemn same-sex sexuality.

The clearest reference to marriage and celibacy in the Christian scriptures is in the first letter of Paul to the Corinthians where he made clear how squeamish he was about heterosexuality: "It is good for a man not to touch a woman. Nevertheless, to avoid fornication, let every man have his own wife, and let every woman have her own husband."[1] In Paul's world it would be better if everyone was unmarried like himself,[2] as "those who marry will have affliction in regard to the flesh, and I would spare you that."[3] He therefore recommends virgins should not marry[4] and widows should not remarry.[5] The Apostle Paul was clearly not a family values voter.

The Romans worshiped multiple gods like Jupiter, Neptune, Mars, and Venus, a practice Christians condemned and labeled pagan. As Paul wrote to a group of Romans who had been Christians but reverted back to their pagan religious customs, "For this cause God gave them up unto vile affections: for even their women did change the natural use into that which is against nature: And likewise also the men, leaving the natural use of the woman, burned in their lust one toward another; men with men working that which is unseemly, and receiving in themselves that recompense of their error which was meet."[6] This sounds like strong stuff in English but in the original Greek "vile affections" was not a statement against passion or lust. "Vile affections" was a reference to the frenzied rituals of wine, drugs, sex, and music the Romans observed as part of their religious rites. These older Roman traditions had women cutting their hair short and men growing their hair long as signs of devotion to their gods. Men and women cross-dressed, and men were castrated to serve as prostitute eunuchs in their temples, all examples of "changing the natural use" of the body in ways Paul considered inappropriate for the newly emerging Christian community. In the same way, "against nature" meant differing from the ordinary or beyond the ordinary realm of experience. One liberal interpretation of this scripture might say: "Do not get so drunk and high that you have sex that is not even in your nature, with straight men and women all over each other and everyone feeling terrible afterwards." From sex-phobic Paul this actually sounds like pretty solid advice.

The other two scriptures Paul wrote against homosexuality offer even clearer examples of problematic translations. As he wrote to the people of Corinth: "Know ye not that the unrighteous shall not inherit the kingdom of God? Be not deceived: neither fornicators, nor idolaters, nor adulterers, nor effeminate [makakoi], nor abusers of themselves with mankind [arsenokoitai] Nor thieves, nor covetous, nor drunkards, nor revilers, nor extortioners, shall inherit the kingdom of God."[7] That Paul is uncomfortable with effeminate men does not seem surprising given his own ambivalence around sex. It is hard to imagine Paul as overly masculine. But the Greek word makakoi can refer to all kinds of behaviors like cowardice and laziness, and not just effeminacy. Arsenokoitai, on the other hand, refers to the sacred temple prostitutes of Christianity's neighboring religions, or male prostitutes in general, or those who sexually abused boys. What arsenokoitai does not refer to is adults in loving same-sex relationships.

Arsenokoitai shows up again in 1 Timothy: "Knowing this, that the law is not made for a righteous man, but for the lawless and disobedient, for the ungodly and for sinners, for unholy and profane, for murderers of fathers and murderers of mothers, for manslayers, for whoremongers, for them that defile themselves with mankind [arsenokoitai], for menstealers, for liars, for perjured persons, and if there be any other thing that is contrary to sound doctrine."[8] Again, not as clear-cut in two thousand year old Greek as it sounds in the English translations.

The only other scripture in the New Testament referring to same sex-attraction is even stranger. In the gospel of Jude it says, "Even as Sodom and Gomorrah, and the cities about them in like manner, giving themselves over to fornication, and going after strange flesh, are set forth for an example, suffering the vengeance of eternal fire."[9] Given that the men of Sodom wanted sex with angels, calling that flesh strange seems reasonable, like modern people wanting sex with aliens visiting in their UFOs. That said, I see no application to my relationships. As much as I think highly of the men I have dated, not one of them could be mistaken for an angel.

The other three contentious scriptures come from the Hebrew scriptures, but of course the Old Testament is an even tougher read for moderns as it refers to a society so distant from anything we know today. Modern Christians invoking the laws of the Old Testament is a little weird anyway, as the essence of Christianity declares the ancient laws fulfilled in Christ and no longer applicable. Modern Christians do not live the Old Testament's laws of celibacy, marriage, or divorce. Modern Christians do not kill their non-virgin brides on their wedding night, sell their daughters as sex slaves, own their wives as property, ban divorce from inappropriate spouses, or practice polygamy, no matter how enticing that last one may sound to some Christian men. Modern Christians have updated their marriages, families, and lives to meet modern standards of justice, equality, and respect. Yet those same Christians demand that the Old Testament laws be applied to gay people with all the vigor society can muster.

One of those laws from Leviticus says, "Thou shalt not lie with mankind, as with womankind: it is abomination."[10] That sounds incredibly clear and serious, unless the reader knows the Old Testament well enough to know all the other things labeled abominable, including proud and haughty eyes,[11] seeing a menstruating woman naked,[12] spreading strife among brothers,[13] harvesting the corners of the field,[14] practicing pagan customs[15] (um, like putting up a Christmas tree), shaving or getting a haircut,[16] collecting firewood on Saturday,[17] wearing clothes of mixed textiles,[18] eating shrimp,[19] or touching a dead pig's skin.[20] Jewish Kosher laws came from these same lists of abominations, including the taboo on eating pork or having dairy in the same meal as beef. The Old Testament has 365 of these prohibitions. So fine, I can live with the idea that guy-on-guy sex is an abomination as offensive to the God of the Old Testament as bacon, shrimp cocktails, cheeseburgers, cotton-polyester blends, and footballs.

Another scary sounding scripture says, "If a man also lie with mankind, as he lieth with a woman, both of them have committed an abomination: they shall surely be put to death; their blood shall be upon them."[21] Again with that tough sounding Old Testament language, but other people listed for death include non-believers,[22] people who work on Saturday,[23] adulterous women,[24] men who pull out before orgasm when having sex with their dead brother's wife,[25] people who curse using God's name,[26] witches,[27] fortune tellers,[28] and disobedient children.[29] Blinded by their anti-gay hatred and underlying sex issues, modern Christians blithely commit most of these abominable acts on a regular basis yet claim the two that condemn gay people are among the most important in the Bible.

The easiest way to understand these harsh sounding edicts is to understand the Jewish culture they came from. The Hebrew scriptures are best viewed as the beginning of a long discussion, as seen in the history of Talmud study where the ongoing debate over biblical commentary is an essential part of the faith. Christians, on the other hand, tend to use the Bible to end arguments, as in: "It says so in the Bible, therefore End Of Discussion." A wise Jewish friend taught me a different approach, explaining that when the Hebrew Bible says you should kill someone for an offense, that should be the beginning of a long and thoughtful discussion on morality, community, God, punishment, and everything else that pertains, with plenty of room for compassion, and not be taken as a simplistic dictate to kill. In just that way, Jesus demonstrated a Jewish sense of morality when he told those who felt they had to stone a woman for adultery that the one without sin should cast the first stone.[30] Jesus was demonstrating that the law was where the discussion started, but not necessarily where it ended.

The final scripture used against gay people comes from Deuteronomy and is repeated in Kings: "There shall be no whore of the daughters of Israel, nor a sodomite [*qadesh*] of the sons of Israel."[31] This is a pure mistranslation, as the original Greek *qadesh* was not a reference to the people of Sodom. *Qadesh* referred to the male prostitutes at pagan shrines who did fertility rites and often had ritualistic sex with women. Every use of the word "sodomite" in the English Bible is the medieval translator's mistaken word choice to represent *qadesh*.

That is it, all the anti-gay scriptures. Not one addresses my life, my heart, my relationships, or my ethical questions. I do not go against my sexual nature in sacred frenzies of wine and drugs. I am not a particularly effeminate man, although I pity Paul's uptight self-loathing of the feminine energy in men. I do not work as a temple prostitute, although it sounds like a fascinating career path. I do not follow the Hebraic laws of ritualistic purity or eat a Kosher diet. And I do not crave angel flesh, although frankly, as I have never met a true angel, the possibility remains. If there is a man out there who really is an angel, and finds me interesting, he should call me. I would love to meet over coffee.

Of course now that women are people too, it is important to note that there is not one prohibition on lesbian sex anywhere in the Bible. Not a single mention of female-female sex anywhere in the book. In that typically biblical way Christians teach themselves to overlook, female lives and passions are left out entirely. So if the Bible is truly Christianity's moral guide, then women-on-woman sex appears to have the big green light.

I respect the timeless wisdom of the Bible along with its quirky moral stances on issues that do not exist in the modern world, and of course I love the colorful and often baffling stories. But far too often the Bible gives answers to questions I do not have, while it is silent on the questions I do have. I was born gay, and I have had cancer, and I would not use the Bible as my primary guide for either one. Sometimes it is better to go modern.

For a more dynamic perspective on their faith, Christians like to claim that righteousness comes from living a Christ-like life, but Jesus was not a married man with an office job and a wife and children in the suburbs. The answer to the question "What would Jesus do?" is to never marry, travel constantly, eschew materialism, and spend most days hanging out with twelve men and a prostitute. In other words, his life looked a lot more like mine than it does that of most Christians.

Taking an understanding of Christ's life a few steps further, consider the relationship between Jesus and the Apostle John, or as John called himself, John the Beloved. On Jesus's final day, during the last supper, John laid his head on Jesus's chest. Which of today's Christian churches would allow Jesus and John's act of same-sex tenderness in their pews today? That kind of Christ-like behavior is now banned in almost every church that bears his name. Then, at the end of his life, after being nailed to the cross, Jesus pointed to John and told his mother Mary: "Woman, behold thy son!" and to John: "Behold thy mother!"[32] Consider for a moment what relationship between Jesus and John would make Jesus's mother into John's mother. I know what relationship I would have to have with another man to make his mother into my mother. And it was John, at least according to John's account, who was the first apostle to reach the empty tomb.

I am not saying Jesus was gay. Some people have, but I do not really care enough to take a stand. Knowing the teachings of Jesus, it would hardly surprise me. His life certainly did not exemplify the Thor-like God so many American Christians worship, all brawny and broad shouldered, going into battle with sword in hand. The Jesus I read in the Bible seems more gentle, tender, filled with quirky wisdom, and compassionate in ways more common to gay men, and John the Beloved was central to Jesus's story and life in ways the Bible does not make entirely clear. As with the older story of David and Jonathan, the only thing a modern reader can do is respect the love between Jesus and John chronicled in the scriptures, while resisting the desire to apply modern labels and judgments from so great a distance.

Underlying all the scriptural arguments against homosexuality runs the idea that God only approves of heterosexual relationships. As it says in Genesis, "So God created man in his own image, in the image of God created he him; male and female created he them. And God blessed them, and God said unto them, Be fruitful, and multiply."[33] This scripture does reflects the reality that God, evolution, or Mother Nature created male and female for procreation, but procreation is not the only thing humans do, and clearly male or female are not the only way people are born. This scripture needs to have an asterisk next to it for all the people God created with intersex bodies, non-procreative genitalia, transsexual spirits, or a sense of self that is fuzzy on how the gender binary applies in their lives. Those two human genders are a lovely, beautiful, and even sacred starting point, but ending awareness there is to miss the truth and much of life's beauty. As far as the commandment to be fruitful and multiply, the world's population has more than doubled in my lifetime and is now over seven billion and rising fast. I think humanity has rather over-fulfilled that commandment and needs to pull back a bit before things get worse. Enough with the fruitful multiplication already.

To be relevant to modern lives, religions must address the facts of life as we now understand them. The modern world is, almost by definition, profane, a word that comes from the Latin *pro-* meaning before or in front of, and *fanum* meaning temple. The profane world is everything outside the sanctity of the temple, including all the non-sacred things like money, capitalism, secular laws, and scientific achievements. Humanity will never return to some previous age of uninterrupted communion with the sacred, if such a time ever really existed. For those who want to value the sacred in a modern way, the next necessary step is to re-infuse it into this profane world in a holistic way that embraces the entire yin and yang of life, intertwined and in motion. As it happens, synthesizing apparent contradictions is something at which gay people often excel.

I do not know what thoughtful people can do about religions that are so relentlessly obsessed with gay sex and relationships. My recommendation is some serious prayer and soul searching focused on updating their theology around sexuality and gender to bring it into harmony with adjustments already made for straight people, and stop applying Old Testament laws to people who are not ultra-Orthodox Jews.

In March of 2014, the founding father of the Westboro Baptist church, Fred Phelps, died, after a lifetime of picketing against gay people at over 53,000 events.[34] The gay community did not celebrate. Clearly this was a man deeply tormented around homosexuality, for reasons we can only surmise were personal. A week after his death the Westboro church pulled out their "God Hate Fags" signs and started demonstrating against gay people in their usual way, and they were met by counter-protestors standing on the other side of the street holding a single white banner with words that read: "Sorry for your loss."[35] I know which of those groups looked more Christian to me.

Because this chapter centered on the Christian scriptures, it seems fitting to end with the final instruction Jesus gave to the gathering of his all-male disciples at the last supper, wrapping up his teachings in what many consider the one great commandment: "A new commandment I give unto you, That ye love one another; as I have loved you, that ye also love one another. By this shall all men know that ye are my disciples, if ye have love one to another."[36] Powerful stuff, that.

MEANING

Purpose

> The only way
> to deal with an unfree world
> is to become so absolutely free
> that your very existence
> is an act of rebellion.
>
> ~ *Albert Camus*

WHEN HARRY HAY gathered a few men together to found one of America's first gay rights organizations, he started the meeting with three core questions: "Who are we? Where do we come from? What are we for?"[1] Life is a path, not a destination, so the answers to these kinds of existential questions will always evolve, but here is my crack at it. There is a purpose to being gay, roles we are born to play for the benefit of ourselves, our families, our communities, and the planet. Sexual attraction to people of the same sex may be a flag indicator that an individual differs from the norm, but being gay is about much more than sex.

Viewed with a bit of perspective, gay people often serve as humanity's synthesists, bridges, intermediaries, and border people, walking between worlds and knitting disparate elements together in ways that create the new and exciting. We are the extra adults in the family, loving parents to our children, and vibrant members of our communities. We can also be the tricksters and disrupters of the complacent, the counterbalance to the stolid and square. Applying our sensitivity and outsider perspectives resulted in the greatest stereotype about gay people: our creativity. There is a saying that those who do not procreate, create, and gay people create more than our share of the culture.

Living closer to the fundamental divide of gender, we tend to know more about life on the other side. I know I sometimes feel like the Roman god Janus, from whom we get January, who had two faces, one looking into the future and the other into the past. The difference is that as a gay man I stand in the doorway between the masculine and the feminine, looking both ways at the same time. I may stand more on the masculine and male side, but my life spans into the feminine in ways that even surprise me at times. This ability to stand as a person of one gender reaching out to embrace the qualities of the other may be a core aspect of our creativity. The poet and philosopher Samuel Taylor Coleridge said, "The truth is, a great mind must be androgynous."[2] Psychologist Mihaly Csikszentmihalyi explained part of the reason why: "A psychologically androgynous person in effect doubles his or her repertoire of responses and can interact with the world in terms of a much richer and varied spectrum of opportunities. It is not surprising that creative individuals are more likely to have not only the strengths of their own gender but those of the other one, too."[3]

This non-dualistic both-and quality of gay lives can help us bridge apparent contradictions, making us effective teachers and couples counselors who can speak to both parties from our own experience. This bridging of disparities is why we are often humanity's ambassadors, translators, and mediators, from the US State Department to the Pentagon to corporate personnel offices. One of the tragedies of rejecting gay people from the military was the loss of some of the country's most effective translators in the midst of terrible wars, the exact time when America most needed connectors to hostile nations.[4]

As synthesists, we not only bridge those disparate elements, we can also intermix them, blending and combining them into something new. This is the almost magical ability some gay men have to take in culture and styles, the trendy and the timeless, and then help a middle aged woman pick the perfect dress for her daughter's wedding. The owner of one of the country's poshest retreat spas told me that of all healing professionals she had hired over the years, gay men were the best at combining impeccable service with an acute empathy for what the client was experiencing in the moment. That same quality makes us powerful shamans and comforting nurses. Add more sensitivity to the transcendent, and we become nuns and priests. More connection to nature, and we are gardeners and forest rangers. More people-centered, and we are waiters, stewards, and hosts. Add an aesthetic slant, and we are leaders in fashion, beauty, and entertainment. Mix in more technical minds, and we become software interface designers and technical marketers. The thing all these occupations have in common is the ability to synthesize the various aspects of life into something innovative and tailored to specific human needs.

Living outside the typical duality means gay relationships are often fundamentally different, as we are more likely to see each other as equals, meeting as subject-to-subject, whereas other-sex relations tend to be more subject-to-object. Note the way many straight men view women as sex objects. There is an unfortunate tendency in today's commercialized cultures to view each other as objects that only exist for our pleasure rather than viewing each other as subjects of companionship, love, and support. When I am out socially with my boyfriends, straight women often comment on how beautiful it is to see two men treat each other with love and tenderness, and straight men compliment us on the freedom they observe in our equality-based relationship. Harry Hay felt this subject-subject consciousness could be one of the primary gifts gay people brought to humanity.[5] Heterosexuals have to work out the male-female dynamic for themselves, as it brings its own joys and troubles, but there are practical lessons to learn from same-gender couples about the interplay of love, commitment, and gender roles.

This subject-subject awareness has broader ramifications as well. Every person who can incorporate the natural world as part of the human experience, to be fully included as something of equal value rather than treated as objects to be dominated and exploited, has a better chance of living in prosperous harmony with the only planet humanity has to call home. If the health of the earth is in peril because of human actions, then the people who have mastered non-dualistic thinking may be the salvation of Earth and its inhabitants.

Another upside to being society's sensitive outsiders comes from our role as the harbingers, running ahead and announcing what is coming for everyone. I mentioned the canary metaphor earlier when discussing churches, but I first heard it applied to gay people in the reports of urban studies theorist Richard Florida whose research found that gay people are the canaries of our entire creative age.[6] Just as miners carried canaries into their mines where their singing signaled the mine's air remained healthy, members of the creative class can quickly determine which cities and cultures have an intellectual and artistic environment safe for new ideas and creativity by looking around for the gay people. The more gay people in a city or company, the more obviously creativity and non-conformist thinking are tolerated and embraced, free from the cultural rigidity that kills creativity in its cradle. It is commonly observed that Silicon Valley arose where it did because it is between creatively juicy San Francisco and technically savvy San Jose.

There is an old adage that artists should "Learn the rules well so you can break them effectively," so breaking the rules effectively is practically the definition of creativity. As gay people we break the rules of normalcy by our very existence, which is why creativity is one of our primary gifts. To go one step further with the cliché, it is easier for us to think outside the box because we were born outside the box.

Defining ourselves as people who differ in a fundamental way makes the LGBT community the catalyst for new possibilities, but that also means we tend to trip up the rigid and bland, like the mythical coyote of Native American legend who comes into the story to mess things up when authority gets too complacent. The kind of people who cling to society's norms and declare all the old habits sacred are the same people who get peevish when those norms are subverted, so of course gay people upset them. There are reasons organizations like the Mormon and Catholic churches neglected their charge to care for the poor, the sick, and the dying to put their political capital into fighting gay people. We were anathema to their means of holding power — not to their Christian values as charged by Jesus, but to their style of organizational control that required all of life to fall under their neatly outlined authority. Gay people pop up in the center of that kind of tidy certainty like Bugs Bunny, the prankster who makes the guy with the gun look the fool.

If homophobia is the irrational fear of gay people, then there are, in fact, rational reasons to fear us. We do threaten the rigid, the simple-minded, and the narrow. Gay people threaten authoritarian governments and simplistic ethical systems because we demonstrate by our very existence that there are multiple correct answers to life's deepest questions. Every individual who skips across the color spectrum can be seen as threatening by those who cling to black and white. Every person who learns the depths of their own truths threatens those who believe truth resides in a pamphlet, a slogan, an ideology, or a book. There are perfectly good reasons to fear gay people for the unexpected surprises our queer perspectives bring, and the power, spirituality, and exuberance we contribute to the world. But that fear of gay people, based on our power as disrupters, is profoundly, and deeply, rational.

Disrupting a system, however, is not the same as destroying it. Modern capitalism is based on the idea of creative destruction. Businesses, products, and whole industries are allowed to fade away to make room for newer innovations and approaches. The societies that encourage this process of destruction and rebirth are among the most prosperous. That same creative disruption is needed in the ways cultures treat women, minorities, foreigners, people of differing religions, and all the varieties of gender and sexualities. While tradition is a great starting point, it is only through the process of constructive change that a new and better future can arise.

Of course after the disassembling process comes the essential next step of consolidation and reform, and the act of re-integration also requires the creative. Luckily, the same people who know how to disrupt a system often know how to put it all back together again in newly empowered ways, and gay people excel at constructive creativity as well.

It is my deepest belief that we stand at the crossroads of the modern dilemma. With the Enlightenment, mankind separated out the distinctions between body, mind, and spirit, resulting in the rise of democracy and capitalism over theocracy and kings. Building on that success, the great task of society today is to reweave all the disparate aspects of body, mind, and spirit back together. It is like the Swiss cuckoo clock someone gave me when I was a child. I immediately took it apart, fascinated by the beautifully machined mechanisms, but I could not get it back together, destroying something beautiful in the process. Modern society disassembles human lives in similar ways, catering to our needs, desires, and beliefs beyond any reasonable standard, while the core of our humanity shrivels and slowly dies. Putting gay people back into our natural roles as healers, caregivers, teachers, creators of beauty, and priests may be an important step towards building a culture that reunifies body, mind, and spirit back into a healthily working whole.

Every young gay person learns that the rules of religion and society may be great in the abstract but wrong in the specific, so we choose to follow our souls over the dictates of a society gone wrong. As Socrates said, the unexamined life is not worth living,[7] and no openly gay person gets to live an unexamined life. Fate requires us to work out our moral truths outside the default paths, and integrity makes us strive to live from those truths. Every human being who lives an examined and authentic life infuses themselves and all of humanity with an expended sense of depth, meaning, and purpose. This was a solitary task for many gay people back in the days when society did not understand us, but today we are ending that ignorance and moving forward into a future where communal support and broader nurturance are available. As Harry Hay said so many years ago, "No boy or girl, approaching the maelstrom of deviation, need make that crossing alone, afraid, and in the dark ever again."[8]

If I have done my job right, I have mapped the dark forest and highlighted some of the trails out of the old mindsets and into new paradigms where everyone — straight, gay, lesbian, bisexual, asexual, pansexual, cisgender, gender non-conforming, and so many more — will be able to continue humanity's progress and chart their own courses into the light of a better day.

Dream

> I want to stay
> as close to the edge as I can
> without going over.
> Out on the edge
> you can see all kinds of things
> you can't see from the center.
>
> ~ *Kurt Vonnegut*

I LIVE IN A LITTLE HOUSE on a San Francisco hillside. Looking out my windows I see crisscrossed rows of pastel homes poking out from the trees, the gleaming towers of downtown in the distance. The office where I write is lined with shelves packed with books, art supplies, old journals, photos, and the quirkily soulful art I have collected from my travels around the world. Sitting at my desk I can look out from my computer through the crisp afternoon air and watch the light changing across the city as the sun sets over the Pacific, lighting the few wispy clouds into cotton puffs of burnt orange, the sun's rays reflecting off the skyscraper windows like blinding golden fires.

Modernity is dazzling, and has brought astonishing benefits in science, medicine, individual rights, democracy, and mass prosperity. My handheld phone does things the science fiction of my youth could not imagine. Along with all the benefits, modernity has brought a new set of problems. As individual empowerment grows, the connections between individuals seem to be weakening, and the connections between humanity, the earth, and the sacred have been stretched and disrupted to the breaking point. More and more, people are realizing that something is wrong with modern society, and no one knows quite how to fix it.

The good news is that gay people may be part of the solution. While modernity tends to be technical, secular, and monoculture, the spirits of gay people tend to be sensitive, creative, diverse, and inclusive. Where modernity divides things into atomized parts, queer spirits bridge and synthesize polarities. Rather than representing the dissolution of social structures, as our critics often claimed, gay people can help the unifying forces that pull a complex and increasingly secularized humanity back together into a more harmonious whole with each other, the Earth, and spirit.

When I close my eyes and feel into my life as a gay man in modern America, much of it has been more a nightmare than a dream: a hellish dystopia of religious leaders denying the validity of my existence and calling for my extermination, political leaders rallying their troops by invoking people like me as society's demons, street thugs wanting to bash and kill me in the streets, and families rejecting people like me and tossing us out on the streets to fend for ourselves. Yet history demonstrates over and over that demonizing the wrong things can lead to disaster. Somewhere around the 1200s, the Catholic church started associating witches with cats, declaring that cats were the evil consorts of the devil. Based on this colorful but bizarre superstition, people across Europe killed their cats. Unfortunately, humans domesticated cats in the first place because they killed rats and mice, so when the Black Death arrived in 1347, carried by rats, the vermin thrived because of the absence of cats.[1] Think of that the next time someone jokes about the jinx of a black cat, as that irrational and superstitious fear resulted in the deaths of hundreds of millions of people in wave after wave of epidemics leaving European culture decimated for generations. As the philosopher Friedrich Nietzsche supposedly said, "Be careful, lest in casting out your demon you exorcise the best thing in you." In casting out its gay children, societies across history killed and suppressed some of their most creative and soulful members. The result has been predictably devastating. I see all of that darkness, but the harshness of that reality did not make me a pessimist. As the defiant character of a video game declared, "I survived because the fire inside me burned brighter than the fire around me."[2]

When I close my eyes and let myself dream of a different future, I see parents celebrating the news that their daughter is lesbian, their son is gay, or that their child's sense of labels like son or daughter feels a little fuzzy and interchangeable, because each of these variations offers such a glowing gift in the life of the family and the child. I see Mormons and other fundamentalist parents rising up against their leaders who worship the false idol of family values and stand up for the members of their real families. I see diverse and colorful family trees growing out in every direction, rooted in shared morals and values that directly address the realities of modern life, branching up into variations and configurations previous generations never imagined. I dream of a society celebrating all the people born at the tapering ends of humanity's many spectrums as much as those born in the middle of the bell curves so everyone can grow up feeling "normal" — each individual valued and honored for both their unique gifts and their contribution to the whole.

This book is missing so much. I wish I knew more women's stories, more transgender stories, and more stories of youth. I wish I had room to tell more stories from gay culture — about the importance of Judy Garland, rural gay people, bisexual marriages, underground lesbian house parties, thumping nightclubs filled with dancing gay men, and the grand old queens who so enlivened my younger years. I wish I understood better how to unscramble the mess of our problems — the dangerous worlds of sex and drug addictions, the sticky morass of materialism, and the enduring sense of pain and exclusion that lingers in far too many hearts. I can only experience life through my own two eyes, and I am saddened that the perspective from my one small life keeps me from giving the luscious variations of the LGBT community all it is due. Like the stars and galaxies stretching across the visible sky and far beyond our strongest telescopes, there is too much brightness out there for one man to comprehend.

I take some solace from the old idea that if you give a man a fish he eats for a day, but if you teach him how to fish he eats for a lifetime. In that same spirit, if I tell someone a gay concept that touches their heart they may think about it for a day, but if I teach them how to think through these issues in constructive and healthy ways that ability may last for a lifetime.

Gay people of my generation did an incredible amount of heavy lifting, and now it is time for new and more interesting problems. Gay children raised in gay embracing cultures of the past rose to some of the highest heights in human history, and young people today are growing up in a world increasingly supportive of their queer lives. I do not think it bold to predict that another queer-led renaissance is about to unfold. Who knows what heights gay children raised in healthier environments with modern capabilities can achieve.

This same dream applies to every human being. As Harvey Milk once said, "If a gay person makes it, the doors are open to everyone."[3] Making the world hospitable for those who are curious, funny, eccentric, different, singular, odd, and surprising makes the world a better place for everyone who has their little queer moments.

Modern cultures excel at dividing and naming every aspect of the human condition into smaller and more discrete subsets in the ongoing quest for individual empowerment and prosperity. Having done so well at that task, is time to reweave it all back together, thread by thread, and piece by piece. It is now time to see each individual with respect, and help them find their place in the greater whole. It is time for the modern world to begin to heal.

As someone said at the Stonewall riots, the fags had had it with repression, so we grabbed hold of the world, and transformed it into a place where we, too, could thrive. Now we hand off this radically shifted world to the next generation, and to our children's children, and to all of humanity, so future generations can live and thrive exactly the way God made them — blindingly beautiful, shining brilliant and bright in every color of the rainbow.

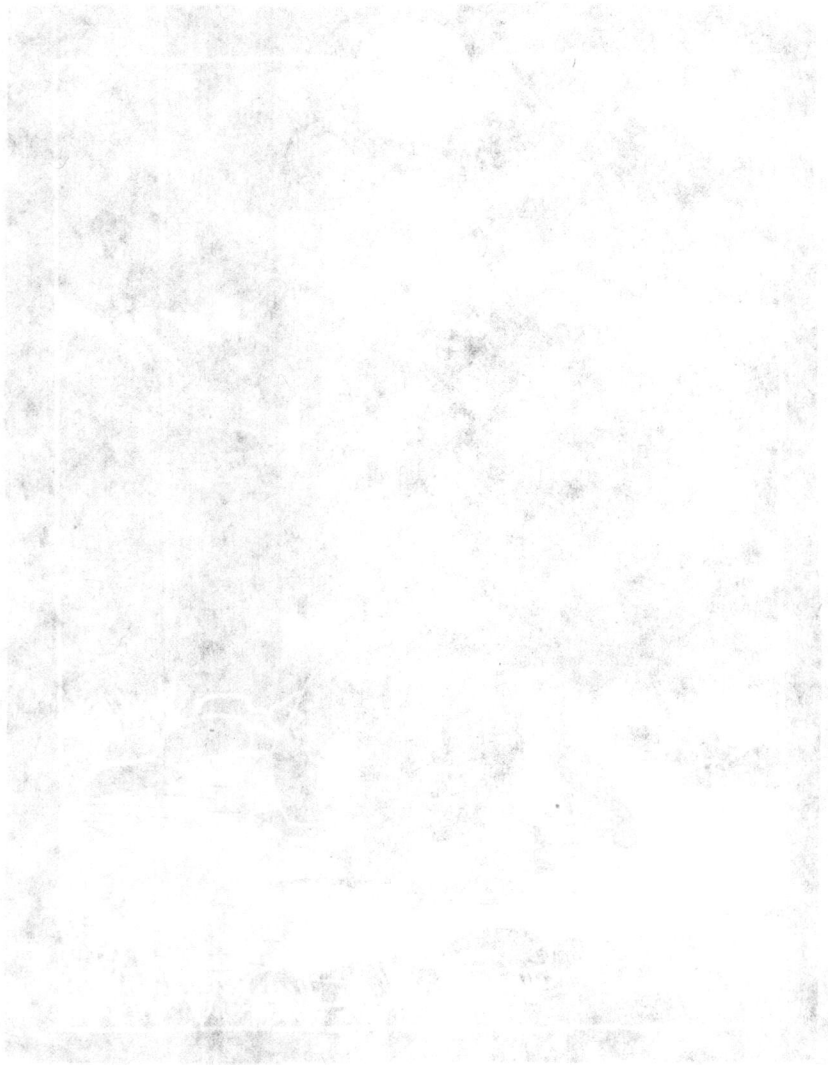

Gatekeepers

Introduced in the chapter on shamans, Malidoma Somé
combines his Jesuit and traditional African educations
to bring an unexpected message to the world about the
importance of gay lives. Here is Malidoma interviewed
by Bert Hoff at the 1993 Mendocino Men's Conference.[1]

Bert: At Conflict Hour you told us that your culture honors gays as
having a higher vibrational level that enabled them to be guardians of the
gateways to the spirit world. You suggested that our Western view limits
itself by focusing only on their sexual role. Can you elaborate for our
readers?

Malidoma: I don't know how to put it in terms that are clear enough for
an audience that, I think needs as much understanding of this gender
issue as people in this country do. But at least among the Dagara people,
gender has very little to do with anatomy. It is purely energetic. In that
context, a male who is physically male can vibrate female energy, and vice
versa. That is where the real gender is. Anatomic differences are simply
there to determine who contributes what for the continuity of the tribe. It
does not mean, necessarily, that there is a kind of line that divides people
on that basis. And this is something that also touches on what has become
known here as the "gay" or "homosexual" issue. Again, in the culture that
I come from, this is not the issue. These people are looked on, essentially,
as people. The whole notion of "gay" does not exist in the indigenous
world. That does not mean that there are not people there who feel the
way that certain people feel in this culture, that has led to them being
referred to as "gay."

The reason why I'm saying there are no such people is because the gay
person is very well integrated into the community, with the functions that
delete this whole sexual differentiation of him or her. The gay person is

looked at primarily as a "gatekeeper." The Earth is looked at, from my tribal perspective, as a very, very delicate machine or consciousness, with high vibrational points, which certain people must be guardians of in order for the tribe to keep its continuity with the gods and with the spirits that dwell there. Spirits of this world and spirits of the other worlds. Any person who is at this link between this world and the other world experiences a state of vibrational consciousness which is far higher, and far different, from the one that a normal person would experience. This is what makes a gay person gay. This kind of function is not one that society votes for certain people to fulfill. It is one that people are said to decide on prior to being born. You decide that you will be a gatekeeper before you are born. And it is that decision that provides you with the equipment (Malidoma gestures by circling waist area with hands) that you bring into this world. So when you arrive here you begin to vibrate in a way that Elders can detect as meaning that you are connected with a gateway somewhere. Then they watch you grow, and they watch you act and react, and sooner or later they will follow you to the gateway that you are connected with.

Now, gay people have children. Because they're fertile, just like normal people. How I got to know that they were gay was because on arriving in this country and seeing the serious issues surrounding gay people, I began to wonder it does not exist in my own country. When I asked one of them, who had taken me to the threshold of the Otherworld, whether he feels sexual attraction towards another man, he jumped back and said, "How do you know that?!" He said, "This is our business as gatekeepers." And, yet he had a wife and children—no problem, you see.

So to then limit gay people to simple sexual orientation is really the worst harm that can be done to a person. That all he or she is is a sexual person. And, personally, because of the fact that my knowledge of indigenous medicine, ritual, comes from gatekeepers, it's hard for me to take this position that gay people are the negative breed of a society. No! In a society that is profoundly dysfunctional, what happens is that peoples' life purposes are taken away, and what is left is this kind of sexual orientation which, in turn, is disturbing to the very society that created it.

I think this is again victimization by a Christian establishment that is looking at a gay person as a disempowered person, a person who has lost his job from birth onward, and now society just wants to fire him out of life. This is not justice. It's not justice. It is a terrible harm done to an energy that could save the world, that could save us. If, today, we are suffering from a gradual ecological waste, this is simply because the gatekeepers have been fired from their job. They have been fired! They have nothing to do! And because they have been fired, we accuse them for not doing anything. This is not fair!

Let us look at the earth differently, and we will find out gradually that these people that are bothering us today are going to start taking their posts. They know what their job is. You just have to get near them, to feel that they don't vibrate the same way. They are not of this world. They come from the Otherworld, and they were sent here to keep the gates open to the Otherworld, because if the gates are shut, this is when the earth, Mother Earth, will shake—because it has no more reason to be alive, it will shake itself, and we will be in deep trouble.

Bert: Christianity has separated spirit from body and spirit from Earth. And earlier you talked to us about Christianity suppressing your culture. So there's a suggestion here that suppression of homosexuality would be the way for the Christians to shut down the gateways, shut down the spirit, and shut down our connection with the Earth.

Malidoma: Yes! That's right! Christianity stresses postponing living on earth, as if we are only here to pack up our baggage and prepare for a life somewhere else "out there." Jesus Christ is right here, man! And of course anyone else who knows more, who knows better, will be suppressed.

And you start with the gatekeepers. You take the gatekeeper and you confuse his mind. You threaten him and you throw him in the middle of nowhere. Then nobody knows where the gate is. As soon as you lose the whereabouts of the gate, then you have a culture going downhill. What keeps a village together is a handful of "gays and lesbians," as they call them in the modern world. In my village, lesbians are called witches, and gay men are known as the gatekeepers. These are the two only known secret societies. These are the only groups that will get together as a separate group and go out into the woods secretly to do whatever they do. And if they find you during their yearly symposium, they have the right to kill you.

Unless they go out on their yearly symposium, the village cannot be granted another year of life. They have to go out to do what they do, in order for the village to feel safe enough to live the way it has lived before. This is why, to me, we're playing with our lives.

Bert:　So our culture may not be granted another year of life.

Malidoma:　That's right! Every year it feels like the number of years that this culture is entitled to live is getting smaller. So God only knows how close to the chasm this culture is. This constantly-reiterated discomfort and hatred for the gay person is again another indication that every year we might as well be prepared for the apocalyptic moment when the stars start to fall to the earth.

You see, unless there is somebody who constantly monitors the mechanism that opens the door from this world to the Otherworld, what happens is that something can happen to one of the doors and it closes up. When all the doors are closed, this earth runs out of its own orbit and the solar system collapses into itself. And because this system is linked to other systems, they too start to fall into a whirlpool. And the cataclysm would be amazing!

Ask the Dogon, they will tell you that. The Dogon. They're a tribe that understands this so well, it's amazing, mind-boggling. And it is a tribe that knows astrology like no other tribe that I have encountered. And the great astrologers of the Dogon are gay. They are gay. There is a dull planet that, in its orbit, is directly above the Dogon village every 58 years. Who knows that, but the gay people.

I mean, I'm not just trying to make gay people look fine. This is the truth, man! I'm trying to save my ass!

Why is it that, everywhere else in the world, gay people are a blessing, and in the modern world they are a curse? It is self-evident. The modern world was built by Christianity. They have taken the gods out of the earth and sent them to heaven, wherever that is. And everyone who aspires to the gods must then negotiate with Christianity, so that the real priests and priestesses are out of a job. This is the worst thing that can happen to a culture that calls itself modern.

Bert:　That theme came up earlier with you and Martín, the Mayan shaman here, that if a modern society wants to shut down another culture they will go out and kill the keepers of the ritual.

Malidoma: Oh, yes! Because they know that this is where the life-pulse of the culture is. This is where the engine room of the tribe is. So if you go and bomb that place, then the whole mechanism shuts down. That's pretty much what's at work in the third world, and what has happened here with the Native American culture. And the thing about it is that humans are going to be begetting gatekeepers, no matter what. This is the chance that we've got. So maybe that means that sooner or later we're going to wake up to the horror of our own errors, and we're going to reconsecrate our chosen people so that they can do their priestly work as they should. Otherwise, I just don't understand. I just don't understand. My position about it is not so much that gays be just forgiven. That's just tokenism. But that they serve as an example of the wrong, or the illness, that modernity has brought to us, and that we use that to begin working at healing ourselves and our society from the bottom up. That way, by the time we reach a certain level, all the gatekeepers are going to find their positions again. We cannot tell them where the gates are. They know. If we start to heal ourselves, they will remember. It will kick in. But as long as we continue in arrogance, in egotism, in God-knows-what form of violence on ourselves, no, there's that veil of confusion that's going to continue to prevail, and as a result it's going to prevent great things from happening. That's all I can say about that.

About The Author

Not all those who wander
are lost.

~ *J.R.R. Tolkien*

Preston Grant is a writer, artist, and traveler based in San Francisco. He earned undergraduate degrees from the University of Utah and an MBA from George Washington University, worked in technology and finance, and lived in Salt Lake City, Tokyo, and Washington, DC before returning to life in his native California.

Thank You

Dear Reader,

I had one goal when I started this project — to raise the level of debate by providing the basic information most people were missing. If you feel I succeeded, please pass it along:

- Hand this copy to a friend, no need to buy a new one, just share!

- Gift a copy to someone who might benefit. Maybe drop a copy at your local library.

- Share your reading experience on Facebook or other social media. Word of mouth is incredibly powerful. Linking to www.gayexplained.com provides descriptions and purchasing details.

- Write a review on Amazon, www.amazon.com. This is the #1 place people look for information on books, even when the buy them elsewhere, so your opinion makes a difference.

I also created a thank you page with updated links to resources along with my contact information at www.gayexplained.com/thankyou.

It is my hope that this book touched you in some way, and maybe aided your understanding a bit. I wish you all my best on your own individualistic and queer journey through this adventure we call life. And thank you, I am honored to have walked a bit of the path with you.

– Preston

Acknowledgments

One person stood by me through the long process of creating this book: Kamran Akhavan. His love, kindness, intelligence, and creative genius were invaluable support. He sat through my reading the entire book aloud from cover to cover, helped in the creation of each illustration, reasoned through countless complicated topics with me, and most importantly, provided support through the emotional waves I experienced in getting this done. In many ways I considered Kamran my outrigger, calming the waves when they got rough, and encouraging me to travel farther than I dared to dream. The dual trees of life on the cover of this book are both a design we created together and a symbol of the life we shared. Thank you, thank you, thank you.

Michael Thompson was essential in defining this project and helping it launch. Jathan Gurr was my fellow traveler and mystic cheerleader along the way. George Allen gave practical advice and support at crucial junctions. Every person in my life contributed along the way, huge thanks to all.

A special shout out goes to my test readers who reviewed early drafts and gave crucial feedback, starting with Kamran's mother and a great supporter, Laura Akhavan. Other readers included Marcia Prichas, David Hone, Carl Lindblad, Chris Pryor, Maria Christoff, Ben Ferarri-Church, Phillip Huang, Joan Balderson, Jim Schumacher, Riley Johndonnell, Canyon Jones, Trevor King, and Leo Babauta. Your feedback was invaluable and helped shape the results. Professional editorial help and encouragement from David Colin Carr, Tom Parker, and Renee Auriema, and technical assistance on self publishing from Joan Schwed. A special hug to New York book agent Tory Pryor who believed in the project from the start and worked mightily for its success.

And finally, the gods blessed me with uniquely supportive parents. A heartfelt thanks for all the love you have shared throughout my life. It has not been an easy path for any of us, but you helped me get here. I am deeply and forever grateful.

Notes

TWO **Who I Am**

1.   Spencer W. Kimball, *The Miracle of Forgiveness*, Chapter 6
2.   Stephen R. Covey, *Living the 7 Habits: Stories of Courage and Inspiration*, Simon & Schuster, 1999, p.47

THREE **Who Are We**

1.   Geoffrey Chaucer, *The Canterbury tales, from the text and with the notes and glossary of Thomas Tyrwhitt, condensed and arranged under the text*," D. Appleton & Co., 1856, p.170
2.   Chauncey George, *Gay New York: Gender, Urban Culture, and the Making of the Gay Male World, 1890-1940*, BasicBooks, 1994, p.100
3.   Steve Spencer, "Vicarious/Precarious—Bittersweet Experiences of the London Blitz," *Journal of Social Sciences*, www.united-academics.com, 2 July 2012
4.   Eve Sedgwick, *Epistemology of the Closet*, University of California Press, 1990
5.   Lisa M. Diamond, *Sexual Fluidity: Understanding Women's Love and Desire*, Harvard University Press, 2008, p. 84-85
6.   G. Rieger, J.M. Bailey, and M.L. Chivers, "Sexual arousal patterns of bisexual men," *Psychological Science*, 16, 2005, p.579-584
7.   Diamond, *Sexual Fluidity*, p.67; Christian Rudder, "The Big Lies People Tell In Online Dating," OkCupid, okcupid.com, July 7 2010
8.   G. Rieger, R.C. Savin-Williams, "The Eyes Have It: Sex and Sexual Orientation Differences in Pupil Dilation Patterns," *PLoS ONE*, plosone.org, 2012
9.   Christian Rudder, "The Big Lies People Tell In Online Dating, OkCupid, okcupid.com, July 7 2010
10.   Gary J. Gates and Newport Frank, "Special Report: 3.4% of U.S. Adults Identify as LGBT," Gallup Politics, Gallup.com, October 18 2012
11.   Katy Steinmetz, "How Many Americans Are Gay?" *Time*, www.time.com, retrieved 20 May 2016
12.   Chris, Johnson, "Exit poll: Gay voters made up 5 percent of 2012 electorate," *Washington Blade*, washingtonblade.com, November 7 2012
13.   "Pew Forum on Religion & Public Life: U.S. Religious Landscape Survey," Pew Research, pewforum.org, February 2008
14.   William J. Clinton, "A Place Called Hope," Address Accepting the Presidential Nomination at the Democratic National Convention in New York, 16 July 1992

FOUR **Ancients**

1.   Jessica Kwong, "SF gay history museum finds home, identity," *San Francisco Chronicle*, www.sfgate.com, 12 January 2011
2.   Randy P. Conner, *Blossom of Bone: Reclaiming the Connections Between Homoeroticism and the Sacred*, HarperCollins, 1993, p.23-24
3.   Helena Smith, "2,500-year-old erotic graffiti found in unlikely setting on Aegean island," *The Guardian*, www.theguardian.com, 6 July 2014
4.   Mary Mycio, "The World's Oldest Pornography, *Slate*, www.slate.com, 14 February 2013

5. Emma Blake and A. Bernard Knapp, *The Gendered Sea: Iconography, Gender, and Mediterranean Prehistory*, Blackwell Publishing, 2005

6. "First homosexual caveman found," *The Telegraph*, www.telegraph.co.uk, 6 April 2011

7. Raymond de Becker, *The Other Face of Love*, Neville Spearman, 1967, p.62

8. Greg Reeder, "Same-Sex Desire, Conjugal Constructs, and the Tomb of Niankhkhnum and Khnumhotep," *World Archaeology*, 2, 2000, p.193-208

9. Alan B. Lloyd, *Ancient Egypt: State and Society*, Oxford University Press, 2014, p.86

10. Michael Rice, *Who's Who in Ancient Egypt*, Routledge, 1999, p.194

11. Sam Ro, "The World's Biggest Cities Over Time Since 4000 BC," *Business Insider*, www.businessinsider.com, December 13 2013

12. R.I.M. Dunbar. "Coevolution of neocortical size, group size and language in humans." *Behavioral and Brain Sciences*, 16(4), 1993, p.681-735

FIVE **Shamans**

1. Miller, D. Patrick, "Visions: Malidoma Some," *Mother Jones*, www.motherjones.com, March/April 1995

2. Malidoma Patrice Some, *Of Water and the Spirit: Ritual, Magic and Initiation in the Life of an African Shaman*, Penguin Books, 1995

3. Bert H. Hoff, "Gays: Guardians of the Gates." *M.E.N. Magazine*, menweb.org, September 1993

4. David Abram, *The Spell of the Sensuous: Perception and Language in a More-Than-Human World*, Vintage Books, 1996

5. Mircea Eliade, *Shamanism: Archaic Techniques of Ecstasy*, Princeton University Press, 2004

6. Hoff, "Guardians of the Gates"

7. "The Burning Times," *ReligiousTolerance. org*, www.religioustolerance.org, retrieved 30 June 2014

8. Matthew Dowd "Searching for a Hero/Villain to Unite America," *Huffington Post*, www.huffingtonpost.com, August 25 2014

SIX **Two Spirits**

1. Will Roscoe, *The Zuni Man-Woman*, University of New Mexico Press, 1992

2. Bruce Bagemihl, *Biological Exuberance: Animal Homosexuality and Natural Diversity*, St. Martins Press, 1999, p.237

3. Alvar Nuñez Cabeza De Vaca, *The Journey of Alvar Nuñez Cabeza De Vaca (1542)*, translated by Fanny Bandelier, 1905, retrieved from PBS Archives of the West, www.pbs.org, retrieved 3 Janurary 2014

4. Sabine Lang, *Men as women, women as men: Changing gender in Native American cultures*, University of Texas Press, 1998, p.208-212

5. Ruth Underhill, *Social Organization of the Papago Indians*, Columbia University Press, 1938 cited in Andrew Calimach, "The Two-Spirit Tradition," *The World History of Male Love*, "Homosexual Traditions," www.gay-art-history.org, retrieved 1 July 2014

6. George Devereux, "Institutionalized Homosexuality of the Mohave Indians," *Human Biology*, 9, 1937, p.508-509 cited in Andrew Calimach, "The Two-Spirit Tradition," *The World History of Male Love*, "Homosexual Traditions," www.gay-art-history. org, retrieved 1 July 2014

7. Will Roscoe, "Who are the Native American Two Spirits?," Will Roscoe, www. willsworld.org, retrieved June 9 2013

8. Marc Lacey, "A Lifestyle Distinct: The Muxe of Mexico," *New York Times*, www. nytimes.com, 6 December 2008

9. Bassam Tariq, "Aziz and her dignity," *Boing Boing*, www.boingboing.net, 29 June 2010

10. National Legal Services Authority vs. Union of India, Supreme Court of India Civil Original Jurisdiction Write Petition, No.400 of 2012, Supreme Court of India, 15 April 2014

11. G.G. Bolich, *Crossdressing in Context, Vol. 4: Transgender and Religion*, Psyche's Press, 29 January 2009, p.350

12.   Lauren Greene, "Thai 'Ladyboy' Kickboxer Is Gender-Bending Knockout." *National Geographic*, nationalgeographic.com, 25 March 2004

13.   Schmidt, Johanna. "Redefining Fa'afafine: Western Discourses and the Construction of Transgenderism in Samoa," *Intersections: Gender, History and Culture in the Asian Context*, 6, 2001

14.   Tupuola Terry Tavita, "'You are special', PM tells faafafine," *Savali Newspaper*, www.savalinews.com, 8 June 2011

15.   "Kuma Hina," www.kumuhina.com, retrieved 11 April 2015

SEVEN Amazons

1.   Jose Toribio, *The Discovery of the Amazon, According to the Account of Friar Gaspar de Carvajal and Other Documents*, American Geographical Society, Kessinger Publishing, 2007

2.   Adrienne Mayor, *The Amazons: Lives and Legends of Warrior Women Across the Ancient World*, Princeton University Press, 2014, p.63

3.   Mayor, *The Amazons*, p.415

4.   Linda Grant De Pauw, *Battle Cries and Lullabies: Women in War from Prehistory to the Present*, University of Oklahoma Press, 2000, p.205

5.   Mayor, *The Amazons*, p.427-429

6.   Stanley B. Alpern, *Amazons of Black Sparta: The Women Warriors of Dahomey*, New York University Press, 1998, p.12

7.   Deuteronomy 22:5

8.   Mark Twain, *Personal Recollections of Joan of Arc*, Harper & Brothers, 1896, p.xi

9.   Alexis C. Madrigal, "Q: Why Do We Wear Pants? A: Horses," *The Atlantic*, www.theatlantic.com, 11 July 2012

10.   H.L. Mencken, *Prejudices, First Series*, Knopf, 1920, p.90

NINE Wanderers

1.   Duane A. Smith, *Rocky Mountain mining camps: the urban frontier*, University of Nebraska Press, 1974, p.223

2.   Alexander Saxton, "Blackface minstrelsy," *Inside the minstrel mask: readings in nineteenth-century blackface minstrelsy*, edited by Annemarie Bean, James V. Hatch, and Brooks McNamara, Wesleyan University Press, 1996, p.73

3.   Andy Towle, "Here is a photo of Mormon leader Brigham Young's son in drag," *Towleroad*, www.towleroad.com, August 03 2012

4.   Evelyn A. Schlatter, "Drag's a life: women, gender and cross-dressing in the nineteenth-century west," *Writing the range: race, class, and culture in the women's West*, edited by Elizabeth Jameson and Susan Armitage. University of Oklahoma Press, 1997, p.335

5.   "If There's a Man Among Ye: The Tale of Pirate Queens Anne Bonny and Mary Read," *Smithsonian Magazine*, smithsonianmag.com, 9 August 2011

TEN Ages

1.   William Armstrong Percy, *Pederasty and Pedagogy in Archaic Greece*, University of Illinois Press, 1996

2.   Percy, p.119

3.   Gabrielle Festing, *When Kings Rode to Delhi*, Lancer Publishers, Jul 19, 2008, p.139

4.   W.M. Thackston, Jr., *The Baburnama: Memoirs of Babur, Prince and Emperor*, Random House, 2007, p. 90

5.   Becker, *The Other Face of Love*, p.62

6.   Abu Nuwas, *Le Vin, le Vent, la Vie*, translated by Vincent Mansour Monteil, Sindbad, 1979, p.91

7.   Elizabeth T. Gray, *The Green Sea of Heaven: Fifty Ghazals from the Diwan of Hafiz*, White Cloud Press, 1995, p.59

8.   Becker, *The Other Face of Love*, p.65

9.   *Encyclopedia of Islam and the Muslim World*, MacMillan, 2004, p.316

10.   Najibullah Quraishi, "The Dancing Boys of Afghanistan," PBS FRONTLINE, www.pbs.org, broadcast April 2010

11. Ludwig W. Adamec, *Historical Dictionary of Afghanistan*, Scarecrow Press, 2006, p.470

12. Dharmachari Jñanavira, "Homosexuality in the Japanese Buddhist Tradition," *Western Buddhist Review*, Vol. 13, www.westernbuddhistreview.com, 2001

13. Tsuneo Watanabe and Junichi Iwata, *The Love of the Samurai: A Thousand Years of Japanese Homosexuality*, Heretic Books, 1989, p.113

14. Murasaki Shikibu, *The Tale of Genji*, Editions Artisan Devereaux, 2015

15. Diamond, *Sexual Fluidity*, p. 33

TWELVE **Lovers**

1. Louis Crompton, *Homosexuality and Civilization*, Harvard, 2006, p. 213-214

2. *Gay Histories and Cultures: An Encyclopedia, Volume 2*, George E. Haggerty, Garland Publishing, 2000, p.186

3. Arno Karlen, *Sexuality and Homosexuality*, MacDonald Publishers, 1971, p.229

4. Bret Hinsch, *The Rise of Tea Culture in China: The Invention of the Individual*, Rowman & Littlefield, 2015, p.2

5. Gaspar Da Cruz, *South China in the Sixteenth Century*, Hakluyt Society, 1953, p.224-225

6. Crompton, *Homosexuality and Civilization*, p.214

7. Crompton, *Homosexuality and Civilization*, p.215

8. "Empress Wan Rong — The Last Empress Consort of the Qing Dynasty in China." *Cultural China*, www.cultural-china.com, retrieved 4 January 2014

9. Barbara Demick, "In China, last emperor's family holds rare reunion," *Los Angeles Times*, latimes.com, 28 September 2012

10. Plato, *The Symposium*, translated by Benjamin Jowett, 1939, from The Internet Classics Archive, www.classics.mit.edu, retrieved 1 July 2014

THIRTEEN **Suppressed**

1. Crompton, *Homosexuality and Civilization*, p. 297

2. "Juan II of Castile; Enrique IV of Castile," *Encyclopedia of Homosexuality*, edited by Wayne Dynes, Garland, 1990, p.640-641

3. Javier Cortez and Mario Pecheny, *The Politics of Sexuality in Latin America*, University of Pittsburgh Press, 2010, p.61

4. Richard C. Trexler, *Sex and Conquest: Gendered violence, political order, and the European conquest of the Americas*, Cornell University Press, 1995, p.107

5. Walter L. Williams, *The Spirit and the Flesh*, Beacon Press, 1986, p.137

6. Ian Lumsden, *Machos, Maricones, and Gays*, Temple University Press, 1996, p.46

7. Crompton, *Homosexuality and Civilization*, p.319-320

8. Crompton, *Homosexuality and Civilization*, p. 316

9. Isaac Bonewits, *The Pagan Man: Priests, Warriors, Hunters, and Drummers*, Citadel, 2005, p.155

10. Pete Sigal, "The Politicization of Pederasty among the Colonial Yucatecan Maya" *Journal of the History of Sexuality*, 8 #1, July 1997, p.1-24

11. Sigal, "Politicization of Pederasty"

12. Crompton, *Homosexuality and Civilization*, p. 317

13. Peter Drucker, *Different Rainbows*, Gay Men's Press, 2000, p.44

14. David F. Greenberg, *The Construction of Homosexuality*, University Of Chicago Press, 1990, p.166

15. Greenberg, *The Construction of Homosexuality*, p.165

16. "Mexico," *Encyclopedia of Homosexuality*, p.804

FOURTEEN **Greece and Rome**

1. Editorial Board, "The Many Loves of Hercules," *World History of Male Love, Greek Mythology*, www.gay-art-history.org, 1999

2.   Christopher Harrity, "The Golden Age of Denial: Hercules, the Bisexual Demigod," *Advocate*, www.advocate.com, 14 August 2013

3.   Editorial Board, "Hercules and Hylas," World History of Male Love, *Greek Mythology*, www.gay-art-history.org, 1999

4.   Editorial Board, "Achilles and Patroclus," World History of Male Love, *Greek Mythology*, www.gay-art-history.org, 1999

5.   Crompton, *Homosexuality and Civilization*, p. 73

6.   Thomas K. Hubbard, *Homosexuality in Greece and Rome: A Sourcebook of Basic Documents*, University of California Press, 2003, p.81

7.   Paul A. Rahe, "The Annihilation of the Sacred Band at Chaeronea," *American Journal of Archaeology*, 85, no. 1 (1981): 84

8.   Nicholas J. Saunders, *Alexander's Tomb: The Two Thousand Year Obsession to Find the Lost Conquerer*, Basic Books, 2007, p.26

9.   "Sappho," Poets.org, www.poets.org, retrieved 3 April 2014

10.   Yopie Prins, *Victorian Sappho*, Princeton University Press, 1999, p.129

11.   Jane McIntosh Snyder, *The Woman and the Lyre: Women Writers in Classical Greece and Rome*, SIU Press, 1991, p.18-19

12.   Jim Powell, *The Poetry of Sappho*, Oxford University Press, 2007, p.8

13.   Valerie Estelle Frankel, *From Girl to Goddess: The Heroine's Journey through Myth and Legend*, McFarland, 2010, p.217

14.   Willis Barnstone, *Sweetbitter Love: Poems of Sappho*, Shambhala, 2006, p.xli

15.   Philip Freeman, *Julius Caesar*, Simon & Schuster, 2008, p.33

16.   David Fredrick , "Look Who's Laughing at Sex: Men and Women Viewers in the *Apodyterium* of the Suburban Baths at Pompeii," *The Roman Gaze: Vision, Power, and the Body*, The Johns Hopkins University Press, 2002, p.149-181

17.   Brian Harvey, "Graffiti from Pompeii," *Pompeiana.org*, www.pompeiana.org, retrieved 3 April 2014

18.   Andy Towle, "Robertson: USA heads for 'garbage heap of history' over gay rights,"

TowleRoad, www.towleroad.com, 18 June 2009

19.   Crompton, *Homosexuality and Civilization*, p.151

FIFTEEN **Bible**

1.   "faggot (n.2)," *Online Etymology Dictionary*, www.etymonline.com, retrieved January 4 2014

2.   Crompton, *Homosexuality and Civilization*, p.248

3.   Genesis 19:1-29

4.   Crompton, *Homosexuality and Civilization*, p.247

5.   Laurie Goodstein, "Falwell: blame abortionists, feminists and gays." *The Guardian*, theguardian.com, September 19 2001; "Hagee Says Hurricane Katrina Struck New Orleans Because It Was 'Planning A Sinful' 'Homosexual Rally'," *Think Progress*, thinkprogress.org, April 23 2008

6.   Genesis 19:1-5

7.   Alex Ginsberg, "Cop used baton to sodomize man: NYPD witness," *New York Post*, www.nypost.com, 1 February 2010

8.   Will Storr, "The rape of men: the darkest secret of war," *The Guardian*, www.theguardian.com, 16 July 2011

9.   Genesis 19:6-8

10.   Genesis 19:30-38

11.   Matthew 10:12-15 (NIV)

12.   Ezekiel 16:49 (NIV)

13.   Jude 6-7

14.   1 Corinthians 11:10

15.   Hebrews 13:2

16.   Crompton, *Homosexuality and Civilization*, p.137

17.   John Ebenezer Honeyman Thomson, *The Temple Dictionary of the Bible*, Dent, 1910, p.765

18.   1 Samuel 16: 18

19.   1 Samuel 16: 12

20.   1 Samuel 16: 23

21.   1 Samuel 18:27

22.   1 Samuel 18:4

23.   1 Samuel 20:30-32

24. 1 Samuel 20:41

25. 2 Samuel 1:25-27

26. Ruth 1:16-17 (NIV)

27. Genesis 2:24; Ruth 1:14

SIXTEEN **Renaissance**

1. Psalm 104:5 (NIV)

2. Michael Brooks, 13 *Things That Don't Make Sense: The Most Baffling Scientific Mysteries of Our Time*, Profile Books, 2010, p.81

3. Bernard Berenson, *The Florentine painters of the Renaissance*, G.P. Putnam's Sons, 1896, p.67

4. Giorgio Vasari, *The Lives of the Artists*, Penguin Books, 1965, p.270

5. Crompton, *Homosexuality and Civilization*, p.265

6. Giorgio Vasari, *Lives of the Most Eminent Painters, Sculptors, and Architects*, Volume 2, George Bell & Sons, 1907, p.252-253

7. Crompton, *Homosexuality and Civilization*, p.265

8. Crompton, *Homosexuality and Civilization*, p.287

9. Sherwin Nuland, *Leonardo da Vinci: A Life*, Penguin, 2005

10. John Addington Symonds, *The Life Of Michelangelo Buonarotti*, Kessinger Publishing, 2004, p.40

11. Ascanio Condivi, *The Life of Michelangelo*, Louisiana State University Press, 1976, p.106

12. Becker, *The Other Face of Love*, p.116

13. Michelangelo, *Love Sonnets and Madrigals to Tommaso De'Cavalieri*, translated by Michael Sullivan, Peter Owen, 1998

14. George Bull, *Michelangelo: A Biography*, Macmillan, 1998, p.322

15. Romain Rolland, *The Life of Michael Angelo*, E.P. Dutton, 1912 , p.92

16. Becker, *The Other Face of Love*, p.116

17. Howard Hibbard, *Michelangelo*, New York, 1974, p.229

18. Giovanni Dall'Orto, "Michelangelo Buonarroti," *Babilonia*, 85, January 1991, p.14–16

19. Eliakim Littell, "Vittoria Colonna," *The Living Age*, Volume 167, Living Age Company, Incorporated, 1885, p.14

20. Jed Perl, "Michelangelo's Most Haunting Drawing Comes to New York," *New Republic*, newrepublic.com, October 3 2012

21. "Roman baths inspired Michelangelo's Last Judgment," CBC News, cbc.ca, November 14 2010

22. Vasari, *The Lives of the Artists*, p.69-70

23. Crompton, *Homosexuality and Civilization*, p.254

24. Crompton, *Homosexuality and Civilization*, p.257

25. Leonard Dudley, *Information Revolutions in the History of the West*, Edward Elgar Publishing, 2008, p.103

26. Fiona Graham, "To the manor bought". BBC News, www.news.bbc.co.uk, June 5 2008

27. David Moore Bergeron, *King James and Letters of Homoerotic Desire*, University of Iowa Press, 1999

28. John Boswell, *Christianity, Social Tolerance, and Homosexuality: Gay People in Western Europe from the Beginning of the Christian Era to the Fourteenth Century*, University of Chicago Press, 2009, p.231

29. Nigel Saul, *Richard II*, Yale University Press, 1999, p.332

30. Steven Leigh Morris, "Royal Pains: King Richard II and Power," *LA Weekly*, www.laweekly.com, August 8 2007

31. Kirsten Cronn-Mills, *Transgender Lives: Complex Stories, Complex Voices*, Lerner Publishing Group, 2014, p.39

32. For more, see Michael Joseph Gross, "The Vatican's Secret Life," *Vanity Fair*, www.vanityfair.com, December 2013

SEVENTEEN **Greats**

1. Walt Whitman, *Leaves of Grass: The First Edition (1855)*, Digireads.com Publishing, 2008, p.85

2.   Whitman, *Leaves of Grass, First Edition*, p.5

3.   Walt Whitman, *Leaves of Grass: The Death Bed Edition*, Digireads.com Publishing, 2008, p.233

4.   Whitman, *Leaves of Grass, Death Bed Edition*, p.91

5.   Whitman, *Leaves of Grass, Death Bed Edition*, p.88

6.   Rictor Norton, "Walt Whitman, Prophet of Gay Liberation", *Gay History and Literature*, 18 November 1999, retrieved from www.rictornorton.co.uk 10 August 2014

7.   Walt Whitman, *Leaves of Grass: The Death Bed Edition*, Digireads.com Publishing, 2008, p.98

8.   Whitman, *Leaves of Grass, Death Bed Edition*, p. 98

9.   Jonathan Ned Katz, *Love Stories: Sex Between Men Before Homosexuality*, University of Chicago Press, 2003, p.111

10.   Tripp, p.39-43 (Spelling and capitalization modernized by the author)

11.   Herman Melville, *Moby Dick: Or The Whale*, Scribner, 1902, p.13

12.   Tripp, p.47-48

13.   Jonathan Ned Katz, *Love Stories: Sex Between Men Before Homosexuality*, University of Chicago Press, 2001, p.9

14.   Carl Sandburg, *Abraham Lincoln: The Prairie Years*, Harcourt Brace & Company, 1927, p.264

15.   Dinitia Smith, "Finding Homosexual Threads in Lincoln's Legend," *New York Times*, nytimes.com, 16 December 2004

16.   Smith, "Finding Homosexual Threads in Lincoln's Legend," p.392

17.   Larry Flynt and David Eisenbach, *One Nation Under Sex: How the Private Lives of Presidents, First Ladies and Their Lovers Changed the Course of American History*, Macmillan, 2011, p.50

18.   George Ticknor Curtis, *Life of James Buchanan: fifteenth President of the United States, Volume 1*, Harper & Brothers, 1883, p.519

19.   S.I. Salamensky, *The Modern Art of Influence and the Spectacle of Oscar Wilde*, Palgrave Macmillan, 2012, p.141

20.   Salamensky, *The Spectacle of Oscar Wilde*, p.142

21.   Michael S. Foldy, *The Trials of Oscar Wilde Deviance, Morality and Late-Victorian Society*, Yale University Press, 1997, p.47

22.   Gyles Brandreth, *Oscar Wilde and the Murders at Reading Gaol: A Mystery*, Simon and Schuster, 2013, p.238

23.   Oscar Wilde, *De Profundis*, Victoria Institutions, 2008, p.11

24.   Ashley H. Robins, *Oscar Wilde, the Great Drama of His Life: How His Tragedy Reflected His Personality*, Apollo Books, 2011, p.143

25.   Paul Russell, *The Gay 100: A Ranking of the Most Influential Gay Men and Lesbians, Past and Present*, Kensington Books, 2002, p.117-120

26.   David Hilliard, "Newman, John Henry," *Who's who in Gay and Lesbian History: From Antiquity to World War II*, edited by Robert Aldrich and Garry Wotherspoon, Psychology Press, 2002, p.384-385

27.   Tim Jeal, *Baden-Powell: Founder of the Boy Scouts*, Yale University Press, Feb 12, 2007, p.94

EIGHTEEN   Heroes

1.   Kenneth Borris, *Same-Sex Desire in the English Renaissance: A Sourcebook of Texts, 1470-1650*, Routledge, 2003, p.107-108

2.   D. Michael Quinn, *Same-Sex Dynamics Among Nineteenth-Century Americans: A Mormon Example*, University of Illinois Press, 2001, p.269

3.   Quinn, *Same-Sex Dynamics*, p.415

4.   Katherine Joslin, *Jane Addams: A Writer's Life*, University of Illinois Press, 2004, p.11

5.   Ace Collins, *Stories Behind the Hymns That Inspire America: Songs That Unite Our Nation*, Zondervan, 2009, p.25

6.   "America the Beautiful," words by Katharine Lee Bates 1895, melody by Samuel Ward 1882

7. Judith Schwarz, "Yellow Clover: Katharine Lee Bates and Katharine Coman," *Frontiers: A Journal of Women's Studies*, 4:1, Spring 1979, p.59–67

8. Jennie Rothenberg, "But Were They Gay? The Mystery of Same-Sex Love in the 19th Century," *The Atlantic*, theatlantic.com, September 7 2012

9. James R. Mellow, "The Stein Salon Was The First Museum of Modern Art," *New York Times*, nytimes.com, December 1 1968

10. Elizabeth D. Heineman, "Sexuality and Nazism: the Doubly Unspeakable?" *Sexuality and German Fascism*, edited by Dagmar Herzog, Berghahn Books, 2005, p.35

11. Kate Connolly, "Germany remembers gay victims of the Nazis," *The Guardian*, www.theguardian.com, 27 May 2008

12. George Dyson, *Turing's Cathedral: The Origins of the Digital Universe*, Vintage, 2012

13. Leigh Eason, "Gay, Black, and Quaker: History catches up with Bayard Rustin," *Religion Dispatches*, www.religiondispaches. org, 25 June 2012

14. Joseph Lelyveld, *Great Soul: Mahatma Gandhi and His Struggle with India*, Knopf, March 29 2011, p.89

NINETEEN Liberation

1. Susan Stryker and Jim Van Buskirk, *Gay by the Bay: A History of Queer Culture in the San Francisco Bay Area*, Chronicle Books, 1996, p.30

2. Stryker and Buskirk, *Gay by the Bay*, p.29-30

3. Allen Ginsberg, *Howl and Other Poems: Pocket Poets Number 4*, City Lights Books, 1956, p.9

4. Ginsberg, *Howl*, p.13

5. Catherine A. Davies, *Whitman's Queer Children: America's Homosexual Epics*, Bloomsbury Publishing, 2012, p.112

6. George Judson, "Naked Lunches and Reality Sandwiches: How the Beats Beat the First Amendment," *New York Times*, www. nytimes.com, 1997

7. Randy Shilts, *The Mayor of Castro Street*, St. Martin's Press, 1982, p.47-48,52

8. Shilts, *The Mayor of Castro Street*, p.57-58

9. Eric Slade, *Hope Along the Wind: The Life of Harry Hay*, documentary film, 2002

10. Betsy Kuhn, *Gay Power!: The Stonewall Riots and the Gay Rights Movement, 1969*, Twenty-First Century Books, 2011, p.42

11. Frank Kameny, "Gay is Good, Godly and American," Letter of the Week, *WND*, www.wnd.com, 7 October 2009

12. Jonathan Rauch, "A Pariah's Triumph— and America's," *The Atlantic*, www.theatlantic. com, December 2006

13. David Carter, *Stonewall: The Riots That Sparked the Gay Revolution*, Macmillan, May 25, 2010, p.150-151,205

14. Eliel Cruz, "Remembering Brenda: An Ode to the 'Mother of Pride'," *The Advocate*, www.advocate.com, 17 June 2014

15. Will O'Bryan, "Gay Is Good: How Frank Kameny changed the face of America," *Metro Weekly*, www.metroweekly.com, 4 October 2006

16. Laura Hibbard, "Leonard Matlovich Tombstone: Gay Vietnam Veteran's Grave Resurfaces In Reddit Online Discussion," *The Huffington Post*, www.huffingtonpost.com, 2 May 2012

17. Betsy Kuhn, *Gay Power!: The Stonewall Riots and the Gay Rights Movement, 1969*, Twenty-First Century Books, 1 January 2011, p.103

18. Shilts, *The Mayor of Castro Street*, p.374

19. Molefi K. Asante and Abu Shardow Abarry, *African Intellectual Heritage: A Book of Sources*, Temple University Press, 1996, p.775

20. Elijah Wald, *Josh White: Society Blues*, Routledge, Dec 16, 2013, p.42

21. Arnold Rampersad, *The Life of Langston Hughes: Volume II: 1914-1967, I Dream a World*, Oxford University Press, Nov 30, 2001, p.336

22. Henry Louis Gates, Jr., *Tradition and the Black Atlantic: Critical Theory in the African Diaspora*, Basic Civitas Books, 2010, p.57

TWENTY AIDS

1. "Timeline: HIV & AIDS," John Pickrell, *New Scientist*, newscientist.com, September 4 2006

2. Randy Shilts, "In Cold Blood," *Mother Jones Magazine*, November 1987, p.46

3. Jon Cohen, *Shots in the Dark: The Wayward Search for an AIDS Vaccine*, W.W. Norton & Company, January 2001

4. Karen Ocamb, "Ronald Reagan's Real Legacy: Death, Heartache and Silence Over AIDS," *FrontiersLA*, frontiersla.com, 6 February 2011

5. Matthew Gallaway, "A Chat With Fran Lebowitz," *The Awl*, www.theawl.com, 2 October 2012

6. Helen Briggs, "HIV 'may have an ancient origin'," BBC News, bbc.co.uk, January 25 2013

7. Daniel K.W. Chu, et al, "MERS Coronaviruses in Dromedary Camels, Egypt," *Emerging Infectious Diseases*, 20:6, www.cdc.gov, June 2014

8. Karen J. Carlson, Stephanie A. Eisenstat, and Terra Diane Ziporyn, *The New Harvard Guide to Women's Health*, Harvard University Press, 2004, p.546

9. Roy Greenslade, "Liberace, the Daily Mirror and a libel trial fiasco…," *The Guardian*, www.theguardian.com, 12 June 2013

10. John Gallagher, "Silence = Stigma," *The Advocate*, 7 February 1995, p.31

11. Dana Milbank, "A Senator's Wide Stance: 'I Am Not Gay,'" *The Washington Post*, wwww.washingtonpost.com, 29 August 2007

12. "HIV infection rate in the US falls by a third in a decade," BBC, www.bbc.com, 19 July 2014

13. Anthony S. Fauci, "No more excuses. We have the tools to end the HIV/AIDS pandemic," *Washington Post*, www.washingtonpost.com, 8 January 2016

14. Ashley H. Robins, *Oscar Wilde — The Great Drama of His Life: How His Tragedy Reflected His Personality*, Apollo Books, 2012, p.132

TWENTY-ONE Now

1. Maureen, Dowd, "An Odd Couple Defends Couples That Some (Oddly) Find Odd," *New York Times*, www.nytimes.com, January 16 2010

2. *Tora! Tora! Tora!* Quotes, IMDb, www.imdb.com, retrieved 11 March 2016

3. "2014 MTV/David Binder Research Study," MTV's Look Different, www.research.lookdifferent.org, 2014, retrieved 11 April 2015

TWENTY-TWO Seeing

1. Maria Popova, "Isaac Asimov on Science and Creativity in Education," *Brain Pickings*, www.brainpickings.org, retrieved 11 August 2014

2. Jacques Steinberg, "After Press Dinner, the Blogosphere Is Alive With the Sound of Colbert Chatter," *New York Times*, www.nytimes.com, 3 May 2006

3. Roughgarden, *Evolution's Rainbow*, p.26-27

4. W.J. Tennent, "A note on the apparent lowering of moral standards in the Lepidoptera," *Entomologist's Record and Journal of Variation*, 99, 1987; p.81–83

5. Antoine de Saint-Exupéry, *The Little Prince*, Harcourt Brace Jovanovich, 1971 p.87

6. Gil Troy, *Moynihan's Moment: America's Fight Against Zionism as Racism*, Oxford University Press, 2013, p.194

7. Isaac Asimov and Robert Silverberg, *Nightfall*, Random House, 9 November 2011. p.93

TWENTY-THREE Animal Sexuality

1. Edward H. Jeter, "Seagulls and Crickets," *Mormonism: A Historical Encyclopedia*, edited by W. Paul Reeve and Ardis E. Parshall, ABC-CLIO, 2010, p.111

2. Geoff R. MacFarlane, Simon P. Blomberg, and Paul L. Vasey, "Homosexual behaviour in birds: frequency of expression is related to parental care disparity in the sexes,"

Animal Behaviour, 80(3), September 1 2010, p.376

3. Bagemihl, *Biological Exuberance*, p.415
4. Anne Perkins and Charles E. Roselli, "The Ram as a Model for Behavioral Neuroendocrinology," *Hormonal Behavior*, 52(1), June 2007, p.7-77
5. Bagemihl, *Biological Exuberance*, p.221
6. Bagemihl, *Biological Exuberance*, p.82
7. Bagemihl, *Biological Exuberance*, p.221
8. Bagemihl, *Biological Exuberance*, p.378-381
9. Bagemihl, *Biological Exuberance*, *p.415*
10. Bagemihl, *Biological Exuberance*, p.413-416
11. Bagemihl, *Biological Exuberance*, p.432-5
12. Bagemihl, *Biological Exuberance*, p.427-430
13. Bagemihl, *Biological Exuberance*, p.391-393
14. Bagemihl, *Biological Exuberance*, p.269
15. Ryan Christopher, "7 Things Bonobos Can Teach Us About Love and Sex," *Psychology Today*, Febrary 15 2012
16. Joan Roughgarden, *Evolution's Rainbow*, University of California Press, 2009, p.157-8
17. Roughgarden, *Evolution's Rainbow*,p.157
18. Bagemihl, *Biological Exuberance*, p.276-335
19. Brandon Keim, "Whales Might Be as Much Like People as Apes Are," *Wired*, www.wired.com, 25 June 2009
20. Bagemihl, *Biological Exuberance*, p.339-348
21. Jennifer Viegas, "Dolphins - Living Loose in the Ocean," *Discovery News*, news.discovery.com, March 27 2012
22. Bagemihl, *Biological Exuberance*, p.342-347
23. Bagemihl, *Biological Exuberance*, p.350
24. Bagemihl, *Biological Exuberance*, p.374-377
25. Bagemihl, *Biological Exuberance*, p.33-4
26. David E Featherstone et al, "A glial amino-acid transporter controls synapse strength and courtship in Drosophila," *Nature*

Neuroscience, www.nature.com, 9 December 2007, p.54-61
27. Shasha Zhanga et al, "Serotonin signaling in the brain of adult female mice is required for sexual preference," *Proceedings of the National Academy of Sciences*, www.pnas.org, 30 April 2013
28. Jon Mooallem, "Can Animals Be Gay?" *New York Times*, www.nytimes.com, 31 March 2010
29. Bagemihl, *Biological Exuberance*, p.488
30. "Long-lost study reveals 'sexual depravity' in penguins," ABC, www.abc.net.au, 12 Jun 2012
31. Bagemihl, *Biological Exuberance*, p.524-527
32. Bagemihl, *Biological Exuberance*, p.657-663

TWENTY-FOUR **Animal Gender**

1. Stephen R. Palumbi and Anthony R. Palumbi, *The Extreme Life of the Sea*, Princeton University Press, 2014, p.141-142
2. Roughgarden, *Evolution's Rainbow*, p.30-35
3. Roughgarden, *Evolution's Rainbow*, p.75-93
4. Roughgarden, *Evolution's Rainbow*, p.38-39
5. Helen Thompson, "In This Community of Brazilian Cave Insects, Females Wear the Penises, Literally," *Smithsonian Magazine*, www.smithsonianmag.com, 17 April 2014
6. James Gorman, "Amorous Squid Seeks Partner: Any Sex Will Do," *New York Times*, www.nytimes.com, 20 September 2011
7. Rolanda Lange et al, "Female Fitness Optimum at Intermediate Mating Rates under Traumatic Mating," *PLOS One*, www.plosone.org, 22 August 2012
8. Ella Davies, "Antarctic molluscs 'switch sex'," *BBC Nature*, www.bbc.co.uk, 11 September 2012
9. Katherine Harmon, "No Sex Needed: All-Female Lizard Species Cross Their Chromosomes to Make Babies," *Scientific*

American, www.scientificamerican.com, 21 February 2010

10. Brian Switek, "Virgin births seen in wild vipers," *Nature*, www.nature.com, 12 September 2012

11. David M. Hillis, "Rare gene capture in predominantly androgenetic species," *Proceedings of the National Academy of Sciences of the United States of America*, www.pnas.org, 27 April 2011

12. Christopher Jobson, Spectacular Genetic Anomaly Results in Butterflies with Male and Female Wings, *Colossal*, www.thisiscolossal.com, 28 April 2014

13. David George Haskell, "Nature's Case for Same-Sex Marriage," *New York Times*, www.nytimes.com, 29 March 2013

14. Roughgarden, *Evolution's Rainbow*, p.27

TWENTY-FIVE Evolution

1. Walter D. Koenig, *Population Ecology of the Cooperatively Breeding Acorn Woodpecker*, Princeton University Press, 1987

2. Paul L. Vasey, "Pre- and Postconflict Interactions Between Female Japanese Macaques During Homosexual Consortships," *International Journal of Comparative Psychology*, 17(4), 2004, p.351-359

3. Nathan W. Bailey and Marlene Zuk, "Same-sex sexual behavior and evolution," *Trends in Ecology & Evolution*, Volume 24, Issue 8, August 2009, p439-446

4. John Cloud, "Why Some Animals (and People) Are Gay," *Time*, www.time.com, 19 June 2009

5. Hans Van Gossum et al, "Reversible switches between male–male and male–female mating behaviour by male damselflies," *Biology Letters*, 1(3), www.ncbi.nlm,nih.gov, 22 Sep 2005, p.268–270

6. Sarah Spickernell, "Homosexuality 'is an essential part of evolution', say scientists - in hunter-gatherer days, it was an advantage to be bisexual," *City A.M.*, www.cityam.com, 25 November 2014

7. Bagemihl, *Biological Exuberance*, p.261

TWENTY-SIX Genetics

1. "No Single Gene For Eye Color, Researchers Prove," *Science Daily*, www.sciencedaily.com, February 25, 2007

2. J. Michael Bailey and Richard C. Pillard, "A Genetic Study of Male Sexual Orientation," *Archives of General Psychiatry*, 48, December 1991, p.1089-1096

3. S. Hu et al., "Linkage between sexual orientation and chromosome Xq28 in males but not in females," *Nature Genetics*, 11, 1995, p.248-256

4. G. Rice et al., "Male homosexuality: absence of linkage to microsatellite markers at Xq28," *Science*, 284, 1999, p.665–667

5. Andy Coghlan, "Largest study of gay brothers homes in on 'gay genes'," *New Scientist*, 15:48, www.newscientist.com, 17 November 2014

6. Megan Erickson, "Dirty Minds: The Neurobiology of Love," *Big Think*, www.bigthink.com, March 11 2012

7. Jason Koebler, "Scientists May Have Finally Unlocked Puzzle of Why People Are Gay," *US News & World Report*, www.usnews.com, December 11 2012

8. S. Bocklandt et al., "Extreme skewing of X chromosome inactivation in mothers of homosexual men," *Human Genetics*, 118, 2006, p.691–694

9. Randy Dotinga, "Moms' Genetics Might Help Produce Gay Sons," *HealthDay News*, www.healthday.com, 21 February 2006

10. Clara Moskowitz, "Why Gays Don't Go Extinct," *LiveScience*, www.livesience.com, 17 June 2008

11. Sergey Gavrilets and William R. Rice, "Genetic models of homosexuality: generating testable predictions," *Proceedings of the Royal Society B: Biological Sciences*, 273, 2006, p.3031–3038

12. Natalie Wolchover, "Why Are There Gay Men?," *LiveScience*, www.livescience.com, 11 June 2012

13. Simon LeVay, "The Paradox of Gay Genes," *Huffington Post*, huffingtonpost.com, 12 October 2012

14.   R.C. Pillard and J.M. Bailey, "Human sexual orientation has a heritable component," *Human Biology*, 70, 1998, p.347–365

15.   "The 'liberal gene': An instant guide," *The Week*, theweek.com, 29 October 2010

16.   Springer, "Prevalence of homosexuality in men is stable throughout time since many carry the genes: Computer model sheds light on how male homosexuality remains present in populations throughout the ages," *ScienceDaily*, sciencedaily.com, 12 April 2016

TWENTY-SEVEN **Physiology**

1.   R. Blanchard and A.F. Bogaert, "Proportion of homosexual men who owe their sexual orientation to fraternal birth order: an estimate based on two national probability samples," *American Journal of Human Biology*, 16, 2004, p.151–157; R. Blanchard, "Quantitative and theoretical analyses of the relation between older brothers and homosexuality in men," *Journal of Theoretical Biology*, 230, 2004, p.173–187

2.   Simon LeVay et al., "A Difference in Hypothalamic Structure Between Heterosexual and Homosexual Men," *Science*, June 1991

3.   Ivanka Savic-Berglund and Per Lindström, "PET and MRI Show Differences in Cerebral Asymmetry and Functional Connectivity Between Homo- and Heterosexual Subjects," *Proceedings of the National Academy of Sciences of the United States of America*, June 16, 2008

4.   "Gay Men's Bilateral Brains Better at Remembering Faces, Study Finds," *ScienceDaily*, sciencedaily.com, 24 June 2010

5.   M.L. Lalumière, R. Blanchard R, and K.J. Zucker, "Sexual orientation and handedness in men and women: a meta-analysis," *Psychological Bulletin*, 126(4), July 2000, p. 575-92; B.S. Mustanski, J. Bailey, and S. Kaspar, "Dermatoglyphics, handedness, sex, and sexual orientation," *Archives of Sexual Behavior*, 31, 2002, p.113–122; R.A. Lippa, "Handedness, sexual orientation, and gender-related personality traits in men and women," *Archives of Sexual Behavior*, 32, 2003,

p.103–114; R. Blanchard et al, "Interaction of fraternal birth order and handedness in the development of male homosexuality," *Hormones and Behavior*, 49, 2006, p.405–414

6.   S. Marc Breedlove et al, "Finger-length ratios and sexual orientation," *Nature*, 404, 2000, p.455–456

7.   J.A.Y. Hall and D. Kimura, "Dermatoglyphic asymmetry: Relation to sex, handedness and cognitive pattern," *Behavioral Neuroscience*, 108, 1994, p.1203-1206

8.   J.T. Martin and D.H. Nguyen, "Anthropometric analysis of homosexuals and heterosexuals: implications for early hormone exposure," *Hormones and Behavior*, 45, 2004, p.31-39

9.   Anthony Bogaert, "The Relation Between Sexual Orientation and Penile Size," *Archives of Sexual Behavior*, June 1999

10.   Dennis McFadden and Edward G. Pasanen, "Comparison of the auditory systems of heterosexuals and homosexuals: Click-evoked otoacoustic emissions," *Proceedings of the National Academy of Sciences*, 95(5), March 1998, p.2709-2713

11.   "Are Lesbians Earmarked?" *The Advocate*, 14 April 1998, p.14

12.   Qazi Rahman et al, "Sexual orientation-related differences in prepulse inhibition of the human startle response," *Behavioral Neuroscience*, 117(5), October 2003, p.1096-1102

13.   Ivanka Savic and Per Lindström, "PET and MRI show differences in cerebral asymmetry and functional connectivity between homo- and heterosexual subjects," *Proceedings of the National Academy of Sciences of the United States of America*, www.pnas.org, 16 June 2008

14.   Charles Wysocki, et al, "Preference for Human Body Odors Is Influenced by Gender and Sexual Orientation," *Psychological Science*, 16(9), September 2005, p.694-701

15.   Amar J.S. Klar, "Excess of counterclockwise scalp hair-whorl rotation in homosexual men," *Journal of Genetics*, 83(3), December 2004, p.251

16.   John H. McDonald, *Myths of Human Genetics*, Sparky House Publishing, 2011, p.40-45

TWENTY-EIGHT **Psychology**

1.   J.M. Bailey and K. Darwood, "Behavioral genetics, sexual orientation, and family," *Lesbian, gay, and bisexual identies in families: Psychological perspectives*, Oxford University Press, 1998, p.3-18

2.   "Submission to the Church of England's Listening Exercise on Human Sexuality," Royal College of Psychiatrists, rcpsych.ac.uk, retrieved 4 January 2014

3.   Hollingsorth v Perry, 570, US, 12-144

4.   Evelyn Hooker, "The adjustment of the male overt homosexual," *Journal of Projective Techniques*, Vol. 21, 1957, p.18-31

5.   Richard A. Lippa, "The Gay-Straight Divide," National Sexuality Resource Center (NSRC), nsrc.sfsu.edu, 8 April 2008, retrieved 28 August 2009

6.   Frank Vyan Walton, "Boies: Under oath is a lonely place to Lie!" *Daily Kos*, www. dailykos.com, 8 August 2010

7.   Alex Dobuzinskis, "Former foe of gay marriage in California now favors unions," *Chicago Tribune*, chicagotribune.com, 23 June 2012

TWENTY-NINE **Cures**

1.   Jeff Laver, "Mormon & Gay," *Affirmation*, affirmation.org, October 2000

2.   Benedict Carey, "Psychiatry Giant Sorry for Backing Gay 'Cure,'" *New York Times*, www.nytimes.com, 18 May 2012

3.   Dave Rattigan, "Joseph Nicolosi Responds to Exodus Reparative Therapy Claims" *Ex-Gay Watch*, exgaywatch.com, 19 July 2012

4.   Jim Burroway, "Kirk's Life Has Now Been Used For Good, to Help Save Lives of Kids 'Just Like Him'" *Box Turtle Bulletin*, www. boxturtlebulletin.com, 1 October 2012

5.   "Position Statement on Psychiatric Treatment and Sexual Orientation," American Psychiatric Association, www.psychiatry.org, December 1998

6.   "Psychologists Reject Gay 'Therapy'," *New York Times*, nytimes.com, 5 August 5 2009

7.   Steve Lee, "35 years of prayer couldn't get rid of my homosexuality. My name is Steve and I am an Ex Mormon," *YouTube*, www. youtube.com, 8 July 2011

THIRTY **Homophobia**

1.   Henry E. Adams et al, "Is homophobia associated with homosexual arousal?" *Journal of Abnormal Psychology*, 105(3), August 1996, p.440-445

2.   *Ibid.*

3.   Joshua G. Rosenberger JG et al, "Sexual behaviors and situational characteristics of most recent male-partnered sexual event among gay and bisexually identified men in the United States." *The Journal of Sexual Medicine*, Volume 8, Issue 11, November 2011, p.3040–3050

4.   Robin Bell, "Homosexual men and women". *BMJ*, bmj.com, 318(7181), February 13 1999, p. 452–455

5.   "Nancy Elliott, Anti-Gay Lawmaker, Describes Anal Sex During Public Hearing: 'Wriggling' Around 'In Excrement,'" *Huffington Post*, www.huffingtonpost.com, 10 April 2010

6.   Selcuk Sirin et al, "Differential Reactions to Men and Women's Gender Role Transgressions: Perceptions of Social Status, Sexual Orientation, and Value Dissimilarity," *The Journal of Men's Studies*, 12(2), 2004, p.119-132

7.   Miller McPherson et al, "Social Isolation in America: Changes in Core Discussion Networks over Two Decades," *American Sociological Review*, 71:June:335-375, 2006

8.   Lisa Wade, "American men's hidden crisis: They need more friends!" *Salon*, www.salon.com, 7 December 2013; and Katy Waldman, "Society Tells Men That Friendship Is Girly. Men Respond by Not Having Friends," *Slate*, www.slate.com, 9 December 2013

THIRTY-ONE Healing

1. Ken Wilber, *A Brief History of Everything*, Shambala Publications, 1996, p.230-232
2. *Wikiquote*, www.en.wikiquote.org, sources quote to Arthur H. Secord, "Condensed History Lesson", *Readers' Digest*, 38(226), February 1941

THIRTY-TWO Love and Sex

1. Robert A. Johnson, *Inner Work: Using Dreams and Active Imagination for Personal Growth*, Harper & Row, 1988
2. Stuart Timmons, *The Trouble With Harry Hay: Founder of the Modern Gay Movement*, Alyson Publications, 1990, p.36
3. Dan Savage, "Wiggle Room," *Savage Love*, www.thestranger.com, 25 February 2010
4. Christian Rudder, "Gay Sex vs. Straight Sex, *OKTrends*, blog.okcupid.com, 12 October 2010
5. Ayako Miyashita and Gary J. Gates, "UPDATE: Effects of Lifting Blood Donation Bans on Men who Have Sex with Men," Williams Institute, www.williamsinstitute.law. ucla.edu, September 2014
6. Mary Emily O'Hara, Rejoice, lesbians: 'bed death' isn't actually a thing, The Daily Dot, www.dailydot.com, 7 April 2015
7. Charlotte Alter, "Exclusive: Millennials More Tolerant of Premarital Sex, But Have Fewer Partners," *Time*, www.time.com, 5 May 2015
8. Dan Avery, "Lounge Legend Tony Bennett Owes His Enduring Fame To A Homesick Gay Couple," *Queerty*, www. queerty.com, 22 February 2012

THIRTY-THREE Gender

1. Amanda Schaffer, "Pas de Deux: Why Are There Only Two Sexes?," *Slate*, slate. com, September 27 2007; Laurence D. Hurst, "Why are There Only Two Sexes?"; *Proceedings of the Royal Society B: Biological Sciences*, 263(1369), p.415; E.S. Haag, "Why two sexes? Sex determination in multicellular organisms and protistan mating types,"

Seminars in cell & developmental biology, 18(3), 2007, p.348-9
2. Anne Fausto-Sterling et al, "How sexually dimorphic are we? Review and synthesis," *American Journal of Human Biology*, 12, 2000, p.151-166
3. Mike Hurst, "Caster Semenya has male sex organs and no womb or ovaries," *Daily Telegraph*, www.dailytelegraph.com.au, 11 September 2009
4. "Report Says Stella Walsh; Had Male Sex Organs," *The New York Times*, nytimes.com, 23 January 1981
5. Amanda Schaffer, "Gender Games," *Slate*, www.slate.com, 25 July 2012
6. Richard E. Jones and Kristin H. Lopez, *Human Reproductive Biology*, Academic Press, 2013, p.87-102
7. Ben Mauk, "Why Do Men Have Nipples?," *LiveScience*, www.livescience.com, February 01, 2013
8. Richard E. Jones and Kristin H. Lopez, *Human Reproductive Biology*, Academic Press, 2013, p.87-102
9. Chuck Hadad, Susan Chun, and Dana Ford, "Transgender ex-Navy SEAL lives in 'gray world,'" *CNN*, www.cnn.com, 4 September 2014
10. Heather Havrilesky, "The Bruce Jenner Interview Was a Triumph," *New York Magazine*, www.nymag.com, 25 April 2015
11. Rachel McRady, "Laverne Cox: Bruce Jenner Told Me the Diane Sawyer Interview 'Is Like Another Gold Medal,'" *US Magazine*, www.usmagazine.com, 27 April 2015
12. "Lana Wachowski receives the HRC Visibility Award," Human Rights Campaign YouTube video, www.youtube.com, 24 October 2012
13. Tracy Baim, "Second Wachowski filmmaker sibling comes out as trans," *Windy City Times*, www.windycitymediagroup.com, 3 August 2016
14. Luke Brinker and Carlos Maza, "15 Experts Debunk Right-Wing Transgender Bathroom Myth," Media Matters for America, www.mediamatters.org, 20 March 2014

15. Katharine Hepburn and Susan Crimp, *Katharine Hepburn Once Said...: Great Lines to Live By*, HarperCollins, 2003, p.30

THIRTY-FOUR Authenticity

1. J. Krishnamurti, "On Right Livelihood," *J. Krishnamurti Online*, www.jkrishnamurti.org, retrieved 31 March 2016

1. George Chauncey, *Gay New York*, Basic Books, 1994, p.6-8

2. "Robert Eichberg, 50, Gay Rights Leader," *New York Times*, nytimes.com, 15 August 1995; Rob Eichberg, *Coming Out: An Act of Love*, Dutton, 30 October 1990

3. Oscar Wilde, *The Picture of Dorian Gray*, Plain Label Books, 1945, p.40

4. Susie Steiner, "Top five regrets of the dying," *The Guardian*, theguardian.com, February 1 2012

THIRTY-FIVE Ethics

1. William Saletan, "Sodom and Greensboro," *Slate*, www.slate.com, 8 May 2012

2. Judith Martin, *Miss Manners Rescues Civilization: From Sexual Harassment, Frivolous Lawsuits, Dissing, and Other Lapses in Civility*, Crown Publishers, 1996, p.174

3. George Lakoff, *Moral Politics: How Liberals and Conservatives Think, Second Edition*, University of Chicago Press, 2010, p.33-36

4. Robert Barnes, "Supreme Court asked to revive Virginia's anti-sodomy law," *Washington Post*, www.washingtonpost.com, 18 August 2013

5. James Boswell, *The Life of Samuel Johnson, Volume 1*, Routledge, Warne, and Routledge, 1865, p.274

6. Luke 10:25-37

THIRTY-SIX Military

1. Brendan McGarry, "Troops oppose repeal of 'don't ask,'" *Military Times*, www.militarytimes.com, 26 December 2008

2. "Supporting the 1993 Law that Protects Morale and Readiness," *Flag &*

General Officers for the Military, www.flagandgeneralofficersforthemilitary.com, retrieved 14 August 2014

3. Fran Lebowitz, *Public Speaking*, documentary, directed by Martin Scorsese, HBO, www.hbo.com, 2010

4. Lila Shapiro, "One Year Out: An Assessment of DADT Repeal's Impact on Military Readiness," Palm Center, University of California Los Angeles Law School, 20 September 2012

5. "We're Gay, Get Over It," *Marine Corps Times*, www.militarytimes.com, 13 September 2011

6. Elisabeth Bumiller, "Marines Hit the Ground Running in Seeking Recruits at Gay Center," *New York Times*, www.nytimes.com, 20 September 2011

THIRTY-SEVEN Children

1. Maria Cora, *Queer Ancestors Project*, Author's notes, November 2012

2. William Saletan, "A Liberal War on Science?" *Slate*, www.slate.com, 14 June 2012

3. C.J. Patterson and R.E. Redding, "Lesbian and gay families with children: Implications of social science research for policy," *Journal of Social Issues*, 52(3), 1996, p.29-50

4. J.L. Wainright, S.T. Russell, and C.J. Patterson, "Psychosocial adjustment, school outcomes, and romantic relationships of adolescents with same-sex parents," Child Development, 75(6), November-December 2004, p.1886-1898

5. Wainright et al, 2004

6. J.M. Bailey et al, "Sexual orientation of adult sons of gay fathers," *Developmental Psychology*, 31(1), January 1995, p.124-129

7. Fiona L. Tasker and Susan Golombok, *Growing up in a lesbian family*, Guilford Press, 1997

8. Michael J. Rosenfeld, "Nontraditional families and childhood progress through school," *Demography*, 47(3), August 2010, p.755-775

9. "Children raised by same-sex couples healthier and happier, research suggests," ABC, www.abc.net.au, 4 July 2014

10. Eyal Abraham, "Father's brain is sensitive to childcare experiences," *Proceedings of the National Academy of Sciences of the United States of America*, 111:27 p.9792–9797, www.pnas.org, 1 May 2014

11. Colleen Hoff et al, "The impact of parenting on gay male couples' relationships, sexuality, and HIV risk," *Couple and Family Psychology: Research and Practice*, 1(2), June 2012, p.106-119

12. "ASA Files Amicus Brief with U.S. Supreme Court in Same-Sex Marriage Cases," American Sociological Association, press release, 28 February 2013

13. Daniel Hernandez, "Mexican singer Paquita la del Barrio on gay adoption: 'It's better that the child die,'" *Los Angeles Times*, www.latimes.com, 17 March 2010

14. Post on *Boy, Interrupted*, redzilla.org.uk, retrieved 6 January 2014

15. Jessica Garrison, "A Prop. 8 fight over schools," *Los Angeles Times*, www.latimes.com, 19 October 2008

16. Nicolas Ray, "Lesbian, Gay, Bisexual and Transgender Youth: An Epidemic of Homelessness" National Gay and Lesbian Task Force, thetaskforce.org, 2006

17. Alex Morris, "The Forsaken: A Rising Number of Homeless Gay Teens Are Being Cast Out by Religious Families, Rolling Stone, www.rollingstone.com, 3 September 2014

18. L. Tom Perry, "Why Marriage and Family Matter—Everywhere in the World," The Church of Jesus Christ of Latter-Day Saints, www.lds.org, April 2015

19. Tad Walch and Lois M. Collins, "LDS Church leaders mourn reported deaths in Mormon LGBT community," *Deseret News*, www.deseretnews.com, 28 January 2016

20. John Dehlin and Matt Long, "Child Abuse in the Church," *Infants on Thrones*, www.infantsonthrones.com, 2 February 2016

21. Matthew 7:15-17

22. Lindsey Tanner, "What leads gay, straight teens to attempt suicide?," *Seattle Times*, seattletimes.com, 17 April 2011

23. Lisa Foderaro, "Private Moment Made Public, Then a Fatal Jump," *New York Times*, www.nytimes.com, 29 September 2010

24. "Suicide Risk and Prevention for Lesbian, Gay, Bisexual, and Transgender Youth," Suicide Prevention Resource Center for the U.S. Department of Health and Human Services, sprc.org, 2008, p.15

25. Peeter Värnik, "Suicide in the world," *International Journal of Environmental Research and Public Health*, 9(3), March 2012, p.760–71

THIRTY-EIGHT Marriage

1. John 1:1-11

2. Saint Thomas Aquinas, *The "Summa theologica" of St. Thomas Aquinas, Part 3, Issue 5*, R. & T. Washbourne, 1922, p.290

3. Caleb H. Johnson, *The Mayflower and Her Passengers*, Xlibris Corporation, 27 December 2005, p.83

4. Andy Towle, "Anti-Gay Catholic Blowhard Bill Donohue: Marriage is 'Not About Love': Video," *Towleroad*, www.towlroad.com, 12 April 2013

5. Marc Malkin, "Colin Farrell Mocks Catholic Church's Opposition to Gay Marriage — Watch Now," *E! Online*, www.eonline.com, 8 June 2015

6. "The Potential Budgetary Impact of Recognizing Same-Sex Marriages," Congressional Budget Office, cbo.gov, June 21, 2004, p.1

7. "Bill Maher: Kim Davis = Christian Sharia," Joe.My.God., www.joemygod.com, 12 September 2015

8. Jonathan Rauch, "The Great Secession," *The Atlantic*, www.theatlantic.com, 25 June 2014

9. Edward McClelland, "States That Allow Same-Sex Marriage Have Lower Divorce Rates," NBC Chicago, www.nbcchicago.com, 27 June 2013

10. James Fallows, "No One Asked Me, but ... (Obama on Same-Sex Marriage)," *The Atlantic*, www.theatlantic.com, 9 May 2012

11. Pam Spaulding, "Tobias Wolff (and Lou Dobbs!) slay NOM's Gallagher on DOMA,"

The Bilerco Project, www.bilerico.com, 21 August 2009

12. Peter Sagal, "Samuel Johnson on Same Sex Marriage," www.petersagal.com, 8 April 2009

13. Tara Parker-Pope, "Gay Marriage: Same, but Different," *New York Times*, www.nytimes.com, 1 July 2013

THIRTY-NINE Religion

1. "A New Generation Expresses its Skepticism and Frustration with Christianity," Barna Group, www.barna.org, 24 September 2007

2. Emily Fetsch, "Are Millennials Leaving Religion Over LGBT Issues?" Public Religion Research Institute, www.publicreligion.org, 13 March 2014

3. "Survey Charts Dramatic Change Toward Marriage Equality," Greenberg Quinlan Rosner Research, www.gqrr.com, 27 March 2014

4. Dan Harris, "Haggard Admits Buying Meth," ABC News, www.abcnews.go.com, 3 November 2006

5. Catherine Deveney, "Cardinal Keith O'Brien: how Britain's Catholic leader fell from grace," *The Observer*, www.theguardian.com, 2 March 2013

6. Jeremy Hooper, "Video: Amendment 1 pastor gives parents 'special dispensation' to use violence against LGBT kids!!!," *Good As You*, goodasyou.org, 1 May 2012

7. Isolde Raftery and James Eng, "Standing ovation greets Pastor Charles Worley, who made anti-gay statements," *NBC News*, www.nbcnews.com, 27 May 2012

8. Dan Savage, "O They Will Know We Are Christians…" *The Stranger*, www.thestranger.com, 30 May 2012

9. "Peter Lucas Moses, North Carolina Man, Pleads Guilty In Deaths Of Woman And Boy He Thought Was Gay," *Huffington Post*, www.huffingtonpost.com, 11 June 2012

10. Michelangelo Signorile, "Arizona and Uganda: How the Same Groups Spread the Same Hate Around the Globe," Huffington Post, www.huffingtonpost.com, 25 February 2014; Jeremy Hooper, "The next anti-LGBT export target: Peru," GLAAD, www.glaad.org, 17 March 2014

11. Kevin Kloosterman, "Op-ed: Queer Eye for the Mormon Bishop Guy," *The Advocate*, advocate.com, July 13 2012

12. Willa Paskin, "Your God Is Too Small," *Slate*, www.slate.com, 6 March 2014

13. Rachel Donadio, "On Gay Priests, Pope Francis Asks, 'Who Am I to Judge?'" *New York Times*, www.nytimes.com, 29 July 2013

14. Antonio Spadaro, "A Big Heart Open to God," *America*, www.americamagazine.org, 30 September 2013

15. Philip Pullella, "Church should not fear change, pope says at synod close," Rueters, www.reuters.com, 20 October 2014

16. Carol Glatz, "If laws don't lead people to Jesus, they are obsolete, pope says," *Catholic News Service*, www.catholicnews.com, 13 October 2014

FORTY Scripture

1. 1 Corinthians 7:1-2

2. 1 Corinthians 7:6

3. 1 Corinthians 7:28, translation from James D.G. Dunn, *The Theology of Paul the Apostle*, Eerdmans Publishing Co. quoted in "Was Paul Against Sex?" *Beliefnet*, www.beliefnet.com, retrieved 19 August 2014

4. 1 Corinthians 7: 38

5. 1 Corinthians 7: 39-40

6. Romans 1:26-27

7. 1 Corinthians 6:9-10

8. 1 Timothy 1:9-10

9. Jude 1:7

10. Leviticus 18:22

11. Proverbs 6:16-17

12. Leviticus 18:19

13. Proverbs 6:16-19

14. Leviticus 19:23

15. Leviticus 18:30

16. Leviticus 19:27

17. Numbers 15:32-36

18. Deuteronomy 22:11

19. Leviticus 11:10-12

20. Leviticus 11:8

21. Leviticus 20:13

22. Deuteronomy 17: 2-5

23. Exodus 35:2

24. Leviticus 20:13, Leviticus 21:9, Isaiah 14:21

25. Genesis 38:6-10

26. Leviticus 24:16

27. Exodus 22:17

28. Leviticus 20:27

29. Deuteronomy 21:18-21

30. John 8:7

31. Deuteronomy 23:17; 1 Kings 14:24, 15:12, 22:46; 2 Kings 23:7

32. John 19:26-28

33. Genesis 1:28

34. Daniel Burke, "Westboro church founder Fred Phelps dies," *CNN*, www.cnn. com, 25 March 2014

35. "Counter protestors surprise Westboro church members with 'Sorry for your loss' sign at Lorde concert following death of founder," *Daily Mail*, www.dailymail.co.uk, 23 March 2014

36. John 13:34-35

FORTY-ONE Purpose

1. Harry Hay, *Radically Gay*, edited by Will Roscoe, Beacon Press, 1 June 1997, p.181

2. Samuel Taylor Coleridge, *Specimens of the Table Talk of the Late Samuel Taylor Coleridge: In Two Volumes*, Volume 2, Murray, 1835, p.96

3. Mihaly Csikszentmihalyi, *Creativity: Flow And The Psychology of Discovery and Invention*, Harper Perennial Modern Classics, 2013, p.71

4. Stephen Benjamin, "Don't Ask, Don't Translate, *New York Times*, www.nytimes.com, 8 June 2007

5. Peter Hennen, *Faeries, Bears, and Leathermen: Men in Community Queering the Masculine*, University of Chicago Press, 15 November 2008, p.76-80

6. Richard Florida, "The Rise of the Creative Class," *Washington Monthly*, www. washingtonmonthly.com, May 2002

7. Thomas C. Brickhouse and Nicholas D. Smith, *Plato's Socrates*, Oxford University Press, 1994, p.201

8. John D'Emilio, *Making Trouble: Essays on Gay History, Politics, and the University*, Routledge, 4 February 2014, p.30

FORTY-TWO Dream

1. Emily Zeugner, "Feline geneticist traces origin of the cat," *USA Today*, www.usatoday. com, 9 June 2008

2. "Joshua Graham," *Fallout Wiki*, www. fallout.wikia.com, in reference to the video game *Fallout: Las Vegas*, retrieved 1 December 2014

3. Randy Shilts, *The Mayor of Castro Street: The Life and Times of Harvey Milk*, 1982, p.363

Gatekeepers

1. Bert Hoff, "Gays: Guardians of the Gates, An Interview with Malidoma Somé," *M.E.N. Magazine*, www.menweb.org, September 1993. Copyright © 1993, 1997 by Bert H. Hoff. Used with permission

Index

Symbols

9-11 attacks 92
69 223, 224
1492 75, 100

A

Aboriginal Australians 70
Absaroka Amazon 45
Achilles 85, 87
   and Patroclus 85
A Clockwork Orange 12
acorn woodpeckers 171
Addams, Jane
   and Mary Rozet
      Smith 117
Addaura caves 32
Adonis 85
adoptions 170, 201, 258
   and Dan Savage 262
Adriatic 92
Afghanistan 65
Africa 37, 52, 149, 156
age-differing relationships
   See older-younger
   relationships
Age of Flowers 78
AIDS 131–138, 149, 200,
   220
   and Memorial Quilt 3–6
AIDS Memorial Grove 137,
   142
AIDS Memorial Quilt 3–6
Ai, Emperor of China 71
Akhenaten, Pharaoh of
   Egypt 34–35
Aladdin 64
albatross 160–161
Alexander I, Emperor of
   Russia 107

Alexander the Great 87, 254
   and Hephaestion 87
Ali Baba and the Forty
      Thieves 64
Amazon jungle 49–50, 158
Amazon river dolphins 158
amazons 49–54
   and Diana 84
   Aztec 78
ambassadors 290
American Sociological
      Association 257
America the Beautiful 117
anal sex 206, 222, 224 See
   also sex
ancestors See queer ancestors
androgen insensitivity
      syndrome 230
androgens See hormones
androgyny 40, 46, 236
And Tango Makes
      Three 162
angels 93, 94, 280
Angels in America 133
animals
   and gay label 150
   and gender 164–168
   and sexuality 153–163
   sex with 247
Anne, Queen of Great
      Britain 107
antagonistic selection 172
Antarctic mollusc 167
anti-gay conservatives
      See social conservatives
ants 165
APA, American Psychiatric
      Association 201
Apollo 84

and Hyacinth 84
Apple Inc. 262
apricot trees 168
Aquinas, Thomas 265
Arabian Nights 64
Arabs 64, 65
Arcadia 85
Argentina 266
arsenokoitai 280
Artemis 84
asexuality
   in animals 155, 170, 229
   in humans 56, 294
asexual reproduction 167
Asimov, Isaac 147, 152
Athens 36, 62, 86
attraction-repulsion 205
Augean stables 85
Augustine, Saint 95
Australia 70, 161
Australian black swans 161
authenticity 239–241 See
   also coming out
auto da fé 77
Avalokitesvara 46
aversion therapy 12–15 See
   also cures
Avian flu 135
Aztecs 78

B

Babur, Zahir-ud-Din 63
bacha bazi 65
Baden-Powell, Lord
      Robert 114
Bagaos 87
Bagemihl, Bruce 163
Bailey, Michael 178, 180
Baker, Josephine 129

bakers 269
Balboa, Vasco Núñez de 77
Bali 40
baptism 268
The Baptism of Christ 102
Barbary Coast 122
Bates, Kathy Lee
   and Katherine
      Coman 117
Bathsheba 97
Beard, Charles Austin 213
bears 202
Beat movement 125
Beautiful Boxer 47
Beck, Kristen 233
bees 164–165, 166, 170
beetles 171
"be fruitful, and
   multiply" 284
Beijing 36
Belgium 266
bell curves 297
Benin 52
Bennett, Tony 227
berdache 44 See also transgender; two spirits
Berenson, Bernard 101
Berlin 230
bestiality 247
Bey, Hakim 173
Bible 92–99, 278–285
   and flat earth 101
   and lesbian sex 283
   and polygamy 267
   as addiction 221
   King James version 95,
      106
bighorn sheep 154
bilateral gynandro-
   morphia 167
binary, gender See gender
biological sex 236
birds 160–162, 167, 171
bisexuality
   and evolution 172
   attractions 23
   definition of 19

in animals 155, 157,
   158–159, 160
in plants 168
bison See buffalo
Black Cat bar 123
Black Death 296
Blackfoot tribe 45
"black Sparta" 52
Blankenhorn, David 197
Bletchley Park 119
bodhisattva 46
bodies, human See physi-
   ology
Boies, David 196, 197
bone lengths 183, 185
Bonnard, Pierre 118
Bonny, Anne 59
bonobos 157, 171
   and clitoris location 157
border people 290
The Bostonians 117
Boston marriages 117–118
bottlenose dolphins 158, 171
Boulder Outdoor Survival
   School 209
Boy Scouts 114, 115
Bracci, Cecchino dei 104
brains
   male-female 183
   structure of 183–185
Brazil 62, 218, 266
Brazilian cave flies 166, 167
bridges 290
Briggs initiative 128
brimstone 266
Brokeback Mountain 59
Brooklyn 227
Bruno, Friar Giordano 276
Bryant, Anita 128, 155
bubonic plague 296
Buchanan, President
   James 112
   and William Rufus
      King 112
Buddhists 46, 66
buffalo 156, 163, 171
bullfrogs 166

Buonarroti, Michelangelo
   See Michelangelo
burial customs 33
Burkina Faso 38
Burroughs, William S. 123
bushido 66
Bush, Laura 160
butterflies 167

C

cactus buck deer 155
Caesar, Emperor of Rome
   Julius 89
Calafia, Queen of
   California 51
California 51, 58, 59, 92,
   118
   name origin 51
Caligula, Emperor of
   Rome 89
Callisto 84
Canada 266
canaries
   in churches 276
   of creative age 292
canary-bird fish 166
Caprotti, Gian
   Giacomo 102
Caribbean 75
Carvajal, Gaspar de 49–50
Casas, Friar Bartolomé de
   las 78
Castro neighborhood 125,
   128
Catholic League 265
Catholics
   and cats 296
   and marriage 268
   and priest sexual
      abuse 274
   and Sappho 89
   and sexuality 136, 189
   and tricksters 292
   as Other 207
   gay 107, 114, 274
cats 296
Cavalieri, Tommaso
   dei 103–104

cave drawings 32 *See also* petroglyphs
cave flies 166, 167
Cayo Puto 77
celibacy 56
Central Park Zoo 162
Cesena, Biagio da 105
Chanca, Diego Álvarez 75
Chardin, Teilhard de 15
Chaucer, Geoffrey 107
cherry trees 168
Chicago 117
chickens 168
child abuse *See* children; sexual ethics
children 255–263 *See also* children, gay
  abuse of 65, 194, 260
  and two parents 256, 263
  gay threat to 194
  of gay parents 255–258
  of straight parents 257
  sex and 246, 258–259, 259
children, gay *See also* children
  abuse of 259, 260
  and adoption 258
  and gender 236
  and suicide 261–263
  future of 298
  helping 262
chimpanzees 157
China 33, 90, 92
  and Confucian family values 69
  and female warriors 51
  and gay love 71–72
  and Guanyin 46
Chin dynasty 78
choice hypothesis of gay 148
Christians *See also* Bible
  and Dark Ages 90
  and gayness of anti-gay leaders 274
  and genocide 77
  and international prosletizing 275
  and martyrs 277

and Old Testament 281–282
  and shamanism 39
  and Sodom 92
  and Spanish conquistadors 94
  and the profane 284
  and witches 42
  burning the gay 91–92
  conquest of Americas 75
  dominance of 272
  effects of being anti-gay 273
  future of 277, 285
  gay as canaries for 276
  North Carolina examples of 274
  Spanish Inquisition 76
  tolerance from Vatican 276
  viewing tolerance as persection 268
Christina, Queen of Sweden 107
Christopher Street Liberation Day March 126
chromosomes and sex determination 230
Churchill, Sarah 107
Cicero 86
cichlids 166
circus 58
cisgender 294
  word origin 232
The City of God 95
civil rights, African American 119
Civil War 110, 111
clams 167
Clementi, Tyler 261
Cleveland, President Grover 43
clitorises
  hyena 166
  location in humans 157
Cloud Atlas 234
clownfish 165, 166
Colbert, Stephen 149
Coleridge, Samuel Taylor 290

Colonna, Vittoria 104
Columbus, Christopher 75, 100
Coman, Katherine 117
coming out 239–241
  phrase origin and usage 240
  spiritual act 277
concentration camps, gay people in 118
concubines 264
confirmation bias 149–150
Confucian ethics 69
Congo 93
Coñori, Amazon queen 50
consenting adults *See* sexual ethics
conservatives, anti-gay *See* social conservatives
Constantinople 51
conversion therapy *See* cures
Copernicus, Nicolaus 90, 101
Corinth 279, 280
Cortés, Hernán 51, 76
Cory, George 227
Council of Trent 105
Cowboys Are Frequently Secretly (Fond of Each Other) 59
cows 155, 264
coyote 292
crabs 167
creativity 101, 290, 292, 296
crime against nature *See* laws, anti-gay
Cross, Douglas 227
cross-dressing
  and history of pants 53
  and Joan of Arc 53
  female as male 53, 59
  male as female 59
  Mayan 78
Crow tribe 45
Cruz, Friar Gaspar da 72
crystal methamphetamine 274

Csikszentmihalyi,
Mihaly 290
cures 198–203 *See
also* aversion therapy
Czech Republic 33

D

Dagara people 38, 38–39
Dahomey amazons 52
damselflies 172
Dance-Along
Nutcracker 123
Dark Ages 101
Darwin, Charles 169
Daughters of Bilitis 123
David, King of Israel 95–97
and Jonathan 95–97, 99,
113, 279
Oscar Wilde on 113
sculpture of 103
da Vinci, Leonardo
See Vinci, Leonardo da
deer 154, 155, 166
DeGeneres, Ellen 129
Delphi 86
Denmark 266
Depp, Johnny 59
De Profundis 114
Derickson, David 111
devil 296
Diamond, Lisa 188
Diana 84
dildos 223
Dionysus 85
dishonorable discharge 122
disrupters 290, 292–294
distant father theory 193
dolphins 158–159, 171
Donohue, Bill 265
Don't Ask, Don't Tell
See military
Douglas, Lord Alfred 113,
114
Douglas, Marquess of
Queensberry John
Sholto 113
Dowd, Maureen 140
Doyle, Peter 109

drag 126, 236 *See also* cross-
dressing
at Stonewall 125–126
dragonflies 160, 163
dresses *See* cross-dressing
Dunbar-Nelson, Alice 129
dung flies 171
Dyson, George 119

E

Earth 101
earthquakes 266
The Ecology of Magic 40
Edward II, King of
England 107
Egypt 34, 51, 89, 98, 189
clothes of 53
Eichberg, Rob 240
elders, gay 133
elephants 156
Eliade, Mircea 40
Elizabeth I, Queen of
England 106
elms 168
Empire and political
homophobia 78
England 52–53, 119, 177,
266
Enigma code 119
Enlightenment 107, 293
Epaminondas 86
Epic of Gilgamesh 33
epigenetics 172, 173,
178–179
word origin 178
epi-marks 179
Escalante River 210
estrogen *See* hormones
ethics
and 'crime against
nature' 249
and privacy 248
Confucian 69
sexual *See* sexual ethics
Ethiopia 275
Eurystheus, king of
Tiryns 85
evolution 169–173

and advantages of same-sex
couples 161
and survival of human
species 70
Evolution's Rainbow 165
Exodus International 200
eye blinks 183, 186
eye connections 221
Ezekiel, Prophet 95

F

fa'afafine 47, 70
faggot, word origin 91
"the fags have had it with
oppression" 126
families *See also* children;
children, gay; parents;
parents, gay
as anti-gay concept 263
future of 297
in Confucian China 69
traditional 38, 68–70, 70,
256
Farrell, Colin 266
fashion 291
fathers, theory of distant 193
femininity *See* masculinity-femininity spectrum
Fields, Annie 118
"fight, flight, or mate"
response 184
Finding Nemo 165
finger lengths 183, 185
fingerprints 183, 185
Finland 266
flamingos 162
floods 266
Florida 44
Florida, Richard 292
flour beetles 171
Fon people 52
foreplay 223, 224
foreskins 96
France 52–53, 266
Francis I, King of
France 103
Francis, Pope 276, 277
Frederick the Great 107

Freud, Sigmund 103
fruit flies 160

G

Galileo, Galilei 90, 101
Gandhi, Mahatma 119, 120
    and Hermann
        Kallenbach 120
Ganymede 84
Gap Inc. 262
Garland, Judy 297
gatekeepers 38–39, 41,
    301–305
Gates, Henry Louis Jr. 129
Gaugin, Paul 118
gay
    and LGBT acronym 19
    applied to animals 150
    word origin and usage 16,
        18
gay bars 140
gay children See children;
    children, gay
gaydar 221
gay elders 133
gay gene 178, 179, 181
gay history See history, gay
"Gay is Good" 125
gay liberation 121–130
    today 141
"gay lifestyle" See choice
    hypothesis of gay
gay neighborhoods 140
Gay Pride parades 66, 126,
    140, 205, 274
gay-straight marriages 256
gender 164–168, 228–238
    and chromosomes 230
    and intersex 230–232
    and sexuality 236, 237
    and sexual repro-
        duction 165, 229
    experiences of 236
    in nature 164–168
    in toddlers 236
    physical 230
    spectrum 237
    yin-yang symbol of 237
genderqueer 236

genealogy 177
genetics 149, 177–181, 189
    and asexual repro-
        duction 167
    and chickens 168
    and evolution 172–173
    and sexuality 172–173,
        177–181, 180
    research fears 149
    word origin 177
genitalia
    ambiguous 46, 230, 231
    and hijras 46
    formation of 232
    intersex 230
Genji, Hikaru 66
genome 178
Germany 118
Gidlow, Elsa 118
Gilgamesh 33
gingko trees 168
Ginsberg, Allen 122
Giovio, Paolo 103
giraffes 156
Glassgold, Julia 201
goats 155, 264
gobies 166
God and gods See also Jesus
    of Nazareth
    ancient 33, 73
    and AIDS 132, 135,
        135–136
    and Bible scriptures 279,
        281–282, 283
    and Catholics 276, 277
    and China 72
    and choice
        hypothesis 189, 251, 277
    and 'crime against
        nature' 249
    and David 96, 97
    and flat earth 101
    and Frank Kameny 124
    and gay cures 200
    and human physi-
        ology 230
    and Joan of Arc 52
    and Marriage 266
    and monotheism 39, 40

and Mormons 12, 140,
    154, 260
and nature 153, 163, 164,
    167, 168, 170
and Ruth 97
and Sappho 88
and Sodom 92, 93, 95
and Westboro Baptist
    church 272–273, 285
Aztec 78
Greek 84–85, 88
Mayan 78
Roman 279, 290
spirit of 37, 62, 112, 298
word usage 17
"God Bless Us Nelly
    Queens" 123
"God Hates Fags" 285 See
    also Westboro Baptist
    church
Golden Fleece 85
Golden Gate Park 218
Golden Rule 250
gold rush 58, 121
Goliath 96
Good Samaritan 250
Google 262
gorillas 218
graffiti 32, 90
Grant, Preston
    and abuse 12–15,
        211–212
    and AIDS 3, 134, 137
    and Bible scriptures 95,
        282
    and Christianity 277
    and dancing bear 202
    and desert survival 209
    and Mormons 7, 15, 16
    and relationships 61,
        217–220
    as author 5, 16, 294, 295,
        307
    family of 7–8, 8, 177
    masculinity-femininity
        of 228
    photo of 307
    youth of 8–17, 127
gray whales 159

Great Barrier Reef
gobies 166
Greece 83–89
and Amazons 51, 52
and graffiti 32
and Italian Renais-
sance 101
and pederasty 62, 65, 66
clothes of 53
gods of 84–85, 290
human origin story 73
Greene, Billy 110
Greenland 266
Greenwich Village 125
Gregory VII, Pope 89
Grimké, Angelina Weld 129
gross indecency
and Alan Turing 119
and Oscar Wilde 113, 119
Gros Ventre tribe 45
Guanyin 46
gynandromorphia 167

H

Hafiz 64
Haggard, Ted 274
Haight Ashbury 125
hair swirls or whorls 187
Hall, Radclyffe 118
Hall, Thomas/
Thomasine 231
Hamlet fish 166
Hammon, Mary
Vincent 116
handedness 183, 184
handkerchief 107
Han dynasty 72
Hao, Fu 52
happiness 247
harbingers 292
Haring, Keith 240
Harlem Renaissance 129
Hathaway, Anne 106
Hatshepsut, Pharaoh of
Egypt 35
Havana 77
Hawaii 48, 160
Hay, Harry 221, 291, 294

and Mattachine
Society 123, 289
healers 294
healing 209–213 See
also psychology
Heimbach, Dr. Daniel 247
Helms, Senator Jesse 132
Henry IV, King of Spain 76
Hephaestion 87
Hercules 84
and Hylas 85
and King Eurystheus 85
heretics 76
hermaphrodites 166, 173
Hermaphroditus 85
hermits 56
hijras 45–46
Hindus 223
hippies 125
history, gay 31–32, 35–36
See also individual topics
by name
HIV See AIDS
Hoff, Bert 301–305
Hollywood 262
Holocaust 92
homeless youth 259
Homer 85
homophobia 204–208
and advanced societies 78
rational reasons for 293
Hood, Robin 58, 106
Hooker, Dr. Evelyn 195
hookups 226
hormones
and bisexuality 172
and epigenetics 179
and gender determi-
nation 230
and smell attraction 186
estrogen 230
in animals 160
testosterone 179, 187
horses 155, 245
House of David 97
Howard, Brenda 126
Howl 122
HPV, Human

Papillomavirus 136
HRC, Human Rights
Campaign 234
Hughes, Langston 129
hugs 263, 266
Hull House 117
Hurricane Katrina 92
husband 264
Hyacinth 84
hyenas 166
Hylas 85
Hymn to Aphrodite 89
hypothalomus 183

I

Iceland 266
identical twins 178
"if it feels good, do it" 247
I Have a Dream speech 119
Il Divino 103
I Left my Heart in San
Francisco 227
Iliad 85
Incas
and temple prostitutes 76
empire and
homophobia 78
Spanish conquest of 49
India 45–46, 120, 223
Indonesia 40
initiation rituals 32
inner ear clicks 183, 186
Inquisition 77
insects 160
intermediaries 290
intersex 230–232, 236
and hijras 46
Mother Nature as 173
Isabella, Queen of Spain 76
Isherwood, Christopher 195
"I sing the body
electric" 108
Islam
and Dark Ages 90
and Inquisition 76
and love of boys 64–66
and Queen Calafia 51
and shamans 39

as Other 207
Israelites 95–96
itches 226
It Gets Better Project 261

J

Jackson, President
  Andrew 112
James, Henry 117
James VI and I, King
  of England and
  Scotland 106
  and George Villiers 106
  and King James version of
    Bible 106
Jane Addams 117
Japan 122
  and older-younger relation-
    ships 66
  clothes of 53
Japanese cherry
  blossoms 168
Japanese macaques 171
Jason and the Argonauts 85
Jenner, Caitlin/
  Bruce 233–234
Jesus of Nazareth
  and Christlike life 283
  and Golden Rule 250
  and John the Beloved 283
  and last supper 283
  "cast first stone" story 282
  in pants 53
  lineage of 97
  "love one another" 285
  on homosexuality 278
  on sin of Sodom 94
  sexuality of 283
Jewett, Sarah Orne 118
Jews See also Bible
  and Nazis 118
  and Spanish Inqui-
    sition 76
  as Other 207
  in Egypt 98
  US population of 25
Joan of Arc 52–53
John II, King of Spain 76
Johnson, Robert 129

Johnson, Samuel 250
John the Beloved 283
Jonathan 95–97, 99, 113
Jones, Cleve 3
Joseph 98–99, 279
Jung, Carl 229
Jupiter 279

K

Kachina 44
Kallenbach, Hermann 120
Kameny, Frank 124, 127
Kangjiashimenji petro-
  glyphs 32
Kaposi's sarcoma 132
kathoey 47
Khan, Genghis 94
"Kill the Gays" laws 275
King James Version of the
  Bible 106
King, Martin Luther 119
Kloosterman, Kevin 275
Kolhamana Kachina 44
kouros 84
Kramer, Larry 133
Krishnamurti, Jiddu 240
Kushner, Tony 133

L

labels 19–22
  and shifting gay-straight
    distinctions 141
ladyboys 47
Lakota 44
The Last Emperor 72
The Last Judgment 103, 105
The Last Supper 101
laws, anti-gay 249–250
  current 250
  "Kill the Gays" 275
Laysan albatross 160–161
"learn the rules well, so you
    know how to break them
    effectively" 292
Leaves of Grass 108, 110
Lebowitz, Fran 253
Legionnaires disease 132
lemon trees 168

lesbian sex See sex, lesbian
lesbian, word origin 88
Lesbos 88
LeVay, Dr. Simon 183
LGBT acronym 19
Liberace 137
liberation See gay liberation
Library of Alexandria 89
Lincoln, Abraham 110–111,
    112
  and Billy Greene 110
  and Captain David
    Derickson 111
  and Joshua Speed 111
Ling, Duke of Wei 72
lions 149, 150, 156
The Little Prince 152
lizards 166, 167
lobsters 167
Locke, Alain 129
London 36, 59
Los Angeles 123
  and AIDS 132
Lot 93, 94
Louisiana 60
love and sex 217–227, 227
"love of the cut sleeve" 71
"love of the shared
    peach" 72
"love that dare not speak its
    name" 113
Ludwig II, King of
  Bavaria 107
Luther, Martin 90, 101
Luxembourg 266
Lyon, Phyllis 123

M

macaques 171
Macedonia 87
Maddow, Rachel 130
mahu 48
Maine 117, 266
makakoi 280
male-female binary
  See gender
Maleficent 42
Malidoma See Somé,

Malidoma

manatees 159

Manet, Édouard 118

The March of the
Penguins 162

Marian, Maid 58

Marine Corps Times 253

marine mammals 158–159

Marquess of Queensberry
rules 113

marriage 264–271
gay-straight 68–70
Mayan 78
secular versus
religious 268

Mars 279

Martin, Del 123

Martin, Judith 247

Maryland 266

masculinity-femininity
spectrum 232, 236

Massachusetts 266

Matlovich, Leonard 127

The Matrix 234

Mattachine Society 123

Mazarine Blue butter-
flies 151

McDowell, Malcolm 12

McKay, Claude 129

meaning See purpose

Melville, Herman 110

Melzi, Count Francesco 102

mermaids 151, 159

MERS, Middle East Respi-
ratory Syndrome 135

Mexico 45, 78, 266

Mexico City 77

Meyer lemons 168

mice 160, 296

Michelangelo 103–105
and Cecchino dei
Bracci 104
and David sculpture 95
and Gherardo Perini 103
and Oscar Wilde 113
and Vittoria Colonna 104

military 58, 252–254 See
also Alexander the Great;

Sacred Band of Thebes
helped create gay
community 122

Military Times 252

Milk, Harvey 128, 298

Milky Way galaxy 101

Millay, Edna St.
Vincent 118

Miller, Kenneth 197

Miller, Terry 261

Ming dynasty 72

Minos 105

minstrels 57–60

Miss Manners 247

Moby Dick 110

Mojave 45

Mona Lisa 101

monastic life 56

monks 55–56

monogamy 219

Monterey Bay
Aquarium 151

Mormon crickets 154

Mormons
and blacks 268
and child abuse 260
and gay animals 154
and gay cures 202
and geneology 177
and guns 155
and HPV 136
and NARTH 196
and polygamy 267
and Preston Grant 7–17,
18, 210
and Proposition 8 140
and sex 248
and sexuality 117, 189,
193, 275–276
and suicide 202, 260
and tricksters 292
anti-gay pronouncements
of 12, 260
future of 297
in Angels in America 133
pioneers 153
US population of 25

Morocco 151

Moscone, George 128

Moses 98

Mother Nature 173, 230,
284

Mother of Pride 126

mothers of gay men 179

mothers, over-protective
theory of 193

Mount Olympus 84

Moynihan, Daniel
Patrick 152

MRSA, Methicillin-re-
sistant Staphylococcus
aureus 135

Muay Thai 47

Mulan 52

mule deer 154, 155

muxes 45

myths
and animals 159, 292
and children 259
and religion 83
biblical 93
Greek 73, 85
in the Americas 77
modern 59, 133, 154
of California 51

N

Naked Lunch 123

Names Project See AIDS
Memorial Quilt

Naomi 97, 99

NARTH, National Associ-
ation for Research &
Therapy of Homosexu-
ality 196, 201

nasal sex 158

National Association of
Evangelicals 274

National Coming Out
Day 240

natural law 265

natural selection
See evolution

nature versus nurture 179

Navajo Nation 45, 155

Navratilova, Martina 129

Nazis 118, 119, 230
Neferkare, Pharaoh of
Egypt 34
Nefertiti, Queen of
Egypt 34–35
Nelson, Willie 59
Neptune 279
Nero, Emperor of Rome 89
Netherlands 266
Newman, Cardinal John
Henry 114
New Orleans 92
New York City
and AIDS 132, 133
Central Park Zoo
penguins 162
gay history of 21
Gay Pride parades 126,
127
police sodomy in 93–94
Stonewall rebellion 125
townhouses of 70
New Zealand 266
Niankhkhnum and Khnum-
hotep 34
Nicolosi, Dr. Joseph 200
Nicomedes IV, King of
Bithynia 89
Nietzsche, Friedrich 297
Nigeria 275
nipples, male 232
Noah 93, 167
non-dualism 237, 290 *See*
also yin and yang
The Normal Heart 133
Norman, Sarah White 116
North Carolina 132
Norway 266
Nugent, Richard Bruce 129
nuns 40, 56, 291
nurses 291
The Nutcracker 123
nut trees 168
Nuwas, Abu 64
nymphs 84

O

Oakland 118

Oaxaca 45
O'Brien, Cardinal Keith 274
observer bias 149–151
O'Donnell, Rosie 129
Of Water and the Spirit 38
Ojibway 44
OKCupid 23, 225
Okinawa gobies 166
Oklahoma 253
older brother effect 182
older-younger relation-
ships 61–67
Oscar Wilde on 113
Olson, Ted 196
Olympics 230, 233
opposite sex 16
oral sex 223, 224, 226
Oregon 261
Orman, Suze 130
other-sex 16
otoacoustic emissions
See inner ear clicks
overdominance 172
over-protective mother
theory 193
Ovid 166

P

pagans 279
Pan 85
Panama 77
pansexuality 173, 294
pants 53 *See also* cross-
dressing
Papago 45
parents *See also* children;
children, gay
and AIDS Memorial
Quilt 4
and effective
parenting 194
celebrating gay
children 297
gay 256–257, 257
heterosexual 257
single 256
Paris 38, 52
Passover 99

patlacheh 78
Patroclus 85, 87
Paul, Apostle 279
peach trees 168
Pearl Harbor 122
Pearson, Carol Lynn 200
pederasty 62, 65, 66 *See*
also older-younger
relationships
pedophilia 62, 65 *See*
also sexual ethics
penguins 162
penises
and sex 223
petroglyphs of 32, 33
sizes of 183, 186
Pentagon 290
perineal raphe 232
Perini, Gherardo 103
Persians 64, 65
persimmon trees 168
petroglyphs 32, 33 *See*
also cave drawings
Phelps, Fred 285
pheromones, response
to 183, 186
Philalexandros *See* Alexander
the Great: and
Hephaestion
Philip II, King of
France 106
Philip II, King of
Macedonia 87
Philistines 96
physiology 182–189
bone lengths 183, 185
brain structures 183,
183–185
brain symmetry 183
eye blinks 183, 186
fears of researching 188
finger lengths 183, 185
fingerprints 185
hair swirls or whorls 187
handedness 183, 184
hypothalami 183
inner ear clicks 183, 186
of gay male bodies 187

of lesbian bodies 188
older brother effect 182
penis sizes 183, 186
response to phero-
  mones 183, 186
response to sweat 183, 187
Picasso, Pablo 118
Pietà 103
pigs 155
Pillard, Richard 178, 180
Pine Leaf, woman chief 45
pink dolphins 158
pink flamingos 162
pink triangle 118
pirates 59
Pirates of the Caribbean 59
Pitcairn Islands 266
Pixar 165
Pizarro, Francisco 76
plague, bubonic 296
plants 168
Plato 73, 83, 86, 113
Plutarch 84
pneumocystis
  pneumonia 132
Poland 230
Polo, Marco 92
polygamy
and gay marriage 267
in Bible 98, 281
in China 72
Mormon 267
pomegranate trees 168
Pompeii 89
pornography
and aversion therapy 13
and bisexuality 23
and conservative percep-
  tions 249
as coping mechanism 211
effect of 226
gay male 223
Portugal 266
post-decadent 227
priests 291, 294
primates 157–158, 171
prison effect 199
promiscuity 225–226 See

also sex
Proposition 8
and George Rekers 201
and Mormons 140
effects of 140
trial of 196–197
Prove It On Me Blues 129
Provincetown, Massachu-
  setts 205
psychology 149, 193–197
  See also healing
PTSD, post-traumatic stress
  disorder 14
Purple Heart 233
purpose 40, 289–294
Puyi, Emperor of China 72,
  73

Q

qadesh 95, 282
queen bees 164–165, 170
queer ancestors
African 39
and gay-straight
  marriages 69, 70
and minstrels 57, 60
and Monks 55, 56
as lovers 71, 74
definition of 36
suppressed 75
Queer Eye for the Straight
  Guy 275
quince trees 168

R

racists 250
rainbows 266, 298
Rainey, Gertrude "Ma" 129
Raleigh, Sir Walter 106
rape
as act of violence 93–94
threat of gay 99
Ratjen, Hermann/Dora 230
rats 296
Rauch, Jonathan 269
reaction formation 205
Read, Mary 59
Reagan, Ronald 132
reality

and nature 173
and optimism 297
and religion 277, 284
and science 147, 149, 151,
  152
Rekers, Dr. George Alan 201
religion 83
Renaissance
and Dark Ages 90
and Diana 84
future 129, 298
Harlem 129
Italian 100–107
Renoir, Pierre-Auguste 118
RentBoy.com 201
reparative therapy See cures
Republicans 137, 261
Richard II, King of
  England 107
Richard I, King of
  England (Richard the
  Lionheart) 106
and Philip II of
  France 106
Ride, Sally 130
Robertson, Pat 90
role playing 224
romance 227
Rome
and Amazons 51
and Diana 84
and Ovid 166
and pederasty 66
and Renaissance 101
and Sappho 89
clothes of 53
emperors of 89
fall of 90
gods of 279
population of 36
sexuality in 89–90
Romeo and Juliet 265
Romero 218–219, 222
Roscoe, Will 45
Roughgarden, Joan 165
Roxanne 87
Royal College of Psychia-
  trists 195

Rubens, Sir Peter Paul 84
Rufus, King William 112
Rufus, William 106
Rushdie, Salman 268
Russia 115, 189, 275
  and Pyotr Ilyich
    Tchaikovsky 114
Rustin, Bayard 119, 120
Rutgers University 261
Ruth 97–98, 99, 279
  and Naomi 97–98, 99,
    279

S

Sacred Band of
    Thebes 86–87, 254
Sagan, Carl 101
sailors 58, 59, 221 See
    also pirates
Saint-Exupéry, Antoine
    de 152
salmon 166
Salt Lake City 117, 154,
    267, 307
Samoa 47
Samurai 66
Sandburg, Carl 111
San Francisco
  and AIDS 132
  and gay liber-
    ation 121–123
  and Oscar Wilde 113
  and Preston Grant 8, 218,
    295
  and Silicon Valley 292
  as gay mecca 125
  Gold Rush 58
  parenting in 255
Sappho 88–89, 123
Sarria, Jose 123
Saul, King of Israel 96–97
Savage, Dan 261
science 147, 149, 152, 189
Scotland 177, 266
Scott Antarctic
    Expedition 162
Seagull Monument 154
seagulls 154, 163

seas slugs 167
sea turtles 170
self-polinating trees 168
Serengeti 149
sex 217–227
  anal See anal sex
  and overabundance 226
  gay male 223–226
  lesbian 222–223, 226
  relationships
    without 218–220, 219
sexual ethics 245–247
sexual fluidity 188
sexually antagonistic
    selection 172
Shakespeare, William 84,
    105
  Oscar Wilde on 113
shamans 37–42, 301–305
  and purpose 291
  in Africa 38–39
  in Americas 77, 78
  Joseph 98
  petroglyphs of 33
shame 211
sheep 154, 155, 264
shepherds 155
shudo 66
sickle cell disease 172
side-blotched lizard 166
Silicon Valley 292
sin See choice hypothesis
    of gay
Sinbad 64
single parents 256
Sissy Man Blues 129
Sistine Chapel 103, 104
slaves 264
Slovenia 266
S&M 224
Smith, Bessie 129
Smith, Mary Rozet 117
social conservatives
  and AIDS 132, 135
  and children 259, 261
  and Christians 276
  and culture wars 207
  and ethics 247, 248

and marriage 268, 270
and military 253
and Proposition 8
  trial 196–197
and sex 224, 247, 248, 249
genetic origins of 180
healing of 250
social relations and same-sex
    sexuality
  in animals 157, 171
  in humans 171
Socrates 294
Sodom
  references to 205, 279,
    280
  story of 92–96, 99
sodomites
  and Oscar Wilde 113
  and scriptures 282
  in Americas 76, 77, 79
  in China 72
  word usage 95
sodomy 77
Solomon, King of Israel 72,
    97
Somé, Malidoma 37–39, 41,
    301–305
South Africa 230, 266
Southeastern Baptist
    Theological
    Seminary 247
Southern Baptists 189, 247,
    268
  population of 25
Southern Christian
    Leadership
    Conference 119
Spain
  and Americas 49–50,
    75–79
  and Inquisition 76
  and marriage 266
sparrows 166
Sparta 52, 86
Speakes, Larry 132
Speed, Joshua 111
spinner dolphins 158
Spitzer, Dr. Robert 200

squid 166, 167
Star of David 118
stars 91
startle response See eye blinks
STDs See also AIDS and lesbians 135
Stein, Gertrude 118, 120 and Alice B. Toklas 118
Stephens, Helen 230
Stonewall riots 125–127, 298
"strange flesh" 95, 280
subject-subject conciousness 291
Suburban Baths 89
suicides
  adult 202
  advice to young people 262
  and Preston Grant 14
  child 210, 260–261
Sukel, Kayt 179
Sumeria 33
sunfish 166
"survival of the fittest" See evolution
swans 161
sweat, response to 187
Sweden 266
Swine flu (H1N1) 135
Symposium 83
synthesists 290, 291

T

Taj Mahal 63
Tale of Genji 66
Taliban 65
Taoism 72
Tchaikovsky, Pyotr Ilyich 114
"teach a man to fish" 298
teachers 290, 294
  and America the Beautiful 117
  and gay parents 255, 259
  as role models 194
  ban on gay 128

Temple of Hatshepsut 35
temple prostitutes
  in Bible 95, 279, 280, 282
  Incan 76
  in China 72
Temple Square 154
testosterone See hormones
Thailand 47
Thebes 86–87 See also Sacred Band of Thebes
Theocritus 85
Theodore of Amasea, Saint 92
therapy See also healing
thinking machines 119
"think outside the box" 292
third gender See transgender; two spirits
Thoreau, Henry David 110
Thurman, Wallace 129
Titian 84
Tohono O'odham 45
Toklas, Alice B. 118
Tokyo 15, 66, 307
Tora! Tora! Tora! 140
Tower of Babel 93
transgender 232–238 See also two spirits
  and LGBT 19, 232
translators 291
transvestites 236
tree lizards 166
Trevor Project 262
tricksters 290
Trojan war 85
Troy 86, 87
Tuck, Friar 58
Tum, Nong 47
Turing, Alan 119, 120
turtles 170
Tutankhamen, Pharaoh of Egypt 34–35
twelve tribes of Israel 95
Twinkie defense 128
twins studies 178
two spirits 43–48 See

also transgender
Guanyin-Avalokitesvara 46
  in Americas 76, 77
  in Hawaii 48
  in petroglyphs 32
  in Samoa 47
  in Thailand 47
  Navajo 155

U

U-boats 119
Uganda 189, 275
United Kingdom 274
United States of America 230
  and World War II 122
  Walt Whitman on 108
Upanishads 204
Uruguay 266
US Mail 125
US Marines 254
US National Institute for Mathematical and Biological Synthesis 179
US Navy SEALs 233, 254
US State Department 290
US Supreme Court 250, 257
Us versus Them 207
Utah 59, 208, 209
  and animals 153–156, 166
  and polygamy 267
  and Preston Grant 7, 9, 12, 228
  and sexuality 117

V

Vaca, Álvar Núñez Cabeza de 44
Vasari, Giorgio 102
Vatican See Catholics
velvet-horn deer 155
Venice 91–92
Venus 279
Vere, Robert de 107
Verrocchio, Andrea del 102
"vile affections" 279
villages 36, 68
Villiers, George 106
Vinci, Leonardo da 101–103

and Count Francesco
  Melzi 102
and Francis I of
  France 103
and Gian Giacomo
  Caprotti 102
Virginia 249–250
Vitruvian Man 101

W

Wachowski, Lana 233–234
Wachowski, Lilly 233
Wales 266
walruses 158
Walsh, Stella 230
wanderers 57–60
Washington, DC 16, 220,
  249, 273, 307
water buffalo 156
Waters, Ethel 129
wave-particle duality 151
wedding cakes 269
We Shall Overcome 126
Westboro Baptist
  church 272–273, 285
West Indian manatees 159
We Were Here 133
We'wha 43–44, 47
whales 158, 159
"What would Jesus do?" 283
whiptail lizard 167
White, Dan 128
White House 3, 112
White Night riots 128
white-tailed deer 154, 155
white throated sparrows 166
Whitman, Walt 108–110
  and Peter Doyle 109
Wilber, Ken 212
Wilde, Oscar 112–114, 138,
  241
  and Lord Alfred
  Douglas 113
William II, King of England
  (William Rufus) 106
William the Conqueror 106
witches 42, 296
"woman trapped in a man's

body" 233
woodpeckers 171
Woolf, Virginia 118
World War II 118, 122, 227
wrasses 166
Wright, iO Tillett 26

X

Xochiquetzal-Xochipilli 78

Y

Yamamoto, Admiral
  Isoroku 140
Yang. Princess Pin 52
Yellow Emperor 72
yin and yang 237
Young, Brigham 59
Young, Brigham Morris 59
Yucatan 78

Z

Zapotec 45
zebras 170
Zephyr 84
Zeus 73, 84
Zion National Park 154
Zuk, Marlene 157
Zuni 43–44, 45